Playwrights for Tomorrow

VOLUME 1

American Power two one-act plays

BY JAMES SCHEVILL

Ex-Miss Copper Queen on a Set of Pills

BY MEGAN TERRY

A Bad Play for an Old Lady

BY ELIZABETH JOHNSON

And Things That Go Bump in the Night

BY TERRENCE MCNALLY

EDITED, WITH AN INTRODUCTION, BY ARTHUR H. BALLET

PLAYWRIGHTS FOR TOMORROW

A Collection of Plays, Volume 1

THE UNIVERSITY OF MINNESOTA PRESS · MINNEAPOLIS

Library of Congress Catalog Card Number: 66-19124

PUBLISHED IN GREAT BRITAIN, INDIA, AND PAKISTAN BY THE OXFORD UNIVERSITY PRESS, LONDON, BOMBAY, AND KARACHI, AND IN CANADA BY THE COPP CLARK PUBLISHING CO. LIMITED, TORONTO

INTRODUCTION by Arthur H. Ballet *page 3*

AMERICAN POWER by James Schevill *page 7*
THE SPACE FAN *page 13*   THE MASTER *page 43*

EX-MISS COPPER QUEEN ON A SET OF PILLS
by Megan Terry *page 73*

A BAD PLAY FOR AN OLD LADY
by Elizabeth Johnson *page 107*

AND THINGS THAT GO BUMP IN THE NIGHT
by Terrence McNally *page 159*

Playwrights for Tomorrow

VOLUME 1

PLAYWRIGHTS FOR TOMORROW

Arthur H. Ballet

OF THE artists who band together to share the theatrical experience, the playwright's lot is the loneliest and perhaps the most difficult. In modern America, he generally writes in a vacuum, deprived of colleagues, of intellectual stimulation, and of meaningful theatrical contact.

This isolation of the writer is disastrous. Historically, the important contributions to theatre have come from writers who were intimately involved as artists and as people with a specific theatre or at least with an individual school of ideas and practice.

The plight of the new writer is especially critical. There is ample assurance that he can, alone at his typewriter, turn out a script. But unless he can then work within that creative bond of writer, director, actor, and audience which results in a living play, his talent will not be developed, his potential will remain unrealized. He must be allowed to try this and then that, to rework and start afresh. Yet he is engaging in an art that, in the present day, does not permit failure, whose audience judges each aspiring effort with finality. What is desperately needed is the opportunity for many writers to have their work for the theatre tried out, developed, viewed, and evaluated. Only in this way can we hope for a vital, relevant theatre.

Once the commercial theatre and local repertory companies could and did chance it with new writers. Today, costs are prohibitive in the commercial theatre, local repertory is turning more and more to "safe classics," and university and collegiate theatres are too frequently bent on emulating commercial success. There is no room for the experimental writer, for the beginner who might *learn* to be a good playwright.

In foolhardy fashion, fresh theatre in this country has survived in a single city, New York. Here new plays are welcomed and given their hour upon the stage — albeit dogged by struggles with standards set by the countinghouse, audiences who seek solely to be diverted, unions which are preserving a battle station of protectivity long outdated, and artists who are self-centered rather than art-centered. The miracle is that any new play is ever produced in this bedlam, let alone that significant new drama can emerge. Nonetheless, it has been the New York theatre, and, regrettably, the New York theatre almost alone, which has had the courage to present new playwrights, to experiment with form and meaning, and to underwrite changes in the status quo.

The provincial theatre has for the most part been precisely that: provincial, either sacrosanctly re-presenting the "classics" of a foreign heritage or righteously bringing to the hinterlands rehashes of the Broadway and off-Broadway success. Instead of providing the lifeblood of the so-called commercial theatre, educational and community theatres too often have bled it. Despite elegantly equipped playhouses and well-attended productions, they have failed to venture very far afield and consequently are insignificant except as rerun houses. Secure in their audiences and successes, they have retreated from artistic honesty and experimentation with the lament that "the audiences will not accept new plays." They refuse to recognize that the only important theatre in the country, that which is in New York, has survived — haphazardly to be sure — *only* on new plays.

At the same time, dramatists by the hundreds have gone unproduced, unseen, and unheard because they do not measure up to a New York producer's estimate of what will "go." And the producer is not to be blamed for his judgment; his risk will be enormous and he must rely, however mistakenly, on his own taste and estimate of what will work and what will not. Simultaneously, the writer lucky enough to get a New York hearing risks his whole career in that single hearing, for the unreasonable and catastrophic alternatives of smash hit or utter failure face him — and both success and failure on the gargantuan scale of Broadway are too frequently catastrophic for the new writer as a creative artist. There is no in-between, no chance to consider his work in terms of a company of actors, a theatre, and a community, no chance to rewrite on the basis of audience and player reactions. At best, a play is produced; it is seldom developed.

PLAYWRIGHTS FOR TOMORROW

In an attempt to help remedy this bleak situation, the University of Minnesota, in 1963, undertook an experiment with the aid and encouragement of the Rockefeller Foundation. An Office for Advanced Drama Research (O.A.D.R.) was set up with the charge of exploring what helpful relationships might be established between professional playwrights and a thriving center of theatre activity outside of New York City. In the Twin Cities of Minneapolis and St. Paul, there were the Tyrone Guthrie Theatre, the University of Minnesota Theatre, Theatre in the Round Players, Theatre St. Paul, and the Firehouse Theatre — each theatrically knowledgeable and each representative of a variety of dramatic experience. These theatres, together with some twenty other local groups, many equally dedicated and skilled, formed a nucleus on which the O.A.D.R. could rely for support. It is hoped that, in time, most of these theatres, whether professional, semiprofessional, or amateur, will be involved in producing new writers.

University of Minnesota President O. Meredith Wilson named an Executive Committee for the project: Donald K. Smith, assistant academic vice-president of the University of Minnesota, chairman; Oliver Rea and Peter Zeisler, co-managing directors of the Minnesota Theatre Company at the Guthrie Theatre; Willard T. Thompson, dean of the Extension Division of the university; Frank M. Whiting, director of the University Theatre; and Kenneth L. Graham, chairman of the university's Speech and Theatre Arts Department.

As director of the O.A.D.R., I began by asking established theatre people for recommendations of promising young playwrights and then invited submission of scripts from them. Word got around, and other plays began to pour in. All the literally hundreds of manuscripts submitted each year were read carefully. Insofar as possible, the selection of participants was based on their talent for dramatic writing — potential if not always fully realized — and for generating what I can best describe as theatrical excitement. In no case was a *play* selected; my sole concern was the *playwright*. Once chosen, the writer was given the widest possible latitude. He was encouraged to explore his own dramatic efforts freely and honestly, without external pressures. One writer chose to direct her own play; another chose to observe a professional company at work and to perfect, rewrite, and create new plays. With one exception, when a cast and a director were experimentally "imported" from New York, the

5

writers worked with local companies and directors. The plays were circulated to the cooperating theatres, which were free to accept or reject the scripts in terms of their own theatrical goals. Each play developmentally rehearsed under the auspices of the O.A.D.R. was viewed not only by an adequate cross-sampling of local theatregoers, but by guest critics, directors, and actors, brought to the Twin Cities at the playwright's request to help him evaluate his work.

The plays need now to be examined by a wider audience. To that end they are being published in book form. Seven of the first eight playwrights invited to avail themselves of the facilities of the program are represented here and in Volume 2 of *Playwrights for Tomorrow*. (One writer did not wish to have his play published.) The play that concludes this volume — *And Things That Go Bump in the Night* — has already been seen in New York; the published criticism of the play was damning, but the reader, and I sincerely hope other audiences, will judge independently. Megan Terry's newest work has been optioned for 1966 production on Broadway. Since working with the O.A.D.R. on the two one-act plays that appear in Volume 2, Maria Irene Fornés has been given the Obie Award as the outstanding new writer on the 1964 off-Broadway scene, and she is preparing for the production of another of her plays in New York. Each of the playwrights, in short, continues to write and to work productively in the theatre.

The writers were invited to comment on their plays and their experiences with the O.A.D.R., and each has responded in his own way. Their remarks are included here as prefatory notes to the plays.

For the reader who seeks in these plays a connecting thread of commitment, there will be disappointment. They range in theme and subject matter from cosmic apocalypse through social misalliance to personal inadequacy. Some are mature and wise, while others are young and angry. If they share anything it is simply that each represents, I believe, a new and exciting voice in the American theatre.

JAMES SCHEVILL

American Power

TWO RELATED ONE-ACT PLAYS

to Eric Bentley

American Power by James Schevill was performed on August 16, 1964, at the Tyrone Guthrie Theatre, Minneapolis. It was directed by Edward Payson Call.

Cast of Characters for THE SPACE FAN

MELINDA	Yvonne McElroy
INVESTIGATOR	Charles Cioffi

Cast of Characters for THE MASTER

THE MASTER	Gordon Howard
THE CANDIDATE	Jennifer Warren
THE ASSISTANT	Willis Sherman

PLAYWRIGHT'S PREFACE

To REHEARSE a new play at leisure under professional conditions . . to change one's play in rehearsal from a desire to experiment and not from commercial pressures . . to work closely with a good director and trained actors in the development of a script, exchanging ideas, trying possibilities — these are ideals seldom achieved in American theatre but brought closer to realization by the playwriting project sponsored by the Office for Advanced Drama Research at the University of Minnesota. To be sure they have not been realized completely as yet, but at least a start has been made.

The constant criticism is heard that "there are no good new plays," but it is my own belief that what is really lacking is the opportunity for experienced writers with high standards to work out their plays in a creative atmosphere with a director and actors. Unlike a novel or a poem, a play can never be finished without the theatrical experience. So it is wrong to expect brilliant plays from writers who have little sense of actors or stage. Note, however — I say experienced *writers*, not necessarily experienced *playwrights*. Many would-be playwrights mask what is actually their inability to write well by protesting that the theatre demands an absolutely specialized handling of the word. Certainly the playwright must have a sense of the physical word — the word suited to gesture and action. But he must also have a sense of standards and a knowledge of relationship between the arts, which the experienced writer should possess. The great fault of our theatre today is its isolation. Painting, sculpture, poetry, the novel, music, the film, all reveal greater ambitions and higher achievements in general than the theatre today. Yet, if opportunities and the right working conditions were available, many poets and novelists would work eagerly in the theatre. Why? The form comes alive in an exciting immediacy which the word on the page can never match.

My two related one-act plays, called *American Power*, changed completely during rehearsals at the Guthrie Theatre in Minneapolis under Edward Call's dedicated direction. In *The Master*, the Candidate — who had been much more sophisticated and more ambiguous in the San Francisco production at the Actor's Workshop directed by Herbert Blau — suddenly became Miss America. The line of the play, corruption of a sentimental, rather naive, but extremely practical and strong-willed woman by the Master's incessant interrogation and zany revelations, became clearer and easier to follow. The ending, with its eagle dance and marriage ceremony that recapitulated the key satirical points in the play, had greater dramatic force than the rather didactic ending I wrote in San Francisco, an ending influenced by the assassination of President Kennedy which occurred during the final rehearsals.

The second play, *The Space Fan*, I rewrote entirely in rehearsals to create a stronger relationship between the two characters. In my earlier version, the characters of Melinda and the Investigator were more abstract, less related. The actors had trouble playing them. Perhaps I lost some of my intent in rehearsals — the characters became a little less fantastic and strange than I imagined them. But they gained in dramatic clarity. The play acquired a form that could be acted.

Ironically, the chief trouble of the rehearsals was a lack of time to discuss changes adequately and to try alternatives. When one is not sufficiently familiar with actors and director, confidence must be gained. Perhaps I gave in too easily at times. Perhaps the actors and director gave in too quickly at other times. Theatre is the art of creative compromise, but compromise can never be creative unless there is a mutual respect among the participants. That respect can be gained only through a long period of trial and error. Ideally, it would be best if a playwright could go on working with the same actors and director for several plays. Then they would know each other thoroughly — there would be more challenge and response. In any case I learned a great deal during the rehearsals at the Guthrie for which I am grateful to the actors, Yvonne McElroy, Charles Cioffi, Jennifer Warren, Gordon Howard, the direc-

10

tor, Edward Payson Call, the technical staff, and the head of the project, Arthur Ballet.

Here in the United States we see faintly the horizon of a new theatre, yet we draw back from that glow. A paradox: we live in a violent society that lacks the will to risk. I remember an advertisement in the New York subway: "Why risk a kiss before breakfast until you're rid of morning mouth?" That's playing it safe to the point where there may be no kiss of endurance. This unwillingness to risk permeates the arts, particularly the theatre. Is there a relationship between the growing violence of our time and the increasing desire to "play it safe"? Without risk there can be no discovery, and without discovery, life becomes a dead center where the instinct for violence festers. Theatre needs risk because it is the most social, the most institutional of the arts. By its nature it tends toward compromise rather than experiment. It is to be hoped there is risk in these plays, as there was in the production of them. They draw from the techniques of the Theatre of the Absurd, although they are far from Absurdist in nature. They seek to explore the highs and lows of the American comic spirit with all of the over- and under-tones of tragic decisions that confront American power today.

JAMES SCHEVILL

San Francisco, California
June 1965

THE SPACE FAN
A Play of Escape

Cast of Characters

MELINDA
INVESTIGATOR

THE SPACE FAN

The setting is a shed in the backyard of Melinda Davis, a space fan. A clutter of unorthodox space equipment is scattered throughout the shed. The chief item of equipment is a large, homemade space panel with switches and knobs that dominates the center of the stage. A roll of tape protrudes from the left side of the panel. As the play begins, Melinda is pacing up and down in front of the panel. The crackling of a space message is heard, high and eerie music. Melinda begins to rush back and forth adjusting various pieces of equipment. An interfering voice is heard over one recalcitrant piece of equipment: "Charlie, you green? Will you pick up an old lady at the corner of Fourth and Main?" *She bangs the piece of equipment impatiently and the voice stops abruptly. Melinda is middle-aged, fantastic, plain-spinsterish, intense, definitely tuned into space. She is dressed in a cap, a colorful jacket, slacks, and tennis shoes. As the crackling of the space message is heard more intensely, she rushes to the space panel and picks up a homemade microphone.*

MELINDA

(*excited and blissful*) Friendship I . . Friendship I . . Come in, please . . All systems go, Commander? . . Roger. Reading you clearly . . Approaching California coast . . Second orbit . . (*pulls off a piece of tape from the space panel, looks at it, and crumples it up*) Deploy balloon for drag experiment . . Inflating . . Up, up . . Thirty inches, beachball size! . . How's the resistance? None? . . Wonderful

15

space . . No resistance . . Have you exercised yet? . . Still flying by wire? . . Careful . . Not too long . . Don't get cocky in your barber chair . . You'll fall behind in your experiments . . You guys all want to wobble the stick . . That's where the fuel goes . . Try your exercises . . The one with the thick rubber band . . (*stretches an imaginary rubber band*) How's the temperature in your suit? . . Up two degrees? . . Watch it! (*checks anxiously on a piece of equipment*) Stop using your rubber exerciser. Drink plenty of water! . . (*she drinks*) Any trouble drinking? . . Good . . Try some food . . (*she eats*) Squeeze it slowly out of the tube . . Check pressure in the capsule . . Look out for the creeps! . . Over Africa now . . You'll hit Spain in a minute . . Get ready for your Spanish broadcast . . (*a touch of Spanish music is heard through the space sounds and her feet kick out instinctively into a dance for a moment; then she rushes to the side of the stage, picks up a long speaking tube, and calls out*) Ground stations, stand by! (*turns back to the microphone*) Fuel consumption is excessive . . Watch it . . Fly manual control . . What's the matter? . . You sound tired . . Can't read you . . Come in, Commander, come in! . . (*then, with relief*) What were you doing? . . Photographing the cloud cover . . Beautiful, huh . . You've never seen anything like it . . Approaching California coast, final orbit . . You've done it, Commander! That's it! (*lets out a cheer*) Ground stations standing by to fire retro-rockets . . You're not going to use the automatic system? . . It's up to you . . You'll fly the capsule into position by manual and fly-by-wire? . . You're sure you can do it? You know how it wobbles . . (*more and more excited*) Check tilt! . . Thirty-four-degree angle to horizon . . (*checks on a slide rule and leans into the. required angle*) Right . . Ready? . . Ignite retro-rockets! (*then, worried*) What's wrong? . . Damn, they're late! . . Fire! . . 1– 2– 3– 4– 5– . . There! . . Thank God . . (*still alarmed*) Five seconds late . . Can't hear you any more . . Re-entry heat's blacked you out . . Calling recovery ship headquarters! . . recovery ship headquarters! . . Retro-rockets fired five seconds late . . Angle of re-entry smaller . . Space ship may land far beyond target area . . Prepare para-medical units! Friendship I . . Friendship I . . Do you read me? . . Come in, Commander . . Wow, what happened to you? . . God, that was a real cliff-hanger . . (*Still listening, she begins to laugh with relief. After the excitement, she sags into a chair downstage. The Investigator, reserved, dogged in steel-rimmed glasses, dressed in a conservative suit and hat, enters and approaches her.*)

INVESTIGATOR

Excuse me . .

MELINDA

(*still excited, hardly conscious of him*) He's down safely and floating in the tub.

INVESTIGATOR

The tub?

MELINDA

The raft in the sea . . (*then, surprised*) What are you doing here?

INVESTIGATOR

Are you Miss Melinda Davis?

MELINDA

Yes . .

INVESTIGATOR

(*showing her his identification card and then putting it away*) I'd like to ask you a few questions if you don't mind . .

MELINDA

I don't mind . . Who are you? (*the Investigator pulls out his identification card again and she reads*) "William Reynolds . . The Bureau of Space Aeronautics." You're an investigator?

INVESTIGATOR

Yes.

MELINDA

(*looking more closely at his photo on the identification card*) It's not a very good likeness . . What can I do for you?

INVESTIGATOR

(*looking around at the cluttered equipment*) We've been having some trouble with interference on restricted frequencies.

MELINDA

That's a shame.

INVESTIGATOR

Some interference perhaps from your equipment. (*stumbles a little over a piece of equipment*)

MELINDA

Oh, I don't believe in interference.

INVESTIGATOR

(*looking around*) I see . . What are you doing with all this equipment?

MELINDA

Listening.

17

INVESTIGATOR

Listening? To what?

MELINDA

To space.

INVESTIGATOR

What do you hear in space?

MELINDA

Messages.

INVESTIGATOR

What kind of messages?

MELINDA

A new language of sounds and music.

INVESTIGATOR

(*suspiciously*) You mean like a code?

MELINDA

I suppose you could call it that. It has its own secrets, its distances.

INVESTIGATOR

(*crossing to a table and opening his briefcase*) I'd like to ask you some personal questions . . (*She helps him out by cleaning various papers and books off the top of the table. Then she picks up a bottle of vodka and offers him a drink.*)

MELINDA

Would you have a little vodka?

INVESTIGATOR

(*stiffly*) No thanks . . Not when I'm working. (*Melinda pours herself a drink. The Investigator fumbles around in his briefcase, disclosing his unfamiliarity with the job. Finally, he pulls out a piece of paper.*) You were born in Canton, Ohio, the only child of a physician, Dr. Ralph Davis . . Your father was all right, member of the Rotary Club, International Order of Odd Fellows . .

MELINDA

Yes, he was the secretary . .

INVESTIGATOR

(*continuing*) In high school you were something of a prodigy and won all sorts of prizes in mathematics, trig- . . It's kind of blurred . .

MELINDA

Trigonometry . . There was no competition then . .

INVESTIGATOR

You won a scholarship to the University of Chicago . . (*looking at the record*) sciences, humanities . . There's no record of your graduating.

MELINDA

I never believed in graduating, just studying.

INVESTIGATOR

How many years did you study?

MELINDA

Ages, happy ages.

INVESTIGATOR

(*looking at the record*) You studied Russian and other foreign languages in addition to the sciences . .

MELINDA

I was a dabbler in everything, I'm afraid.

INVESTIGATOR

After college you became an exchange student. France, Italy, Greece, Russia . .

MELINDA

Greece was lovely . .

INVESTIGATOR

What were you doing in Russia?

MELINDA

I wasn't a student there really, just traveling. I went to see the place where Pushkin died.

INVESTIGATOR

Pushkin?

MELINDA

The poet. He was an impulsive, handsome young man, part-Negro, the idol of the Tsar's court. He married a beautiful, vain woman who had many admirers. Pushkin was terribly jealous. He discovered that his wife was having an affair. He slapped the offender with his glove and challenged him to a duel. Weapons, pistols, were selected. That morning, as the sun rose through the white birch trees outside of St. Petersburg, Pushkin drove in his carriage to the appointed place. Back to back with his enemy, pistols up, they paced off ten steps, turned and fired!

INVESTIGATOR

(*trying to restrain himself but can't*) Pushkin was killed!

MELINDA

Yes, it created a terrible scandal in the court. All of St. Petersburg turned out for the funeral. People were crying in the streets and reciting Pushkin's verses . . (*recites a couple of lines of Pushkin's poetry and toasts Pushkin with her glass*)

INVESTIGATOR

(*trying to get back to the subject*) I see . . When you came back you worked for the government for a short time?

MELINDA

Yes.

INVESTIGATOR

(*looking at the record*) Research Assistant for the Bureau of Weights and Measures . . How long did you work there?

MELINDA

Seven and a half hours.

INVESTIGATOR

Seven and a half hours! That's not even a full day. Why did you quit?

MELINDA

I couldn't stand weighing and measuring. Besides there was an attractive man next to me. He had the terrible habit of clicking his pen as he weighed and measured. I couldn't stand the work or his clicking. I knew there was no possibility of a closer relationship. So I left . . (*goes behind the space panel*)

INVESTIGATOR

(*clicking his pen unconsciously*) I see . . Have you ever had any visitors here?

MELINDA

(*from behind the panel*) No. You're the first one.

INVESTIGATOR

(*getting up*) You've never had any foreign guests?

MELINDA

I've asked them . . They were too far away . . They couldn't come.

INVESTIGATOR

Have you ever been convicted of a crime in a state or federal court?

MELINDA

(*appearing from behind the space panel in a large hat with flowers and a long-necked oilcan in her hand*) Yes . .

INVESTIGATOR

Yes?

MELINDA

(*as they talk, she oils various pieces of equipment*) Parking meter violations. Fifty-one times . .

INVESTIGATOR

Fifty-one times . .

MELINDA

I can't do anything about it. I hate paying money to machines.

INVESTIGATOR

Do you belong to any international organizations?

MELINDA

I correspond with some.

INVESTIGATOR

You're a corresponding member? What organizations?

MELINDA

No, I simply write to them — scientific organizations, mainly the Federation of International Space Seekers . .

INVESTIGATOR

(*checking in a reference book*) F 14 . . Organizations . . Federation — International — Space — Seekers . . That's not on the list . . They publish any books?

MELINDA

Some technical pamphlets on aspects of space — physics, astronomy, mythology . .

INVESTIGATOR

Mythology?

MELINDA

That's when I first became interested in space . . On top of Mount Olympus, the home of the Greek Gods . .

INVESTIGATOR

Greek gods . .

MELINDA

When I was in Greece I studied with Dr. Andreas Paxanopolous, the head of the Paxanopolous High Energy Communications Institute . . He was an unappreciated genius . .

INVESTIGATOR

(*checking his reference book again*) Wait a minute, please . . F 28 . . Scientists . . Paxan-op-o- . . He's not on the list . . What was he doing?

MELINDA

He discovered an old mythological document. It described Zeus wielding his Awful Thunderbolt to correct wrongs and establish laws . . Dr. Paxanopolous was convinced that the thunderstorms on and around Mount Olympus had special psychological effects . . So together we studied the secrets of thunderstorms in many different places . .

21

INVESTIGATOR

Yeah? . . What happened to this Dr. Paxanopolous?

MELINDA

He died one day in a tragic accident. He fell from an oak tree during a storm . . It was one of the sacred oak trees whose leaves the priests used to interpret the thunderbolt messages from Olympus . . (*reads a message in Greek reverently and toasts Paxanopolous with her glass*)

INVESTIGATOR

I see . . When you came back from Greece you began to build equipment to continue your interest in space . . Would you mind showing me some of your equipment?

MELINDA

Not at all . . (*goes behind the panel and comes out in her working cap to lead him to a machine downstage*) This is designed to sort out the qualities of space sounds much as you might hear different instruments, different ranges, in the orchestra . . I'll pull the switch for the High Range . . (*She does so and listens. The Investigator strains and can't hear anything.*)

INVESTIGATOR

(*shaking his head*) I don't hear anything.

MELINDA

(*explaining*) It's too high a frequency for the normal ear to appreciate . . I've trained myself . . (*looks at him skeptically*) We'll move down a little. I'll try for middle messages . . (*pulls another switch and looks at him with growing resignation and listens a moment*) Too bad . . Nothing in the Middle Ranges . . Down we go, down, nearer to the earth. (*kneels beside him*) The Lower Ranges . . Only two thousand miles above us in space . . (*pulls another switch*) Listen! . . (*a low, soft, gurgling sound comes out*)

INVESTIGATOR

(*smiling suddenly*) Hey, somebody ordered a cab! (*Melinda bangs on the piece of equipment*) I hear something now! (*the sound stops abruptly*) It's gone!

MELINDA

(*explaining*) The messages of space are very brief . . You must train yourself to catch them quickly as the eye catches the swoop of a bird. (*leads him over to another panel with some handles and levers*)

INVESTIGATOR

(*cautiously but more and more interested*) What does this machine do?

MELINDA

It sends up flights of tiny electronic ears to record space messages . . They fly through the air like arrows of light at twice the speed of sound . . Then they hover in space . .

INVESTIGATOR

(*trying to calculate on his fingers*) Twice the speed of sound . .

MELINDA

If you don't mind helping me, it's easier to operate with four hands than two.

INVESTIGATOR

I'll be glad to help.

MELINDA

(*gives him some heavy earphones to put on, which tend to deafen him, so she shouts her instructions louder and louder*) Just hold this lever (*points*) with both hands . . I'll count to three and pull . .

INVESTIGATOR

Pull? . . Right . . (*gives her a thumbs-up signal and bends tensely to his duty*)

MELINDA

(*loudly*) I'll be on these switches over here. (*crosses to the panel*) Ready?

INVESTIGATOR

Ready . .

MELINDA

1– 2– 3– PULL! (*He pulls on the count of two and the lever comes out. He walks over and holds it up apologetically to Melinda just as she is about to command "Pull!"*) I'm sorry . . It doesn't seem to work to-day . . Short circuit in the wiring someplace probably . . You can see why it's only the equipment of a fan . .

INVESTIGATOR

A what?

MELINDA

A space fan . .

INVESTIGATOR

A space fan?

MELINDA

That's right.

INVESTIGATOR

(*laughing with relief*) That puts a different light on things.

MELINDA

What kind of light?

23

INVESTIGATOR

(*smiling*) You know, they thought possibly . .

MELINDA

They thought I was subversive . .

INVESTIGATOR

(*protesting and justifying them*) No, but they can't afford to take chances when it's a matter of security. A fan may be eccentric, but he's normal. A fan is perfectly all right.

MELINDA

Are you calling me eccentric?

INVESTIGATOR

Of course not. I'm a fan like you. A baseball fan.

MELINDA

I suppose there is a distant similarity. But some fans have more ambition, more endurance. The quality of endurance is often the test of the real fan.

INVESTIGATOR

Have you ever sat through a twenty-six-inning game on an empty stomach? That takes quite a bit of endurance from the crowd. But they're always friendly.

MELINDA

A crowd may be composed of fans, but it's not the same thing. The real fan learns to be alone. He has a passion to follow. When the crowd moves in, the pleasure goes out.

INVESTIGATOR

(*dubiously*) I don't know. It's more fun, sharing.

MELINDA

More fun, private.

INVESTIGATOR

More fun, sharing.

MELINDA

(*making a game out of it, insisting*) More fun, *private*.

INVESTIGATOR

Sharing.

MELINDA

Private.

INVESTIGATOR

(*doggedly*) Sharing.

MELINDA

(*taunting him*) Private. You're a socialist!

INVESTIGATOR

(*turning away indignantly*) I hate socialism! Before I go, I'd like to ask you one more question . .

MELINDA

Aren't you a fan of anything besides baseball?

INVESTIGATOR

Well . .

MELINDA

What is it?

INVESTIGATOR

The Civil War.

MELINDA

(*with delight*) You're a history fan!

INVESTIGATOR

(*cautiously*) I'm just a beginner really. I haven't told them at the office.

MELINDA

Why not?

INVESTIGATOR

(*uncomfortably*) They don't like us to have too much of an aesthetic interest.

MELINDA

(*still delighted with the discovery of his fanship*) You belong to all those Civil War book clubs?

INVESTIGATOR

Well, a few . .

MELINDA

And you visit the battlefields!

INVESTIGATOR

(*confessing*) Sometimes . . in summer vacations . .

MELINDA

(*pressing him*) Every summer?

INVESTIGATOR

When I can persuade my wife . .

MELINDA

Your wife?

INVESTIGATOR

(*bitterly*) She doesn't like the Civil War.

MELINDA

(*sympathetically*) That's too bad.

INVESTIGATOR

She says the Civil War is out of date. What's that got to do with the facts of it?

MELINDA

Nothing.

INVESTIGATOR

(*confessing indignantly*) Last night she said the Civil War was boring. She won't go there again this summer. It's too hot in those places for her. She sweats. She can't sleep. She complains about the insects . .

MELINDA

Heat and insects are small deterrents for a real fan.

INVESTIGATOR

(*bitterly*) I've tried to make her one. I've taken her to Shiloh and Gettysburg and Chancellorsville and Bull Run . . I showed her the hills of concealment . . I showed her how they attacked down the slopes . . I showed her the traps in the valleys . . I even showed her the bugle that sounded General Lee's last attack!

MELINDA

I'm sorry.

INVESTIGATOR

(*pulling himself back to the task at hand*) Well, I'd like to ask you one more question . .

MELINDA

Would you rather have Robert E. Lee or Dwight Eisenhower for a general?

INVESTIGATOR

(*protesting*) You can't compare the two. Lee was a cavalry general, not an administrator. Now you take a modern war, it's all over the world. You got all kinds of countries, languages, and weapons to deal with. So you need an administrator like Eisenhower. But Lee, he was a real tactician in the field. He didn't need memoranda and forms and files and . .

MELINDA

I can see you prefer the past . .

INVESTIGATOR

Who said I prefer the past? I'm perfectly content with the present.

MELINDA

Perfectly?

INVESTIGATOR

There is no such thing as perfectly.

MELINDA
There is in space, in the infinity of it.

INVESTIGATOR
Infinity is too much.

MELINDA
Earth is too little.

INVESTIGATOR
Isn't that escaping?

MELINDA
If there is a trap, one has the right to escape.

INVESTIGATOR
I guess so . . Now about my question . .

MELINDA
What are we spending all that money for to reach the moon?

INVESTIGATOR
Scientific research, of course. Please . .

MELINDA
I'll never get to the moon as long as your engineers and mathematicians continue to be so careless.

INVESTIGATOR
(*protesting*) They aren't careless. They're very responsible people . .

MELINDA
Why did they leave a hyphen out of the mathematics on that last Venus shot?

INVESTIGATOR
(*bewildered*) Hyphen?

MELINDA
(*pointing*) Some careless mathematician left a hyphen out of the computer's instructions. This caused it to transmit incorrect steering signals to the spacecraft . .

INVESTIGATOR
(*dazed*) You mean a hyphen . .

MELINDA
(*pushes him downstage into the position of the computer and becomes the spacecraft as she illustrates*) When ground control loses radio contact with a spacecraft antenna, that's an emergency! The antenna is very sensitive. (*imitating the spacecraft antenna, she begins to demonstrate with her hands and arms*) Immediately, the antenna begins to maneuver the spacecraft in an up-and-down "searching" movement. Search! Search, until contact is re-established . .

27

INVESTIGATOR

(*impressed*) That's amazing.

MELINDA

(*excited, continuing*) Automatic radio signals are sent out from the spacecraft. They tell the computer on the ground that this veering, this up-and-down searching movement, is taking place. The hyphen is then fed carefully into the computer and tells the spacecraft not to worry.

INVESTIGATOR

(*fascinated*) You mean a hyphen says don't worry?

MELINDA

Exactly. The omission of the hyphen caused the spacecraft to send out a series of frenzied signals . .

INVESTIGATOR

(*crying out*) What was it signaling?

MELINDA

(*crossing with frenzied signals*) Find me! Find me! Correct my course!

INVESTIGATOR

(*following, intrigued*) Marvelous!

MELINDA

(*sadly, seeing the spacecraft lost above*) But it was no use. The spacecraft was lost.

INVESTIGATOR

(*dazed, echoing her mood, staring up at the destruction*) Because of a hyphen . .

MELINDA

(*vehemently*) Yes, because of carelessness in leaving out a hyphen, eighteen and a half million dollars of spacecraft bound for Venus was blown up in the air.

INVESTIGATOR

(*muttering*) Computers are murder.

MELINDA

You can't blame the computers. It's the people who feed them. A computer must be fed properly, with the proper diet of language, a language never before published in books. Even today, these languages are available only in out-of-the-way places.

INVESTIGATOR

What places?

MELINDA

Mimeographed places, handwritten places . . I wrote to people . .

Many of them answered. They sent me all sorts of scribbled things . . And I scribbled things back to them. Then I began to build my own equipment . .

INVESTIGATOR

(*suddenly remembering his duty as an investigator*) Well, you'll have to be careful about interference . . But I'm sure everything will be all right if you just give me your papers . . Then I can explain about your being a space fan . .

MELINDA

(*staring at him*) You want my papers . .

INVESTIGATOR

It's the easiest way to convince them . .

MELINDA

I don't have any papers.

INVESTIGATOR

I mean the scribbled things you mentioned.

MELINDA

They're only fragments, jottings on backs of envelopes, menus, programs, any odd piece of paper to hand. Most of them aren't even scientific. You couldn't read the handwriting.

INVESTIGATOR

We've got special people for that.

MELINDA

I don't have many left. I throw them away. I don't like a clutter.

INVESTIGATOR

I'll just take what you have. That will satisfy them.

MELINDA

Why should I satisfy them? I give you my word. The scribblings are un-important.

INVESTIGATOR

I'm sorry . . I can't take anybody's word.

MELINDA

You can never trust anyone?

INVESTIGATOR

That would be the end of the investigations.

MELINDA

Never?

INVESTIGATOR

Never.

MELINDA

Never is terribly severe.

INVESTIGATOR

(*defensively*) Maybe a little at first . . You get used to it . . You'd be surprised at how much people tell you is incorrect.

MELINDA

False or incorrect?

INVESTIGATOR

What's the difference?

MELINDA

False is a lie. Incorrect can be a trick of the imagination, don't you think?

INVESTIGATOR

It all comes to the same thing — wrong information.

MELINDA

(*bitterly*) I would hate to live in your world of wrong information. (*She looks at him with scorn and goes off behind the space panel. The Investigator, trying again to fulfill the demands of his job, begins to snoop around the panel as he talks. He pulls out the roll of tape, tries to stuff it under his coat, and discovers this is impossible.*)

INVESTIGATOR

(*loudly*) That's what they taught us to do in our training program. It was full of wrong information. Every teacher had a different method of giving us wrong information. We had to find out the facts.

MELINDA

(*ironically, from behind the panel*) They must have been excellent teachers.

INVESTIGATOR

(*pulls out the tape as he speaks. Melinda appears in a mask above the space panel, looking down at him. He turns away and opens his briefcase, intending to put the tape in it. Behind his back, she pulls the tape back through the panel. He turns around just in time to see the tape disappearing as she reels it in. He jumps for the end of the tape, but it's gone. He turns back and fumbles with the briefcase on his knees.*) I hated them . . My wife made me take the course . . She wanted me to get a white-collar job . . The teachers were always trying to trap us . . One gave the same lecture over and over again . . It sounded true, but it was always a little wrong . . Then he'd test us to see if we caught the error . . He'd say: "If you want to be an investigator, you have to find the one clear, dry place in a sea of mud." (*Melinda, in the mask of the Witch Queen of Space, pounces in on him.*)

MELINDA

(*mocking him as she darts around him*) I'm the Witch Queen of Space!
. . I jam your radio transmission . . I hover over your satellites . .

INVESTIGATOR

(*steps toward her*) Come on, this is no time . .

MELINDA

(*zooming away from him*) I fly away from you on my space scooter . .
The Northern Lights shine between us . . I dazzle your eyes with shoot-
ing stars . .

INVESTIGATOR

(*impatiently*) Don't fool around. I need those papers . .

MELINDA

High up in the Milky Way I build my palace out of Moonshine . .

INVESTIGATOR

Stop it, please . .

MELINDA

I use my Cosmic Ray vision . . The Earthmen disintegrate in their
lies . .

INVESTIGATOR

(*pleading*) I never lied to you! This is my first case. Please, where'd you
hide the papers . .

MELINDA

Look! Where's your space vision? (*points to the back of the stage*) The
papers are hidden on Planet X . .

INVESTIGATOR

(*going in that direction*) You mean back there?

MELINDA

(*mockingly, drawing him downstage*) Gone! . . Someone has moved
them to sanctuary . . Look for them in the third orbit . . (*points at a
drawer*)

INVESTIGATOR

(*moving*) You mean in that drawer? (*goes to the drawer and opens it:
nothing*)

MELINDA

Empty! . . Stolen by the Witch Queen of Space! (*holds up a box high
above her head*)

INVESTIGATOR

Are they in that box? . . Please give them to me . . I'll see that you're
cleared . . I'll tell them that you're all right . .

31

MELINDA

(*jumping on a table and holding the box high above her head*) The Witch Queen of Space holds high the Treasure Chest!

INVESTIGATOR

Give it to me!

MELINDA

The Witch Queen swoops down . . (*swoops down*) and surrenders the Treasure Chest . . (*jams the box into his stomach and he recoils*)

INVESTIGATOR

Thanks . . I'm sorry . .

MELINDA

(*keeping after him*) Fly! Fly away before she claws you!

INVESTIGATOR

(*retreating*) I won't forget this . .

MELINDA

Fly!

INVESTIGATOR

(*getting his hat and briefcase*) I'll tell them you're only a space fan . .

MELINDA

Fly, Master Thief!

INVESTIGATOR

(*as he goes off, pursued by her*) They won't bother you again . .

MELINDA

Fly! (*She chases him off. He hurries out uncomfortably, clutching the box as though it hurts him physically. Melinda stares after him for a long moment. Then she takes off her mask. Her loneliness is apparent. She turns on several switches and moves slowly toward the space panel. The high, eerie music of space is heard. Taking up the microphone at the space panel, she begins to speak. Her soliloquy builds to a high, fantastic intensity.*) Come in, Commander . . You read me? . . All systems Go! . . Blast off! . . Soar, spacecraft! . . Roar like the Saturn rocket for the moon . . Throw out all the earthbound equipment . . You can't come home again . . Float in that weightlessness . . Light as a feather in the winds . . Dead center on course . . Accelerating over Africa . . Approaching Greece . . Come in, Paxanopolous, come in . . Messages sing over your grave . . You taught me about the gods . . This investigator was your Master Thief, your God of Commerce and the Market . . He was your Guide of the Dead . . Why did you send him? . . To bring me to you? . . He's gone now . . We're free . . Rendezvous point coming up . . Spaceships moving together for final voyage . . Equipment working perfectly . . Slow trajectory of approach . . Nearer, nearer . . Touching . . Not even a bump . . So gentle . . Here we are, Paxanopolous, alone in space . . I hear your messages at last . . I hear them sing! . . Do you hear mine? . . I send you the music of space! (*She listens raptly to the high, eerie sounds and music of space. The Investigator has returned at the end of her speech and is also listening. He is angry and tense because he has discovered that the box is empty. His suspicions grow as he hears the equipment working. Finally, he breaks in.*)

INVESTIGATOR

(*rushes to the space panel and takes the microphone away from her*) You tricked me! (*a garbled, protesting Chinese voice is heard and the Investigator says*) That's all right, Mr. Wong. I think we've found the trouble. (*speaks tensely into the microphone*) If anyone is listening, ignore messages from the home of Melinda Davis, 4269 Mira Loma Street! (*hangs up the microphone and rushes around among the equipment, turning off switches haphazardly, and shouting his accusations at Melinda*) Do you realize what you've done? You were responsible for the complaints about interference . . You've been interfering with the lives of other people! Do you know what's happened? . . A Chinese restaurant with radio-dispatched delivery service sent twenty-seven orders of Moo Goo Gai Pan to an empty parking lot! . . Tickets to the church bazaar were delivered to the football stadium! Truckloads of newspapers ended up in a mortuary! . . And that's only local interference . . Who knows what you've done to the international situation? . . And you know damn well there aren't any papers in this box! (*slams the box down*) Now I want your papers! . . Give me your papers! . . Where are they?

MELINDA

(*staring at him calmly*) I'm glad you came back . . You're just in time for the burning.

INVESTIGATOR

What burning?

MELINDA

(*disappears behind the space panel*) I'm going to burn all my papers.

INVESTIGATOR

(*following her around*) You can't do that! It's against the law to burn evidence! You'll never get away with it! (*she reappears again with a large incinerator*) What are you going to do with that?

MELINDA

My burning machine . . You can be a witness . .

INVESTIGATOR

I can't be a witness! . . It's my duty to stop you . .

MELINDA

(*proceeding*) Stop me then . . (*He takes up the incinerator, cradling it protectively in his arms. She takes it away from him and puts it down firmly.*) All you have to do is watch . .

INVESTIGATOR

I can't watch . . I've never watched before . .

MELINDA

Turn your face away . . You won't see the beginning . .

INVESTIGATOR

(*turns his face away and begins to plead again*) Look, you know it isn't my fault . . I didn't want this job . . Give me the papers . . (*she doesn't answer, as she gathers some tattered papers for burning*) It's not safe to burn here . . There are fire laws! . . Please don't burn those papers . .

MELINDA

(*begins to burn her tattered scribblings*) Poor scribblings, preparations, fragments, there's never any completion for you . . I jot you down as numbers, equations . . I line you up as perfect forms, but there are no perfect forms . . Only changing forms . . (*reads a scribbling*) Notes for a London conference: "The tea is lukewarm." (*She lights it with a match and throws it into the incinerator. The lights go down into an increasingly red glow for the burning scene. She picks up an old cardboard menu and reads*) Scribbled on the back of a Parisian menu: "What is the power of thrust necessary for escape?"

INVESTIGATOR

Escape?

MELINDA

(*continuing with the burning ritual*) Burn, symbols! Fly into space! Burn into ashes! Cremate, consume, destroy! (*goes behind the panel and comes back with more papers*) Notes from Russia . .

INVESTIGATOR

No!

MELINDA

Tsarist Russia! Pushkin's vision for the future! (*laughs bitterly and drops the papers into the incinerator; picks up an old envelope*) On a Roman envelope: "Visited the Keats museum . . What a small space to die in" . . Burn the past! Let the future of space glow in the flames! . . (*rushes across the stage to pick up another pile of scribblings*) Asia, too, postcard of a Japanese Zen temple . . (*reads the postcard*) "What is the sound of one hand clapping?" Burn! (*throws the postcard in*) The sound of silence, eternal space . . (*turns to the Investigator*) How can you report unless you participate? . . Do you want to be nothing except an investigator?

INVESTIGATOR

(*uneasily*) Don't be silly . . You can't fool me again . .

MELINDA

Can't you see? There won't be any more interference from the equipment.

INVESTIGATOR

I told you I can't take your word.

MELINDA

You don't have to . . Help me burn . . Then we'll take care of the equipment.

INVESTIGATOR

OK . . (*she leads him over to the incinerator and gives him some papers*)

MELINDA

You know they're of no value now . . Travel notes, musings, old formulas . .

INVESTIGATOR

(*slowly*) Yeah, there's nothing here . . (*reads a scribbling on a postcard*) "How do you like this view of Rio de Janeiro? The sand is so white . . If it were only possible to travel forever" . . (*drops it in automatically and stares at it*)

MELINDA

You see? Long live travel!

INVESTIGATOR

(*automatically*) Long live travel . .

MELINDA

Long live travel to the Civil War sites! (*she throws in some papers and they both circle around the incinerator slowly*)

INVESTIGATOR

(*getting into the spirit*) Long live travel to Gettysburg! (*throws in a scribbling*) Long live Shiloh! (*throws in another scribbling*) Long live Bull Run! (*another scribbling goes in*)

MELINDA

(*laughing as she reads an old postcard*) Postcard from Paris . . "Dear

35

Mother: Why are you such a Puritan that I can't even enjoy Paris?"
(*throws it in*)

INVESTIGATOR

(*laughing with her as he reads an old letter*) How about this one? . .
"As a girl I was always better with facts than boys" . . (*They laugh. As
he drops it in, she cries out*)

MELINDA

Puritan mothers!

INVESTIGATOR

The family is dead!

MELINDA

Burn the past!

INVESTIGATOR

Burn the past!

MELINDA

(*rushes over, gets her large handbag, and cries out*) Burn the present!
(*begins to rummage in the handbag*)

INVESTIGATOR

(*staring at her*) Burn the present?

MELINDA

(*pulling some papers out of the handbag*) Charge accounts . . Last letters from stupid relatives . . (*throws them in*)

INVESTIGATOR

(*impulsively reaches for his wallet and begins to take out various items*)
Detergent housewives who hate the Civil War! (*throws in a photo of his
wife*)

MELINDA

Bank stubs . . savings book . . (*throws them in, as the burning ritual
builds in intensity*)

INVESTIGATOR

Identification card with fingerprints and photo! (*throws it in*)

MELINDA

(*laughing*) It wasn't a very good likeness anyway! . . Life insurance
policy . . Guaranteed payment after death . . (*she drops it in and
they circle gaily around the incinerator*)

INVESTIGATOR

Social Security . . (*drops it in*)

MELINDA

Hospital safety plan . . (*drops it in*)

36

INVESTIGATOR

Civil Service . . (*drops it in*)

MELINDA

Charity donations . . (*throws them in*)

INVESTIGATOR

Investigator Club membership . . (*throws it in*)

MELINDA

Parking meter violations . . (*throws them in*)

INVESTIGATOR

(*caught up in the frenzy, throws in his wallet*) Burn!

MELINDA

(*emptying the rest of the contents of her handbag*) Burn!

INVESTIGATOR

(*tearing off his coat compulsively and stuffing it in*) Burn!

MELINDA

(*stuffing in her handbag*) Escape!

INVESTIGATOR

(*echoing her*) Escape! (*panting, they stare at the flames in the incinerator*)

MELINDA

(*looking at her empty hands*) They're all gone. I'm sorry . . There aren't any more . .

INVESTIGATOR

(*dully, still echoing her*) Gone . .

MELINDA

Would it help if I promise to save them again for next time?

INVESTIGATOR

(*pulling himself together*) There won't be a next time.

MELINDA

There are only next times. I hope they won't make it too difficult for you.

INVESTIGATOR

(*mechanically*) I hope they won't make it too difficult for *you*.

MELINDA

Perhaps I can help. I can show you something that might make it easier for you.

INVESTIGATOR

It doesn't matter.

MELINDA

(*almost timidly*) I'd like to show it to you. All you have to do is put it on.

INVESTIGATOR

Put what on?

MELINDA

(*goes behind the space panel and brings out a helmet*) A helmet.

INVESTIGATOR

What helmet?

MELINDA

A space helmet.

INVESTIGATOR

(*backing away*) Where'd you get that?

MELINDA

It's mine. One day I would like to give it a real test. Try it on.

INVESTIGATOR

I don't think I'd better.

MELINDA

I'll put mine on. We can tune in to each other.

INVESTIGATOR

No thanks. It won't be necessary.

MELINDA

You were making such progress in your investigation. Your report will be incomplete.

INVESTIGATOR

(*reluctantly*) All right. I'll do it. For the report.

MELINDA

For your real work, your real play, for the sacredness of investigation. Relax now . . You'll receive messages through space . . Through the clarity of space . . Weightless messages . . A new clarity and lightness of language . . Polished and pure . . Beyond people . . Beyond confused emotions . . Beyond the force of brutal gravity . . You'll hear the peace of space . . (*a woman's voice is heard singing offstage*)

VOICE

> The shapes our searching arms
>   make in the empty air
>   are women's bodies
> That when the wind and rain
>   possess our sight
> We have that grace to touch,
> Those white shapes to know,
>   and keep a sanity for love.

Slowly, the lights are lowered. From here to the end of the play, the mood is a measured, poignant dance to the high woodwind or elec-

THE SPACE FAN

tronic music. The two voices are heard only on tape. The effect is of communication over a tremendous distance, of a strange, inevitable separation, although they are really very close together.

MELINDA

Can you hear me, Mr. Investigator? Can you hear me?

INVESTIGATOR

I hear you perfectly.

MELINDA

Perfectly?

INVESTIGATOR

Perfectly . . Funny, I've never used that word before.

MELINDA

Watch out. You'll become a space fan, too.

INVESTIGATOR

I feel as if I'm floating.

MELINDA

Higher . . Higher . . You are floating . . In weightlessness . .

INVESTIGATOR

Floating . .

MELINDA

Lie down . . (*he lies down*) Move your arms and legs . . (*he does so*) Raise your feet in the air . . (*he raises his feet in his ordinary brown street shoes*) Your heavy flying boots weigh nothing . . How does that feel?

INVESTIGATOR

Wonderful. No effort at all.

MELINDA

Your life is not just vertical any more. It's horizontal.

INVESTIGATOR

Horizontal is marvelous.

MELINDA

Do you feel the difference? Vertical is a rigid skyscraper.

INVESTIGATOR

Horizontal is a cloud of comfort.

MELINDA

Now you're beginning your space metaphors.

INVESTIGATOR

Horizontal is beyond heaven.

MELINDA

Good . .

39

INVESTIGATOR

Horizontal is the endless glitter of stars, infinite horizons . .

MELINDA

Again!

INVESTIGATOR

Horizontal is the moon of your eyes.

MELINDA

(*gaily*) Again!

INVESTIGATOR

I love space. I love the moon of your eyes. I love you horizontally.

MELINDA

Try to lift your arms. (*he stands up and stretches his arms up*) Higher
. . Higher . . What are you reaching for?

INVESTIGATOR

A world invisible, star beyond star.

MELINDA

Are there any people there?

INVESTIGATOR

I don't see any.

MELINDA

Can you feel any?

INVESTIGATOR

Nothing but stars, cold stars, burning stars.

MELINDA

Time is space, eternal distance.

INVESTIGATOR

It's like a dance. I never danced before.

MELINDA

Neither did I.

INVESTIGATOR

Will you dance with me? (*High woodwinds, flutes and oboes, or high,
eerie electronic sounds until the end of the play. They dance a short,
formal, poignant dance of a meeting that is separation, and a separation
that is meeting.*)

MELINDA

Do you hear music?

INVESTIGATOR

Is that what it's called?

MELINDA

The music of space.

40

THE SPACE FAN

INVESTIGATOR
I never heard such melodies before.

MELINDA
Look out. Look down. Look up. (*he does so*) What do you see?

INVESTIGATOR
Distance. Eternal distance.

MELINDA
Look at your watch.

INVESTIGATOR
It's stopped.

MELINDA
What time is it?

INVESTIGATOR
No time. Time has stopped.

MELINDA
Time is space.

INVESTIGATOR
I can see God now.

MELINDA
What does he look like?

INVESTIGATOR
God is space. (*Silence. The music continues, very high, very distant.*) For the first time in my life, I feel that I've become a real investigator.

MELINDA
You *are* an Investigator.

INVESTIGATOR
(*exultantly*) You're a Space Fan. (*then whispering*) I love you . .

MELINDA
(*whispering*) I love you in space.

INVESTIGATOR
Will you dance with me again, my love?

MELINDA
Yes, my darling. (*They begin to dance slowly, gravely. The lights dim further.*)

INVESTIGATOR
If we could only *never* return to earth . .

MELINDA
That may be possible some day . . (*They continue to dance. As they dance, the woman's voice is heard offstage singing.*)

41

JAMES SCHEVILL

VOICE

> The shapes our searching arms
>   make in the empty air
>   are women's bodies
> That when the wind and rain
>   possess our sight
> We have that grace to touch,
> Those white shapes to know,
>   and keep a sanity for love.

The lights dim slowly to black out.

THE END

THE MASTER
A Play of Commitment

Cast of Characters

THE MASTER
THE CANDIDATE
THE ASSISTANT

THE MASTER

As the lights come up slowly, percussion music is heard played by the Assistant, dressed in a black sweater and pants, who sits on a stand at the rear of the stage. A woman's voice is heard singing:

> The shapes our searching arms
>   make in the empty air
>   are women's bodies
> That when the wind and rain
>   possess our sight
> We have that grace to touch,
> Those white shapes to know,
>   and keep a sanity for love.

The Master and the Candidate enter, cross the stage to the beat of percussion music, bow to each other, and then bow to the audience.

THE MASTER

(*smoking a cigar*) I am the Master.

THE CANDIDATE

I am the Candidate.

> *The Master is dressed in a white robe, the Candidate in a red, white and blue robe. The Master is a heavyset, imposing man, while the Candidate is an attractive young woman, aggressive, yet romantically naive. After the introductions, she sits on a chair at the front of the stage, waiting and preening herself nervously for the examination. The Master goes to his table and chair upstage at stage right. He signals the Assistant who brings a tray of cigars and cigarettes which the Master arranges carefully on the table. Finally, the Master gestures. A bell is rung by the Assistant and the Candidate moves toward the table.*

45

The Master motions to her to be seated. He begins to question her, checking her record sheet before him casually, feeling her out.

THE MASTER

Name?

THE CANDIDATE

Diana Johnson.

THE MASTER

Last name first, please.

THE CANDIDATE

Johnson, Diana.

THE MASTER

Rank?

THE CANDIDATE

Candidate.

THE MASTER

For the degree of mastery. Specific or general?

THE CANDIDATE

General.

THE MASTER

Including religion, physical education, science, war, and the humanities?

THE CANDIDATE

Yes, sir.

THE MASTER

Your Candidate number, please.

THE CANDIDATE

452691 . .

THE MASTER

Good. Do you smoke?

THE CANDIDATE

Please.

THE MASTER

(*unrolling a sign with a vivid illustration and the warning "Smoking Causes Cancer!"*) Help yourself. (*watches her closely as she selects a cigarette, lights it for her*) How many cigarettes do you smoke a day?

THE CANDIDATE

It's hard to say. Half a pack maybe. More if I'm studying.

THE MASTER

It isn't safe. Don't you believe in statistics?

THE CANDIDATE

It depends on the statistics.

THE MASTER
What statistics?

THE CANDIDATE
(*cautiously*) It depends on the relationship.

THE MASTER
On what relationship?

THE CANDIDATE
What the statistics relate to. Objects or subjects.

THE MASTER
You believe in the statistics of subjects?

THE CANDIDATE
Only objects can be measured.

THE MASTER
(*getting up*) Isn't a cigarette an object?

THE CANDIDATE
Yes, but the person smoking is a subject. Pleasure can ignore danger.

THE MASTER
You smoke for pleasure to ignore danger?

THE CANDIDATE
Sometimes. Mainly I smoke because other people smoke.

THE MASTER
(*crossing to her*) You are smoking because I am smoking?

THE CANDIDATE
Yes, sir.

THE MASTER
Exchange smokes. (*gives her his cigar, and takes her cigarette*) You are smoking because I am smoking?

THE CANDIDATE
Yes, sir.

THE MASTER
Is the pleasure greater or lesser?

THE CANDIDATE
Lesser.

THE MASTER
Why? Because of the cigar?

THE CANDIDATE
No, sir. Because I merely smoke to keep other people company.

THE MASTER
You are a conformist?

THE CANDIDATE

Yes, much of the time.

THE MASTER

You think it's always bad to be a conformist?

THE CANDIDATE

(*cautiously*) Sometimes.

THE MASTER

It is bad to be obedient to parents?

THE CANDIDATE

No.

THE MASTER

If you are always obedient to parents, you are a conformist?

THE CANDIDATE

No . . Yes . .

THE MASTER

It is bad to be a conformist?

THE CANDIDATE

Yes and no.

THE MASTER

How much yes and how much no?

THE CANDIDATE

Half and half.

THE MASTER

Instant?

THE CANDIDATE

No, slow. The right balance . . It is hard to tell . .

THE MASTER

Do you believe in Instant Conformity?

THE CANDIDATE

Yes and no.

THE MASTER

(*ordering*) Lie down on your back . . I said lie down on your back!

THE CANDIDATE

(*getting up*) Yes . . (*changing her mind*) and no . .

THE MASTER

You won't obey my order?

THE CANDIDATE

(*unsure*) Is it an order or a question?

THE MASTER

(*ordering, and leaving no doubt by the tone of his voice that it is an order*)

Lie down on your back! (*the Candidate lies down on her back*) You are a conformist.

THE CANDIDATE

I obey orders.

THE MASTER

Lift your feet in the air. (*she does so*) Do the bicycle . . Higher . . Faster. (*she begins to do the bicycle exercise*) Circulation is good for the brain. Enough. Stop exercising. You are a conformist.

THE CANDIDATE

(*panting a little, she stops*) I obey orders.

THE MASTER

Spit on the floor. (*she does so*) Wipe it up.

THE CANDIDATE

How?

THE MASTER

Use your hand. (*slowly, she does so*) You are an Instant Conformist.

THE CANDIDATE

(*bitterly*) I obey orders.

THE MASTER

You hate me?

THE CANDIDATE

Yes and no.

THE MASTER

Kiss me. (*slowly, she goes to him and gives him a short kiss*)

THE CANDIDATE

The kiss of obedience. I obey orders.

THE MASTER

Kiss me again. (*she gives him a short, fierce kiss as he blows a puff of cigar smoke in her face*) Describe the kiss.

THE CANDIDATE

The kiss of hate.

THE MASTER

Is that what you think of a kiss? What is a kiss?

THE CANDIDATE

The highest gift of love.

THE MASTER

Then hate is never part of love?

THE CANDIDATE

Yes and no.

THE MASTER

Give me the kiss of love. (*she gives him a passionate kiss*) Describe the kiss.

THE CANDIDATE

The kiss of love.

THE MASTER

Then love can be a greater affirmation?

THE CANDIDATE

Yes and no.

THE MASTER

Yes and no is a cliché!

THE CANDIDATE

Yes.

THE MASTER

Every cliché is bad.

THE CANDIDATE

No.

THE MASTER

Yes and no is an equivocation. American power does not permit equivocation.

THE CANDIDATE

Yes, sir.

THE MASTER

American power says Yes.

THE CANDIDATE

(*softly*) Yes.

THE MASTER

A loud, affirmative *Yes!*

THE CANDIDATE

Yes.

THE MASTER

In an optimistic, smiling tone!

THE CANDIDATE

(*in an optimistic, smiling tone*) *Yes!*

THE MASTER

Not just once, but several times.

THE CANDIDATE

Yes! Yes! Yes! Yes! Yes!

THE MASTER

Even in the midst of tragedy . .

THE MASTER

THE CANDIDATE

Yes!

THE MASTER

In an optimistic, smiling tone . .

THE CANDIDATE

Yes!

THE MASTER

Yes and no are un-American.

THE CANDIDATE

Yes.

THE MASTER

Yes and no are Zen Buddhism.

THE CANDIDATE

Yes.

THE MASTER

Screw Zen Buddhism!

THE CANDIDATE

Yes.

THE MASTER

The West belongs to Jesus Christ.

THE CANDIDATE

Yes.

THE MASTER

And to the President of the United States.

THE CANDIDATE

Yes.

THE MASTER

And, above all, to the Constitution of the United States.

THE CANDIDATE

Yes.

THE MASTER

No is unconstitutional.

THE CANDIDATE

Yes.

THE MASTER

You will never again say No.

THE CANDIDATE

No . . Yes. (*the Assistant brings a container of coffee with a lid on it and takes the lid off carefully*)

THE MASTER

Take a coffee break. (*the tempo, which has built up rapidly, slows suddenly*)

THE CANDIDATE

(*accepting the coffee*) Thank you, Master.

THE MASTER

Peace is perfect.

THE CANDIDATE

(*echoing him*) Peace is perfect.

THE MASTER

Take a sip. (*she does so*) Pass it to me. (*she gives it to him and he takes a sip*) Peace is perfect. (*he hands it back to her and she takes a sip*)

THE CANDIDATE

Peace is perfect.

THE MASTER

Peace passeth all understanding.

THE CANDIDATE

Yes.

THE MASTER

(*pushing her on*) Peace is beyond all reason.

THE CANDIDATE

Yes.

THE MASTER

Take another sip. (*she takes a sip*) Hand it to me. (*she hands it to him and he takes a sip*) We are at peace. Blessed be the peacemakers.

THE CANDIDATE

Blessed be the peacemakers.

THE MASTER

(*rising and reflecting*) But peace is a difficult word.

THE CANDIDATE

Yes.

THE MASTER

Put on the uniform. (*the Candidate takes off her robe and puts on the officer's jacket*) What rank are you?

THE CANDIDATE

Second lieutenant.

THE MASTER

Shavetail, you call it.

THE CANDIDATE

Shavetail.

THE MASTER

What are the three great principles of an officer throughout history?

THE CANDIDATE

Courage, nobility, generosity.

THE MASTER

In American terms?

THE CANDIDATE

Guts, brass, handouts.

THE MASTER

(*showing her a swagger stick*) I give you a symbol of brass. What is it called?

THE CANDIDATE

Swagger stick.

THE MASTER

(*offering it to her*) Accept it.

THE CANDIDATE

I can't accept it.

THE MASTER

Why not?

THE CANDIDATE

I'm only a second lieutenant. The swagger stick is an optional item of interference.

THE MASTER

According to whom?

THE CANDIDATE

The Commandant of the Marines. He says, "If you feel the need of it, carry it."

THE MASTER

(*commanding*) Feel the need of it!

THE CANDIDATE

(*reaching for it slowly*) Yes, sir.

THE MASTER

Swagger with it. (*she handles it as if it were a baton and swaggers like a drum majorette while the Assistant beats out a march on the percussion*) That is a silly swagger.

THE CANDIDATE

I'm sorry, sir.

THE MASTER

Why do you swagger like a drum majorette instead of an officer?

THE CANDIDATE

I don't have the rank.

THE MASTER

(*reverently, to a shimmer on the percussion, he pulls out a star from a box at the side of the stage*) I promote you. What are you?

THE CANDIDATE

(*looking at the star as he pins it on her shoulder*) A star . .

THE MASTER

A star is the symbol of a general. Swagger with the star like a general! (*she tries unsuccessfully*) With more dignity! You are the master of planning, the great crusader! (*she tries with more dignity*) You are the defender of peace!

THE CANDIDATE

(*at the front of the stage, to the audience*) I swear to defend the country . . (*the Assistant breathes a loud whisper of applause*) with all of the swagger sticks at my command . . (*more applause from the Assistant*)

THE MASTER

(*raising his swagger stick*) Against all swagger sticks?

THE CANDIDATE

(*raising her swagger stick against his*) Against all other swagger sticks!

THE MASTER

(*gesturing upstage*) Through the history of combat? (*he stares at her as she looks at him for a clue*) In the indivisible past?

THE CANDIDATE

(*puzzled*) Invisible?

THE MASTER

(*gesturing as the lights go down a little*) In the forest primeval . . The frontier of promise . . (*the Master begins to test her historically; as usual, she seizes on images of romantic sensuality from which he tries to break her away*) You enter the wilderness . . (*she hesitates and he motions her into the wilderness, repeating*) You hack out your trails of discovery . . (*she hacks out trails of discovery*) What flickers there in the forest? Fire! Fire! (*she kneels like a romantic Indian squaw and twirls her swagger stick as if she were lighting a fire*) Pocahontas, Red Woman of Fire, you swagger in fire everywhere . . (*she rises and dances around in a circle, crying out joyous war whoops which do not please the Master*) No, no! You are a dirty squaw squatting in your crude teepee! (*chastised, she squats down*) You seduce the white man! . . You mix the races. (*she rises and moves forward*) . . You stir up the Melting Pot . . The set-

54

tlers revolt! They send their soldiers into the forest . . They slash down the dark, dripping trees . . (*He moves after her, slashing at her. Startled, the Candidate runs across the stage. She recoils in fear behind a chair, her fingers clutching the back of the chair as if she were a prisoner in a camp.*)

THE CANDIDATE

The Indian is driven out into reserved camps! (*the Master resents this and drives her on*)

THE MASTER

You escape from the reserved camps . . You join the Native Revolutionaries . . You revolt against the Imperial Invaders!

THE CANDIDATE

(*joyfully*) I'm a Minute Man!

THE MASTER

(*pushing her on*) You organize in groups . . You train on raw rations . . You practice guerrilla warfare against the Imperial Invaders! (*the Candidate expands her hypnotic dream of a romantic, revolutionary soldier*)

THE CANDIDATE

"One if by land, two if by sea" . .

THE MASTER

(*taking up a role against her to spur her on*) I take up the sword of the Imperial Invaders . .

THE CANDIDATE

"By the rude bridge that arched the flood" . .

THE MASTER

(*trying desperately to break through*) . . to master the romantic, native revolutionaries!

THE CANDIDATE

(*still happy with her fantasy*) The shot heard 'round the world! (*a shot is heard on the percussion*)

THE MASTER

(*recoiling a little*) The Imperial Invaders found swords of little use in the National Wilderness . .

THE CANDIDATE

The revolutionaries hid behind trees. (*she ducks behind the desk and chair, taking irritating shots from concealment at the Master, which makes him angrier*)

THE MASTER

(*threatening her as he fixes his bayonet in a proud, upright stance*) In our thin red lines we fix bayonets for the charge . .

THE CANDIDATE

(*from her shelter*) The revolutionary sniper in his coonskin shoots you to the ground like flies!

THE MASTER

(*lunging at her in a mechanical march with his bayonet*) Charge! (*His savage charge reveals the intensity of his anger and she is afraid suddenly. He hurts her with his swagger stick in the charge and she lies on the ground, afraid, making the most of her wound.*) Advance! . . Why are you lying there? . . You're in the open line of fire! (*she struggles to get up*) You've stopped the attack . . Are you retreating? . . Does the yellow streak coil up your back? (*she turns a face of aggressive hatred and cleverness to him and rushes toward him where she mimes the burial of her swagger stick and prepares to explode it*)

THE CANDIDATE

(*as the Master looks down, puzzled*) I dig a hole . . Bury my weapon . . (*puts a package in the hole*) Light the fuse . . (*lights the fuse and rushes back upstage*) 5– 4– 3– 2– 1! (*A loud* BOOM *from the percussionist and the Candidate screams at the explosion. The Master jumps with joy, pleased that he's breaking through her fantasies.*)

THE MASTER

Good! . . Dynamite! . . You invent new weapons for defense . . You blow up my last bridge, my fortress, my headquarters . . You flush out my last pocket of resistance . . My ancient redcoats vanish in the distance . . You are victorious! (*the Assistant breathes out applause again, but the Master pushes her on*) You advance to the Civil War! (*suddenly, improvising her new role with the swagger stick, the Candidate takes the side of the romantic South*)

THE CANDIDATE

I parade my colors . . I fire on Fort Sumter! . . I fight for the old plantation, for the mammies who sing us to sleep at night . . All over the South we fight for States Rights! (*she lets out a rebel yell*) Surrender, Yankee! . . Wave your white flag! (*She marches against the Master, singing and whistling "Dixie" — "I wish I was in the land of cotton,"* etc. *The Master is not pleased. Disgusted with her romantic illusion again, he drives her back.*)

THE MASTER

Never, never, never! The house is divided against itself . . Lincoln banishes slavery . . You desert from the South . . You fight for the National Eagle! (*she stares at him, scared and recoiling from her aggression, instinctively seeking some private shelter*) Take cover! . . The secret weapon, the Gatling gun, with its rotating machine barrels, fires at you twelve hundred rounds a minute . . (*she staggers and searches desperately for shelter*) Reinforced by my Sharps Rifles at the Battles of Bull Run . . Run! . . (*she runs and suddenly begins to dig under the table*)

THE CANDIDATE

I escape! I escape from your Civil War! . . I dig underground into the future!

THE MASTER

(*upset, as he thinks she is retreating again into her fantasies*) What are you doing? . . You can't escape . . You can't change wars!

THE CANDIDATE

(*digging and hiding under the table*) I dig my shelter deep underground to coil in against your shells.

THE MASTER

(*furiously*) Come out of there! . . You conceal yourself like a snake! Where are your defensive weapons?

THE CANDIDATE

(*wavering, but clinging desperately to her situation*) I bring in my rations . . (*gets her rations*) My two-thousand-calories-a-day diet of Bulgur Biscuits . . Three and a half gallons of canned water . . (*worried, as she senses his rage*) My sanitation kit, including Purity Plastics for human waste . . (*This uncertainty enrages him further and he stalks around the table preparing to attack her. She waves her swagger stick feebly at him in defense of sanctuary. He presses the button on the end of his swagger stick. Banging on the table with his swagger stick, he climbs up on the table and stamps on it heavily with his foot.*)

THE MASTER

I am the invading fury from the sky — the fire, the gas, the nausea, the heat! . . I filter into your shelter! I vomit all of your Bulgur Biscuits! . . I defecate in your Purity Plastics! I clean out your shelter!

THE CANDIDATE

(*terrified, she rolls out of the shelter and rushes downstage*) Red Alert! . . The enemy attacks! . . I press the button . . (*does so on the end of her swagger stick*) The metal birds rise from their silent cold nests . . They fill the air with the sound and fury of destruction! (*looking up at the excitement of this vision, she recoils suddenly*) Ah, we're all dying . .

THE MASTER

(*going to her*) What is it? Who has killed you?

THE CANDIDATE

(*waving her stick feebly*) The enemies! . . Enemies of the swagger stick . .

THE MASTER

I hear your last wish . .

THE CANDIDATE

Bury me under my swagger stick . . I am in Go condition . . I circle around and around . . around and around . . around and around . . (*struggling back into a state of feminine, public aggression, sensing the Master's intense desire*) I am pursuing . . Happiness! (*dies, disturbed, wondering if she has failed, twitching a little*)

THE MASTER

(*at her feet, contemplating her, wondering about his role as Master*) I bury you with *some* military honors . . The funeral drums pound out their dirge. (*a funeral dirge is heard on the drums*) I plant your swagger stick in the earth to mark the end of your rest. (*plants the swagger sticks together in the shape of a cross between her feet*) You have played out your airy visions of war where all the towers and gates of private fantasies crash down and sleep becomes a radiant dream of dust. Peace . . The Peace that passeth all understanding . . Amen. (*his voice has assumed an Evangelist's intensity as he stares at her, trying to force her toward the eagle's vision of power*) The spirit always moves. Rise! Waste motion is lost devotion. Resurrection! (*she rises slowly as he holds the cross of swagger sticks in his hands, singing* "Mine eyes have seen the Glory," *etc. He speaks sharply.*) What glory do you see?

THE CANDIDATE

(*uncertainly*) A presence . .

THE MASTER

(*impatiently*) Presence?

THE CANDIDATE

(*trembling, staring desperately*) I see . .

THE MASTER

A light?

THE CANDIDATE

(*staring*) Clearer . .

THE MASTER

(*sharply*) A sky? A sun?

THE CANDIDATE

(*staring*) No . .

THE MASTER
A figure?

THE CANDIDATE
Yes . . I think . .

THE MASTER
A face?

THE CANDIDATE
(*staring uncertainly*) I'm not sure . .

THE MASTER
(*impatiently*) Listen!

THE CANDIDATE
(*listening intently*) No words . .

THE MASTER
Music?

THE CANDIDATE
I can't hear!

THE MASTER
(*prodding her into discovery*) Touch!

THE CANDIDATE
No feeling!

THE MASTER
What do you see?

THE CANDIDATE
(*slowly, shuddering*) Invisible . .

THE MASTER
(*sharply*) Failure! (*she is huddled tensely in her anguish*) We must change
. . Take off your uniform . . It is time for the autobiography of enlightenment . . Relax . . Take a smoke . .

THE CANDIDATE
(*subdued, humble, taking a cigarette that he lights and gives to her*) Thank
you, sir.

THE MASTER
Sit down . . (*she sits down*) Comfortable? Not too comfortable . . Sit
on the edge of the chair. (*she moves to the edge of the chair; he takes a
cigar*) The story of how I became a Master. (*as he talks and moves
around he smokes and gestures with the cigar*) I began at birth, a baby
of inevitable strength, an extrovert from the start. Naturally, my immi-
grant parents conceived me as a Master. Out of twisted English was to
come a professional man. Everyone has the right to be a Master — if
he has the right equipment: I.Q., Stable Personality, Grit, Will, and the

rest . . I was an ugly boy, staring at success, my ugliness a glare in the mirror. I broke all mirrors! In the dark hours of the morning I sold a city of papers. I earned a banquet, a medal, a round trip to the towers of New York. The skyscrapers shattered my eyes. Man could do that! I sold my way through schools and college in a wonder of facts. My ear was deaf only to foreign languages. I polished my English, my American even more. I learned the morality of manners. I walked on the curb side of women. I studied love with many women until I married one. Came the war. I served as an officer . . I dreamt of far-off victories for which I thirsted at a dried-up desk. After my discharge from the army, I sank and struggled up in quicksand studies. The hooded colors of the Ph.D. flared over my shoulders! At last I was a Philosopher! Money flowed to me through business, government research, the marvelous labyrinths of lucid teamwork. Landlord, I raised my mansion in the suburbs! . . Then one vacation we flew to Europe. My children stared at Old Masters in the museums. They groveled in the beautiful cathedrals and the lobbies of Baroque opera houses. After our return came the awakening, the sense of American power. We were old! Our faces were wrinkled with freedom. It was time to be young again, eternally young, eternally westward. To stop at the halfway house is not the home of the Master. I must teach, not Oriental or European, but risk the extreme like an American! Candidates would come to me like rivers flowing to their goal. Masters would create Mastery! Preserve the republican scepter of achievement! Achieve the proud world of the lonely Master! Let the great rivers of enlightenment — Columbia, Colorado, Hudson, Missouri, Rio Grande, Mississippi — flow with the fury of knowledge in the Master's veins, his mind, his will! *(He crushes out the cigar to end his autobiography and contemplates the Candidate in silence for a moment. Percussion music is heard. Waiting, the Candidate stares at him. He gives no orders. It is up to her. Finally, she begins her autobiography.)*

THE CANDIDATE

My beginning was comfort and security . . We lived in a big house thirty miles away from the city, deep in a lovely woods . . White birch trees glistened along the drive . . The birds of paradise soared out of our garden in their orange flame colors . . My father disappeared down the freeway every morning to his work . . He was a tower of strength in that city . . When he came home tired at night he was received like a king . . His drink was ready . . My mother was dressed up in her pale housecoat . . If he wasn't too tired, he fired up a happy cloud of smoke over the charcoal broiler in the backyard . . He cooked the best steak you ever tasted . . My mother was devoted to her home and children . . She ran everything on the slickest timetable you ever saw, decorating, cooking, buying, visiting her clubs, taking us to ballet lessons after school . . She was artistic too . . She'd always choose a wallpaper that knocked your eye out . . and she had a real touch for antique furniture . . Her favorite possession was her four-poster spool bed with a rose silk canopy . . She used to say, "I feel like a Queen sleeping in that bed!" . . My sister and I invented the games of romance . . We colored boxes into castles . . We turned our pets into knights and lords and princes . . We steamed the bathroom mirrors into reflections of palaces . . There were so many bathrooms in that house . . You could lock the door and be alone with your dreams of beauty. (*pauses and looks at the Master*)

THE MASTER

Continue . .

THE CANDIDATE

When I left home, I wanted to be successful too . . If you want something badly enough you can still get it in this country . . At fifteen I walked down the high school corridor in a tight sweater and the boys whistled at me . . I knew from the mirrors that I had a face and a body . . So I began to enter all of the beauty contests . . In college I was voted Sorority Princess . . Then I won the Annual Rose Competition . . I learned how to walk in a bathing suit with the control that is graceful, but not too sexual . . I learned how to sing popular songs well enough to pass the talent tests . . I learned how to wear clothes and smile at the right people . . After winning the state competition, I walked around in the clouds . . They were going to send me east! . . Suddenly, I was there, in Atlantic City! . . We stayed in a big hotel where we were guarded like crown jewels . . I was first in the bathing suit competition, but only fourth in the talent tests . . The jury asked me questions . . One juror asked: "What would you do if you found your boyfriend with another girl?" . . I answered, "I'd knock him over!" . . I couldn't believe it when they called my name . . I walked down the runway in a daze . . The band was playing . . The crown was on my head . . That was my night of victory! . . I went out to dedicate parking lots . . I modeled and sold the latest fashions . . I waved with mayors and governors in parades . . I cut the ribbons at the openings of new shopping centers . . I learned to dedicate . .

THE MASTER

(*breaking in*) You learned you are the ideal average woman.

THE CANDIDATE

Yes, sir.

THE MASTER

You have lived the ideal average.

THE CANDIDATE

Yes, sir.

THE MASTER

The Master is not average. Begin again.

THE CANDIDATE

I don't understand . .

THE MASTER

Rise above the average! Use your vision!

THE CANDIDATE

How?

THE MASTER

When nothing makes sense, choose American nonsense.

THE CANDIDATE

(*puzzled*) Nonsense?

THE MASTER

Make a choice!

THE CANDIDATE

Give me a clue. (*as the percussionist pounds out the jazz rhythms building up and up in tempo, the Master leads the Candidate through the riddle and the baseball sequence to the image of the eagle*)

THE MASTER

Why does the lonely chicken cross the road?

THE CANDIDATE

(*slowly*) To get . . to the green pastures . .

THE MASTER

Why does the road cross the lonely chicken?

THE CANDIDATE

(*beginning to participate in the game*) To pasture in the green get.

THE MASTER

Why does the cross road lonely on the chicken?

THE CANDIDATE

To green in the pastures gotten!

THE MASTER

Why does the freight train howl in the night?

THE MASTER

THE CANDIDATE

(*moving toward him, as their movements become increasingly dance-like to the jazz rhythms*) To cover the lonely distance.

THE MASTER

Where is the only entrance to the freeway?

THE CANDIDATE

At the door of the cage.

THE MASTER

Between beer and whiskey, where does the drunkard drown?

THE CANDIDATE

(*beginning to be drawn out of herself*) In the glass of himself . .

THE MASTER

(*more exultantly, now that he is beginning to move her out of herself*) What dream does the dreamer dream at Dream Farm?

THE CANDIDATE

The echoing bird is not the real singer.

THE MASTER

How does the blind man cross the road while the deer stands still?

THE CANDIDATE

The music of the feet commands the eye.

THE MASTER

Why is Mary, Mary quite contrary?

THE CANDIDATE

(*faster and faster tempo as the Assistant builds up a jazz salvo on the percussion*) Because she's hairy, hairy, hairy!

THE MASTER

What does the undertaker say to the bones?

THE CANDIDATE

(*breaking out joyfully now*) Rise you old burdens, rise and shine!

THE MASTER

How does the cheese eat the cheeseburger?

THE CANDIDATE

Lettuce to go, pickled with relish!

THE MASTER

When the leaves of the fall *fall*, how does the spring *spring*?

THE CANDIDATE

The jackrabbit jumper is a Jim Dandy!

THE MASTER

What is the pasture of the National Pastime?

THE CANDIDATE

Cows of the world, unite!

THE MASTER

(*satisfied by her progress with the riddles and jazz dance steps, he takes her through a nonsense baseball sequence still leading her to a recognition of the power and force of the eagle*) Fly American!

THE CANDIDATE

(*happily*) Screw Zen Buddhism! (*the Assistant calls out "Hot Dogs! Root Beer!" etc. as the Master picks up a baseball bat and moves toward the plate behind which the Candidate is standing*)

THE MASTER

Play ball! (*the Candidate signals strike one before the Master has swung*) You blind or something? Put on your glasses! (*the Candidate puts on a pair of dark glasses*) That's better. Look 'em over.

THE CANDIDATE

(*as the Master looks at an obviously high ball*) Strike two!

THE MASTER

You're blind as a bat!

THE CANDIDATE

(*wildly*) Strike two and a half!

THE MASTER

(*threatening her with the bat*) You're crazy, you psycho!

THE CANDIDATE

Strike three!

THE MASTER

Who's paying you? What country club are you gonna buy?

THE CANDIDATE

(*jerking her thumb over her shoulder like an umpire*) Out of the game!

THE MASTER

You rich crook!

THE CANDIDATE

Out of the stadium! Out of the city!

THE MASTER

You beer-busted, broken-down bum!

THE CANDIDATE

(*standing up to him*) Out of the country!

THE MASTER

Up the umpires!

THE CANDIDATE

Down the fans!

THE MASTER
(*puts the bat away and laughs suddenly, delighted at her real progress*)
Precise playing.

THE CANDIDATE
Lovely feeling.

THE MASTER
Name projects.

THE CANDIDATE
(*climbing up on the table, approaching the vision of power*) Saint! Midas!
Titan! Mercury! Venus!

THE MASTER
Rise above gravity!

THE CANDIDATE
(*exultantly*) Rule with radiation!

THE MASTER
(*has brought her through the nonsense sequence and brings her now to
the vision of the Eagle of Power*) What is the true American?

THE CANDIDATE
He moves, he flies, he travels forever.

THE MASTER
(*intently*) Describe his motion.

THE CANDIDATE
Restless motion.

THE MASTER
With wings?

THE CANDIDATE
(*crying out*) Eagle wings!

THE MASTER
What kind of eagle?

THE CANDIDATE
(*exultantly*) A Golden Eagle because he flies against the sky. He swoops
in the mountains showing his even black color. When he wheels, the flash
of white of his tail and the mark of gold on his hind neck give him his
grace. No vulture, a Golden Eagle, he soars and hooks into the burning
sky!

THE MASTER
(*commanding*) Show me the flight of the Golden Eagle! (*Slowly the Candidate begins to move her torso. Her neck twitches. She begins to dance
the Flight of the Golden Eagle to percussion music. There is a rising sense
of exhilaration, of soaring upward, of powerful flight. Then the flight be-*

gins to falter and she slips down from the table. Satisfied, he pushes her on to the final test.) Rest . . You have begun. Now you must end . .

THE CANDIDATE

End?

THE MASTER

How does death approach?

THE CANDIDATE

(*staring at him anxiously, she whispers*) In disguise.

THE MASTER

Which disguise?

THE CANDIDATE

The disguise of old age.

THE MASTER

Put on the disguise of old age. (*the Assistant brings her the hat of old age*) You are old, you are sick. What is your disease?

THE CANDIDATE

(*whispering*) It is incurable.

THE MASTER

What is it called?

THE CANDIDATE

Old age.

THE MASTER

(*putting on his hat of old age*) I am old too. Where do we live?

THE CANDIDATE

Away from our children.

THE MASTER

(*they are both playing an old couple, but the Master is still leading her, testing her through the old-age sequence*) We want our independence. We don't want to be a burden to our children.

THE CANDIDATE

We live by ourselves with other old folk in Moon City. We don't let people in Moon City until they're over the hill.

THE MASTER

We can have a lot of fun if we just don't sit down and die.

THE CANDIDATE

We sleep a lot. I can still sleep up a storm, especially if it's raining.

THE MASTER

We see our children once in a while when they come to visit.

THE CANDIDATE

(*as they wander along in their isolation*) We go out to eat once a week at

the Woodthrift — soup, roast beef, carrots, mashed potatoes, pome-
granate jello, and Sanka for a dollar and twenty-five cents.

THE MASTER

Sometimes we go to a prayer meeting.

THE CANDIDATE

Hear a lecture.

THE MASTER

Walk along to see who's old . .

THE CANDIDATE

We're very social in our security.

THE MASTER

At the Senior Citizens' Center, they have square dancing. (*they begin to
dance and they are breathing heavily at the end of a few steps*) It's a leisure world. Old age should be a long vacation.

THE CANDIDATE

A sea voyage!

BOTH

Bon voyage!

THE CANDIDATE

In St. Petersburg, we can have our blood pressure taken for thirty-five
cents in a street-corner booth.

THE MASTER

Or play shuffleboard on 107 courts. (*plays shuffleboard*)

THE CANDIDATE

I like to listen to the free band concerts.

THE MASTER

We love children, but when you get old, you can't have them around all
the time.

THE CANDIDATE

People are growing older. We're very old and we're still alive.

THE MASTER

We can live on less than $5000 a year.

THE CANDIDATE

If we're segregated.

THE MASTER

What we do is sleep good and late.

THE CANDIDATE

Good and late in the morning.

THE MASTER

Sleep is good for old people. Early to bed, late to rise . .

THE CANDIDATE

Makes the old folks old and wise.

THE MASTER

(*cackles*) Sometimes we miss the children . .

THE CANDIDATE

We get lonely for them.

THE MASTER

But we are lonely together.

THE CANDIDATE

We're starting a new life.

THE MASTER

We're together. Forever.

THE CANDIDATE

Forever.

THE MASTER

Forever.

THE CANDIDATE

Forever.

THE MASTER

Forever . . (*The "forevers" get louder and louder until the two are screaming at each other like eagles, then they fade out slowly. There is a long pause.*) Take off the wig! (*she lifts it off slowly and he says exultantly*) Old age flies away from you like the eagle gliding over the white spindrift of the wave! We begin . .

THE CANDIDATE

(*slowly*) We end?

THE MASTER

I am the Candidate.

THE CANDIDATE

I am the Master?

THE MASTER

We begin! We end! (*The Assistant pulls down a window shade on which is painted a large bald eagle staring fiercely at the audience. In one claw is an olive branch, in the other claw the slogan "E Pluribus Unum." The final Eagle Marriage Ceremony begins.*)

THE CANDIDATE

(*with growing recognition*) I am the Mistress . .

THE MASTER

(*bowing*) We Candidates salute you.

THE MASTER

THE CANDIDATE

(*with a growing smile*) I am the Mistress of American Power!

THE MASTER

We honor you, oh Mistress of Power.

THE CANDIDATE

(*with a gesture of power*) Have a cigar. (*the Master selects a cigar*) Sit down. (*knocks the lighter off the table so that he reaches to pick it up*) Light it! (*he does so*) Shoulders back! The proud position! On the edge of the chair! (*he moves to the edge of the chair, sitting there rigidly, puffing out a cloud of smoke*) I can't stand the stink of a cigar. Put it out! (*He crushes out the cigar. She commands in a low, intense voice.*) Fly American Eagle, fly for me! (*She invokes the eagle as the Master rises and the Assistant begins to play the final Eagle Marriage Ceremony on the percussion. The movements of this ritual Eagle Dance are intense and sensuous, but they break out occasionally from the physical sense of a marriage ceremony to repeat earlier satirical elements in the play.*) White Eagle on your high nest in the dead pine tree, fly to me! Lone eagle floating on blocks of ice down rivers, give me your mastery. Fly to me!

THE MASTER

(*moving toward her*) Proud eagle guarding our dream, "Out of the Many, One."

THE CANDIDATE

Bless this search from youth through age to power.

BOTH

To power! To power! To power!

THE MASTER

Bald eagle in your burning flight,
I take this woman to love, honor, and obey.

THE CANDIDATE

I take this man to cherish the mastery of power.

THE MASTER

Obey . .

THE CANDIDATE

Cherish . .

THE MASTER

Obey . .

THE CANDIDATE

Cherish . .

THE MASTER

(*their arms and bodies whirling now in wild, opposed motions, his up and hers down*) Through the bright air . .

THE CANDIDATE

The white clouds . .

THE MASTER

The lightning . .

THE CANDIDATE

The thunder . .

THE MASTER

In the glory of flight . .

THE CANDIDATE

Moving together . . (*they move together*)

THE MASTER

In the dance of flesh . .

THE CANDIDATE

Moving! In the glory of our dancing flesh! (*there is a jazz sequence as they dance together sensuously*)

BOTH

Moving in the glory! Glory! Glory!
Moving in the glory of our dancing flesh!

THE MASTER

Fierce eagle clutching your olive branch,
Bless the power and the glory of our marriage.

THE CANDIDATE

Preening her claws:
Bright eagle with your furious eye,
Tear with your claws for the glory.

BOTH

Tear, tear for the glory!

THE MASTER

Bold eagle bless this union.

THE CANDIDATE

Proud eagle bless this union.

BOTH

In a fierce whisper:
Bless! Bless! Bless!

THE MASTER

As the dance reflects the military sequence and the Assistant plays martial music on the percussion:

70

THE MASTER

Brave eagle with your brilliant eye,
Guard our freedom!

THE CANDIDATE

Fierce eagle in your burning flight,
Guard our freedom!

BOTH

Fiercely:

Freedom! Freedom! Freedom!

THE CANDIDATE

Eagle to eagle . .

THE MASTER

Joined together . .

THE CANDIDATE

Praise the hunting weather!

BOTH

Praise the marriage of power! Praise!

*She has leaped up on him and slides down his side into an embrace
as the play ends with a final salvo on the percussion and an abrupt
blackout.*

THE END

\

71

MEGAN TERRY

*Ex-Miss Copper Queen on a
Set of Pills*

for Barbara Stearns

PLAYWRIGHT'S PREFACE

THE enclosed statement outlines our first experimental steps under the terms of a Rockefeller Foundation Grant. As you may already know, Alan Schneider has nominated you for consideration as a participating writer . ."

No, I didn't know. Crazy to find a letter like that in your mailbox. That was the first letter, received more than a year ago.

Lunch at La Fonda Del Sol. I couldn't eat the Spanish omelet. How do you look like a playwright while pushing peppers and egg around on a plate?

Second lunch at Sardi's. Here I felt at least like a movie playwright. Had to persuade Dr. Ballet that I was worth reading. Hard for writers to talk. Be careful not to talk too much.

"The Executive Committee of this office would like to invite you to come to Minneapolis early next month . . Congratulations." Still gives me a lift.

The jet settled down at the Minneapolis airport where I was met by a young, new Ph.D. who escorted me to the Maryland Motor Hotel and installed me in the Chinese suite. I plugged in the rented electric typewriter which promptly blew all the hotel lights and silenced the air-conditioners. It was August in the Midwest.

The janitor and I figured out a better fuse system, so I got the typewriter going again and revised my long play *Hothouse*. (Since I was deeply committed to the Open Theatre of New York, directed by Joseph Chaikin, I had decided to use my Rockefeller time to rewrite, polish, and copy my existing plays. They were nearly unreadable, except by the most

75

devoted theatre person. The Open Theatre works without money, but to rehearse and put my plays on before an audience we needed copies. We needed many copies. The Office for Advanced Drama Research performed a heroic service. Before I left for home, I had thirty copies of each of my plays.) I revised and polished *Calm Down Mother* and outlined and wrote *Keep Tightly Closed in a Cool Dry Place*. These short plays are now in the repertory of the Open Theatre and had their first public performance March 29, 1965, at the Sheridan Square Playhouse, New York City. I wrote the first draft of a three-act play, but had to burn it. Rewrote, polished, and expanded *Ex-Miss Copper Queen on a Set of Pills*. The results may be read here.

A lot of work done in one month. Thirty days free from nine to five. Free from bills! Free to work. One month. I had to work fast and I did. It was a good test. I set it myself, and thanks to the Rockefeller Foundation and the O.A.D.R. I made it.

To be chosen by people who are not involved with you in any way is a heartening and confirming experience for a writer. It opens up stores of energy you didn't know you had. The entire association with the Office via letters, lunches, and knowing that my work was being read seems to me more meaningful even than the time I spent in Minneapolis writing. I wrote more during that year and a half of this contact than I had in five years previously — if quantity is a valid measure. My attitude toward being eventually recognized as a playwright became more positive, and this feeling was converted into more creative energy. Relatives and friends can help keep a writer going, but to have recognition from outside is especially beneficial and does much to alleviate energy-sapping doubts that plague the artist.

The one criticism I have at present of the O.A.D.R. program is that not enough writers can participate at one time. The cross-pollination that can occur among writers from different sections of the country brought together with professional actors and directors is important. It's hard to find one another in this fast moving world. I met three writers in Minneapolis. Two of them I got to know pretty well, James Schevill and Betty Johnson. I wish I could see productions of all the plays of the project. In this publication we can at least *read* one another's work.

MEGAN TERRY

Georgetown, Connecticut
June 1965

THE PLAY

Cast of Characters

COPPER QUEEN
B.A.
CRISSIE

EX-MISS COPPER QUEEN ON A
SET OF PILLS

The scene opens on a street somewhere on the Lower East Side of New York City. It's about 5:30 A.M. Garbage cans are near the curb ready for the Sanitation Department. There's a slight chill in the air. An old Puerto Rican woman hauls the last can of ash up from the cellar of one of the houses, sets it in its place along the row of other cans, then disappears under the steps of her house. As the light grows stronger we make out the figure of Copper Queen, who is sleeping on the top step of a brownstone stoop. She fights through drugs and drink to wake up.

COPPER QUEEN
(*tries to pull herself to a sitting position, but falls back. She rolls over on her belly and tries to focus her bleary eyes. She thinks she sees a man.*) Hey there, Mister . . this is your dance. Sidewalk's as good a place as any. Say, Mister, you've got my number. You know . . I'm giving it to you . . If you take it I'll let ya buy this little gal a great big drink . . Cig's gone out. Buy me a . . buy me a . . (*Her mind clears a bit more and she sees the sidewalk. She wants to get to it, but it's too far. This makes her angry, but first she tries to talk the sidewalk into coming closer.*) Why hello there . . pleased to see ya. I spot you down there, you sidewalk . . nine million miles away. Sure beats the hell out of me to know why this city builds its sidewalks so far down from the houses. By God . . Only a big city sidewalk would build itself so darn far away from a gal's boot. Swallowed me a blue heaven, man . . Pretty Man . . dance? (*She painfully pulls herself to a sitting position, and*

© Copyright 1966 by Megan Terry.

79

reaches for her bottle of wine. She thinks it's farther from her hand than it actually is, so she reaches beyond it, and works back toward it. She repeats this several times, almost knocking it over.) No you don't. I got ya, thought you'd get away again, I betcha? Can't get away. I take care a the important things. Getting too bright out. You S.O.B. can't make off with my wine. (*It takes two hands and great concentration to get the wine bottle to her mouth. It's without a top.*) Momma needs sugar . . dry . . cut to the rawhide squaw-chewed dust! All right. Git to work. Git to work. Gotta cut outta this here place soon's I can see my way. This ain't no Yellowstone Park, that's for damn sure . . (*laughs and sips some more wine*) All them dresses waitin' to be shown . . I damn well still git myself to work . . In my blue heaven. (*takes a blue pill*) Yeah, but the heaven's in me now, yes it is!

> *Copper Queen is about twenty-six. She wears tight black pants, run-over heels, low-cut blouse, and some tattered scarves. She's half in and half out of a mangy fur coat. Behind the drugs, drinks, and ten years of little sleep lies a beautiful girl. While the Copper Queen sips her wine, two old women enter. One pushes a baby carriage; both search the garbage cans with expert hands and appraising eyes. B.A., the larger of the two women, definitely the manager, wears many watches on each arm. She has three wigs on her head, each a different color and age. She wears one rubber glove and one canvas one. There's a record book chained to her belt and several pens and pencils on cords. The carriage she pushes sports an alarm clock. Several whisk brooms hang on the side of the carriage. The carriage is ancient, but polished and shining. B.A.'s clothes are strange, but they're clean and ironed. Crissie is uncertain of her age, but she does know that she comes from San Francisco. She'd never be seen on any street without her hat and gloves. Like B.A.'s, her clothes are clean and pressed, and she wears one rubber glove, but the other glove is white lace. She moves with delicacy and grace.*

B.A.

Crissie! Crissie Rutherford Denny! What in the name of a snake's insides is this junk you've deposited in my clean carriage?

CRISSIE

Are you calling me, dear? Did you want me, B.A.?

B.A.

What do you think you're trying to do to me!

CRISSIE

I beg your pardon, dear?

B.A.

Don't beg my pardon. Give me an answer.

CRISSIE

What was the question?

B.A.

What is this junk?

CRISSIE

Let me see the item, B.A.

B.A.

Have you lost all your senses. Are you going through this trash properly?

CRISSIE

I'm always proper, B.A.

B.A.

I nearly, I very nearly wrote it down in my record book. Come here! Closer! I want to see your face, hands. Aha! How much eye-opener this morning?

CRISSIE

Hardly a smitch. We were very low.

B.A.

I think you had more than a smitch. I think you finished the jug. Let me smell your breath.

CRISSIE

Please, B.A. That's offensive and hurtful.

B.A.

Hurtful! Look who's being hurtful to *me*. What is this? What is this filthy thing you've carelessly tossed in my carriage?

CRISSIE

Excuse me, B.A. But you promised it would be *our* carriage.

B.A.

What's this cardboard thing? You know I detest cardboard. What is this waxed and runny lice-filled carton?

CRISSIE

Let me see? (*reaches for it*)

B.A.

Don't touch it, you dope. It's covered with germs. (*takes some tongs that hang on the side of the carriage and gingerly fishes the milk carton out of the carriage and throws it into the garbage can*) I'll never get you trained. Why do I keep trying? I'll never get you to understand the true value of anything.

MEGAN TERRY

CRISSIE

Oh, B.A., I know we could use it.

B.A.

Oh yes? How?

CRISSIE

Why I read in last week's lovely issue of *Woman's Day* we found behind the A & P that you just melt lots of different colored candles into one of these empty milk cartons, and then you sprinkle sequins on top, any color you like, and then behold; you have a lovely, lovely Christmas candle that will burn the twelve days of Christmas.

B.A.

At your funeral! Do you realize you could bring typhoid into our home by picking up filth like this? Why you might as well drink water from a toilet.

CRISSIE

I'm sorry, sorry, sorry, B.A. I thought it would be so pretty at mealtimes.

B.A.

We prospect for salable items. Will you get that through your head? I don't bring garbage into our home, and neither do you. We can *buy* a Christmas candle, if you have your heart set on one. But I won't have you endangering your health *or* mine, by such careless . .

CRISSIE

(*starting to cry*) Oh, B.A., please don't raise your voice like that, I can't . .

B.A.

For God's teeth and jawbone, will you stop! This instant! Don't try to shirk your responsibility to our business with a lot of teary . . I'll go back to Alaska . . I'll go back to Alaska and leave you to prospect this whole city . . this whole city . . all by your little dopey self . . all by your . .

CRISSIE

Don't go back to that dangerous country, B.A. . . See? I'm not crying. Earthquakes and polars and . . I couldn't stand it. See . . I'm not crying.

B.A.

What's all that water swimming in your eyes?

CRISSIE

Oh, B.A., I try so hard. I've worked so hard to please you. I've learned so much . . you've truly taught me a great deal . . I was such a tenderfoot when we met . . you've . . I'm so grateful . .

82

EX-MISS COPPER QUEEN ON A SET OF PILLS

B.A.

I wish you'd show it more, then.

CRISSIE

(*plunging into a can*) I'll show you. I'll find treasures all the rest of the morning.

B.A.

You couldn't tell a salable item if it bit you in the behind. (*takes her record book up to write in it; looks at all her watches, adjusts one*) Let's see, we took seven minutes, eighteen seconds for Avenue C, from Fourteenth Street to Eleventh. That's good. That's very good. We're ahead of ourselves by twelve minutes. Best morning's record since the mock air raid of April 13, 1943. (*records the time*)

CRISSIE

I told you. I told you I would, B.A. See here, look, B.A. See, it's a little red jacket. (*Copper Queen puts down her wine at the word "little"*) A dear little child's, little red jacket.

COPPER QUEEN

Child? Dear . . little? . .

CRISSIE

Yes, B.A. A dear little jacket. I can wash it in the boiler room and press it. You'll get us a grand price on Orchard Street.

B.A.

(*plucking the jacket from Crissie and going over it with expert care*) Here . . mmmmmm . . I don't know . . maybe . . Ah . . Sure as hell couldn't wear it down into a mine! Mmmm . . perhaps . . not more than two bits, though. Is this the best you can do?

CRISSIE

Oh a dear little child's jacket as red as this should fetch much more than a quarter, I'd say.

COPPER QUEEN

Was it a boy's or a girl's?

CRISSIE

I said it was a child's, B.A. It's a fine jacket. A little boy I knew in San Francisco had a jacket like that. Do you suppose he lost it?

B.A.

Nonsense. He couldn't have lost it this far . . of course, he might have been visiting the city and lost it . . Did he come to New York often?

CRISSIE

Not often, I think. I think he would not come too often. He was only five.

B.A.

Then it's bound and determined that your friend didn't lose the jacket. So we'll wash it and sell it on Orchard Street. Put it in the carriage.

COPPER QUEEN

He lost it . . a boy . . a little boy lost . . his . . little jacket . .

CRISSIE

See how nicely I fold you, little jacket . . See . . see there, B.A.?

B.A.

Idiot! Don't put it on that side, that's where the blue pants go. Put it on the other side with red top wear.

CRISSIE

I'm so sorry, B.A. I was too excited. Of course I know that red top wear goes here, and blue bottom wear goes there.

B.A.

There, that's better. Balances the color inside the carriage better. I can't have a messy carriage. It'll look like cheap linoleum. Order. We must have order or the carriage will collapse.

CRISSIE

Yes, B.A. See, it's in order now. It's balanced . . perfect . . balance . .

B.A.

(*considers a moment, then rearranges the jacket ever so slightly*) There, that's better. I have an eye for order you know. There. It won't collapse . . I've balanced the carriage. (*pushes the carriage to the next can*)

CRISSIE

It's in order now, B.A.

COPPER QUEEN

(*watching the carriage, fascinated*) A baby . . a baby . . in a buggy . . ride . . (*reaches out and makes an effort to stand, but can't*) Say . . lady . . ladies! . . you there . . Say . .? May I ask you . . with sugar on it . . may I ask . .

CRISSIE

B.A., look at that poor young woman. Look, B.A., that poor young woman, I think she wants to meet us. I'd love to . . I believe she's calling to us . .

B.A.

Pay no attention; we're on a work schedule. The carriage isn't half filled yet.

CRISSIE

I distinctly heard that poor young woman ask . .

EX-MISS COPPER QUEEN ON A SET OF PILLS

B.A.

Just some whore sobering up.

CRISSIE

Oh, the poor little whore.

B.A.

Did you go through all these cans? How about that one? That one on the end?

CRISSIE

I'm just about to, B.A. I was on my way.

B.A.

Get your gloves in there. One twenty-five-cent jacket doesn't get you off the hook for that milk carton.

CRISSIE

Please don't use that carton against me.

B.A.

Don't let it happen again.

COPPER QUEEN

Say lady . .

CRISSIE

We have to speak to her, B.A. She's made the first gesture. It's only common courtesy.

B.A.

To work!

CRISSIE

I was brought up to attend the less fortunate, B.A. There're some things you could learn, too, you know. It's our duty to aid that poor girl.

B.A.

That's no girl. That's a sick whore. We're respectable business women.

COPPER QUEEN

Say there, ladies, may I just ask . . to . . a "red bird" baby . .

CRISSIE

B.A., I must see if I can help . .

B.A.

You stay here, she's more diseased than that filthy milk carton you tried to slip in the carriage.

CRISSIE

Oh, please, B.A.

COPPER QUEEN

May I just have a tiny peek at the . . (*leans over the steps and loses her balance*) Who tipped these stairs!

85

CRISSIE

(*worried, she runs to Copper Queen*) Are you all right, my dear? Here, let me help. There you go. (*steadies her*)

COPPER QUEEN

Much obliged. Just on my way to work . . saw your buggy . .

CRISSIE

Allow me to introduce myself. I'm Crissie Rutherford Denny, and my partner is Miss Mayhew. I don't believe I caught your name.

COPPER QUEEN

I didn't give it. Your partner?

CRISSIE

We're business partners. However, Miss Mayhew is senior partner.

COPPER QUEEN

What line you in?

CRISSIE

We . . we . . 'er, we find things.

B.A.

We're prospectors! We deal in salable items.

CRISSIE

You have no idea how many treasures you can find in the city. Just for the picking.

COPPER QUEEN

Picking! What the hell berries grow on this street?

B.A.

We're business women.

COPPER QUEEN

Some business, picking through crud!

CRISSIE

(*matter-of-fact*) Oh, crud brings a good price, if you know where to sell it!

COPPER QUEEN

How can you drag a poor little baby around while you pick through garbage cans?

B.A.

It's a darn sight more ordered job than whoring.

COPPER QUEEN

(*pulling her ray gun*) Zap! Zap! I've dissolved millions for less than that! (*laughs*)

B.A.

You can't even stand up. Crissie, get away from that mess.

EX-MISS COPPER QUEEN ON A SET OF PILLS

COPPER QUEEN

I'm on my way to work. I work. You're not so smart. I work. Zap! Black-jack! (*takes a pill*)

B.A.

In doorways, at night!

COPPER QUEEN

I got a good job. I'm appreciated. People look at me. What do you get from picking rags?

CRISSIE

We've earned the dearest place. We live in the most secure unit of our building. I've completely redone the inside. It was lots of scrubbing and white tornado, but it was worth it, wasn't it, B.A.?

B.A.

You couldn't never even tell it was ever a coal bin.

CRISSIE

Never, never in a million years. And it's so San Francisco cool in summer. We have so much storage for our treasures.

B.A.

And room for expansion!

COPPER QUEEN

Do you keep a baby in a coal bin? Well blackjack! Why not!

CRISSIE

I'd love you to call on me, my dear. I have the loveliest room all draped in brocade; it completely covers the stone. Keeps dampness out.

B.A.

I've plugged all the rat holes.

COPPER QUEEN

Brocade. Yes, that's it. I wore brocade.

B.A.

Yeah, the latest uniform at the House of Detention. Burlap brocade!

COPPER QUEEN

I did. I had a whole gown of brocade. White brocade.

CRISSIE

White! White for your wedding, dear?

COPPER QUEEN

The contest! Hearts! (*pops another pill into her mouth*)

B.A.

Last time you wore a gown was the day you were born.

87

CRISSIE

You won a contest? I'm honored to meet you. I've never won a contest, but then I've never entered one.

COPPER QUEEN

Copper Queen. Miss Copper Queen of all the dirt you could see on the whole state of Montana. Baby blue heaven . . let's see your baby? . .

CRISSIE

How do you do again. Miss Queen, I'm so very pleased to make your acquaintance. I'm Crissie Rutherford Denny and this is Miss Beatrice Anderson Mayhew.

COPPER QUEEN

And I'm very pleased to meet you, too, little ladies.

B.A.

Where'd you say that contest was?

COPPER QUEEN

Don't talk so fast. Hey baby, boy . . Football! (*calls at carriage and leans toward it as she takes another pill*)

B.A.

She don't know where she is. All right, Miss Crissie Rutherford Denny, you have just ten seconds to live up to your partnership agreement.

CRISSIE

But, B.A. . .

B.A.

March with me now, Crissie . . or I'll cancel your orders. (*goes through the cans, brushing and dusting and wiping things before placing any good item in the carriage; when she does find something good, she writes it down*) We're going to finish up here, and get lickety-split to Avenue D. We're making good time, and I aim to keep it that way. What's this? A nearly new pair of Hart, Schaffner & Marx! That's promising. (*pulls pair of shoes out*) Crissie!

CRISSIE

(*to Copper Queen*) It's not what it used to be, my dear. We do very well, but we have to work fast to earn enough.

B.A.

Another throwaway beer bottle! Plastic and cardboard — the scourge of our times. Once we earned our food on beer bottles alone! The bread, right out of our mouths!

CRISSIE

You know what I saw in a Third Avenue antique shop on Tuesday? A

Prince Albert can! And do you know what they were asking for it? You'll never guess, my dear.

B.A.

Don't tell me, I'll get sick.

CRISSIE

(*sotto voce to Copper Queen*) Two dollars and fifty cents. Two dollars and fifty cents for an old tin tobacco can that we used to pass by.

COPPER QUEEN

(*pounding her temples, beginning to tremble*) Hello, do you have Prince Albert in the can? Well, let him out!

CRISSIE

I understand, my dear. I have days like this, too. Sometimes they last for months.

B.A.

Our partnership is dissolved. Good-bye, Crissie!

CRISSIE

Oh, no.

B.A.

This is it, Miss Denny. I'm leaving. You have one tenth of a second to move your bones, or I'll tell the vacuum cleaner where you are.

CRISSIE

Very good, but you can't trick me that way. I'm coming. I want to come with you, B.A. But I do so enjoy visiting. I haven't had a day off in years.

B.A.

The vacuum cleaner.

CRISSIE

Go ahead and tell the vacuum cleaner, B.A. It can't do anything because it ruined its suction when it tried to swallow my little jade frog.

B.A.

I fixed it, Crissie, and I'll turn it on full power if you don't come immediately.

COPPER QUEEN

I want to see your baby . .

CRISSIE

(*jumping up, tries to shake hands with Copper Queen*) Good-bye, my dear. I must go back to work. It's been so nice to make your acquaintance. If you're ever in San Francisco, I'll take you to lunch at Fisherman's Wharf, and then the opera. Do you like *Der Rosenkavalier*?

COPPER QUEEN

You're such a nice lady . . (*pulls her pillbox out of her coat but can't get it open — pleads sweetly*) Could you please open this little tiny box for me?

B.A.

Oh, Crissie . . oh, Crissie, how you'll cry when you're sucked into the dirt chamber. How black your gloves will get! Where's the . .

CRISSIE

Why, of course, my dear, if you'll pardon my fingers. (*removes her gloves gracefully and opens the box*) What a pretty box. Look, B.A.

B.A.

Mmmhmmm . . At least eighteen dollars. Come on or I'll plug in the cleaner.

CRISSIE

(*opening the box*) What pretty pills. You can't fool me, B.A. There are no electrical outlets on Avenue A.

COPPER QUEEN

(*grabs for pills*) I can't wait any more. I need a set. Stone me honey! Give me blackjack hearts in my blue heaven.

CRISSIE

Pretty pills, B.A. Look at these colors. I know you'd approve of the arrangement. You'd love these colors, B.A. Love them! There's red heart-shaped babies, and black and white clown tinys and long ball-shaped littles and greenies with small colored balls and yellow-jacket bee-like sweeties and blue blue blue . . the color of . . Oops. (*the box spills*)

COPPER QUEEN

My blue heaven . . (*reaches and pills get spilled*) Get them. Give me. I got to have . . I can't make it . .

B.A.

(*shrugs*) She's on goofballs, too, eh?

COPPER QUEEN

Hand them to me. I've got to stay stoned. I can't stand my own company . . the baby . . please lady . . hand me . .

CRISSIE

(*fetching pills*) Here, my dear Miss Queen. How clumsy of me . . I fear in your haste you knocked . .

COPPER QUEEN

Three, give me . . any three as long as they're different colors.

B.A.

Good-bye, Crissie. I'm taking down all that nice brocade when I get home, and you'll have to look at the damp, runny, black, stone walls.

CRISSIE

(*hands pills to Copper Queen*) Here's what I found, my dear . . See, I'm coming now, B.A. Good-bye . . (*makes an effort to shake Copper Queen's hand but she is busily struggling to get the pills in her mouth and wash them down with wine*)

COPPER QUEEN

(*then grabs for Crissie*) You've been so good to me. Let me buy you a drink?

B.A.

A lush, too!

COPPER QUEEN

Let me buy you little ladies a great big drink! (*Crissie, embarrassed, looks to B.A.*) See, got nearly a whole bottle of . . of Chablis. I hate the stuff, but it comes in handy if I run out of . . of . .

CRISSIE

I'm coming with you now, B.A.

B.A.

Is it really wine?

CRISSIE

I believe so. I think I recognize the shape of the bottle.

B.A.

What kind?

CRISSIE

I thought we only had a tenth of a second.

B.A.

What brand of Chablis?

CRISSIE

Gall— Gall— Gallo . . I know that . . They come from the same state as I do. The Gallo brothers. They make lovely wines.

B.A.

It must be filthy.

CRISSIE

B.A., it's nearly a full bottle.

B.A.

Fifth?

CRISSIE

I think it's a full quart.

B.A.

Full?

CRISSIE

Nearly . .

COPPER QUEEN

If you'll let me hold the baby . . just one hold . . just one . . I'll give
you more than a drink . . I'll give you the whole bottle.

CRISSIE

Did you hear, B.A.? She wants to give us the bottle.

B.A.

Give?

CRISSIE

If we let her see the baby.

B.A.

Baby! What baby?

CRISSIE

(*bewildered*) That's right, B.A. We don't have a baby in the carriage.

B.A.

But she doesn't know that.

CRISSIE

(*a bit mournfully*) We'll have to give back the wine.

B.A.

No, we won't. We'll drink the wine. Then we'll let her look.

CRISSIE

But I couldn't deceive *her*, B.A. She trusts me.

B.A.

(*ominously*) Stand still a minute, Crissie.

CRISSIE

No. No. No. Who is it?

B.A.

Mixmaster? I have to place the motor. Yes. It's the mixmaster!

CRISSIE

Not the mixmaster, B.A.! Oh not that.

B.A.

It's coming toward you from behind that last ash can.

CRISSIE

Please turn it off. Pull out the plug, B.A.

B.A.

Will you get the wine?

EX-MISS COPPER QUEEN ON A SET OF PILLS

CRISSIE

Anything. I'll do anything! I can't stand to be whipped into an angel food — not twice in one morning.

B.A.

(*taking a cane from its fitting on the carriage side, she strides to the last ash can and lifts the cane to strike the can*) I, Beatrice Anderson Mayhew, am in command of this street. I hereby turn off all electric current. (*bangs on the can and Crissie relaxes*)

CRISSIE

Oh, thank you, B.A.

B.A.

You can prove your thanks by obeying me.

COPPER QUEEN

If you don't want wine, I'll share my goofballs — pop, pop. (*looks in box*) All gone. All gone, where'd . . I can't last . . got to get to work . . got to connect . . where is he? Why didn't he meet me. Oh God, it'll go away . . it'll go away if I can just . . it'll go away if I can just hold the baby, only for a little while . .

CRISSIE

B.A., the poor little thing . . what shall we do?

B.A.

A moment, a moment till I plan our day. Now let's see? We've covered the *Green*-witch Village area; the mid-East Side, we have three avenues left to go. However, if we fortify ourselves with the wine, we might get ourselves up to Gramercy Park, and that would be good, because there's a *slightly* better class of garbage in that area, and we'd be well ahead of the Sanitation Department. I say we deserve refreshments. We've been out since three.

CRISSIE

But the baby? . .

B.A.

String her along. She'll forget baby . . she doesn't even know her own name.

CRISSIE

(*crossing to Copper Queen*) I want to thank you for your kind offer. We've had an extremely busy morning and we'd certainly enjoy a refreshing pause.

COPPER QUEEN

Sit right down here beside me, little lady from San Fran and Santa Fe. You're like my friend Lucy. She takes care of me. She's a honey. She's

93

comfortable. She comforts me. When I really feel bad she sits on my lap and kisses my new and oncoming wrinkles away . . only you're prettier . . you were . . yes, you are.

CRISSIE

B.A., did you hear? The little whore thinks I'm pretty?

B.A.

Crissie, "whore" isn't exactly a term of affection.

CRISSIE

B.A., did you hear? She says I'm pretty.

B.A.

Pretty broken down and out!

COPPER QUEEN

It's a pleasure to tell you so. They ain't enough pretty people in this universe. Did you ever see such an ugly city? The streets are flooded with uglies. But you, you're pretty. I'm much obliged.

B.A.

Is there wine or is there not, "pretty"? I can't waste precious business time with this bum. Bring that wine here if there is any.

CRISSIE

Of course there's wine. (*handing the bottle to B.A.*) You take the first sip, B.A.

B.A.

Don't mind if I do.

COPPER QUEEN

(*the pills are beginning to work*) Ah . . Yeah, yeah, yeah. That's what I was waiting for. Slow. Don't go by fast this time. Quiet. Make it quiet this time, baby, let me float right off the street and get to work. Oh yeah. Stoning it! Make the ce-ment sidewalk jealous — yeah! Mount Rushmore — that's me!

B.A.

What'll we drink to? We did beat our best time record this morning.

COPPER QUEEN

Pop, Pop . . fly . .

CRISSIE

Don't waste our toast.

B.A.

Yep, that's the only reason I'm allowing a change of schedule. We'll make it up tomorrow. But only because we're ahead of ourselves anyway. Your turn.

94

EX-MISS COPPER QUEEN ON A SET OF PILLS

CRISSIE

(*toasting heroically*) To Beatrice Anderson Mayhew who is in command of this street.

COPPER QUEEN

Drink up, friends, and friends of friends, the end is soon in sight. Everybody drinks. Everybody wins. You're hard to find in this town. I dug you the first I saw you dancing out on the dancing floor.

CRISSIE

Was it a waltz or a mazurka?

COPPER QUEEN

You're like the cute little doll that got left in the rain. Like that doll I had when I lived in the big house with them . . you know them? . . That man and that woman that lived there where I did . . and they, you know, just hardly wouldn't talk to me.

CRISSIE

They wouldn't talk to you either?

COPPER QUEEN

Nope. Not word, one. That whole mountain of copper could have melted into gold and they wouldn't of said a word to me.

CRISSIE

I lived on Nob Hill, and no one spoke to me either, except the ice cream man, and the foghorns in the Golden Bay under the Gateway to the Orient. Sometimes B.A. won't say a word to me, not even if I say — please.

B.A.

(*the wine is beginning to hit her*) Another belt, Crissie?

CRISSIE

I would care for one more swallow, B.A., thank you. This used to be Papa's favorite wine. (*gracefully takes a long swallow*)

COPPER QUEEN

Somebody got a stick? Give me a drag. I can't go that liquor no more. You sip it up, little women, and I'll sing you a little old western song, like they sung it to me in the West. (*sings to the tune of "Streets of Laredo"*)

> And this and the forenoon comes
> To lean against time
> When Gary rides into the West
> Of the High down because we ain't ready
> For the lowdown —
> It is too far to stoop.

So come a ty yi yo — git along little
    girlies
I'll sing you a song that is not of my own
Lie down beside me my fine little girlies
And I'll sing you to heaven that's not
    of my own
But I'll love you and hug you
And pull off your dresses
And curl your hair
And paint your nails
And soothe you and sing you
And kiss all your questions
And I'll save you from nothing —
    no less!

CRISSIE

What a sweet, sweet song . . You have a very nice-sounding voice . . not operatic mind you, but the sound . .

COPPER QUEEN

It was a sound that won me a prize in the talent part of the quest . . O little woman O . . took me a set of pills. I'm stoned out of my head. I feel so cold in this city. Give me some more . . I need a new set . . find me the little black and white ones and the red heart ones and we'll cap it all with a yellow jack. Look down there on that sidewalk. You see any little yellow pills? You do . . yes . . lady — find some! I can't go on like this.

CRISSIE

(tries to look some more) I gave you all I found. (sipping her wine wonderingly) B.A., what's a set of pills?

B.A.

Just a new kind of hophead. I read in the New York Post that these types take sleeping pills and wake-up pills all at the same time, and maybe a Benzedrine chaser. She don't know where she is.

CRISSIE

I'll help find her. Nobody will talk to her, either.

B.A.

Can't say as I blame them. Is this all the wine? Hey, what's the fur she's wearing? That looks like, yes, it's civet cat . . maybe she has some money . . Let's sit beside her. No, not here. You're right, Crissie, maybe we can find her. (they go to Copper Queen and sit one on each side and help her to sit up)

EX-MISS COPPER QUEEN ON A SET OF PILLS

COPPER QUEEN

(*welcoming them, she pulls herself up by flinging an arm around each shoulder*) Hey, that's better, I like warm space. I don't know what it is . . I give them all my money, and still they hurt me. Still they walk out on me. Why do my friends do that? I'm not talking about men, I mean my friends, too. You expect it of men. But friends are supposed to be friendly. I want to help people. But that's the way I am; I'd give away everything I had, only I already did, I already gave it away . . I think I did . . you feel warm . . you're so . . so warm . .

CRISSIE

Poor little thing.

B.A.

(*feeling the coat*) Nice coat . . once!

COPPER QUEEN

I won the contest when I was only seventeen, did you know that?

CRISSIE

A contest? How lovely. Where was it?

COPPER QUEEN

Why it was in Butte. Butte, Montana. Where else?

CRISSIE

Where else? Of course, it was in Montana!

COPPER QUEEN

Of course.

B.A.

(*drinking more wine*) Oh, my God. If it wasn't in New York — why it had to be Montana.

COPPER QUEEN

(*painfully, but bravely, trying to figure it out*) But why do they take my things. I let them stay at my place, and they steal my suitcases. I got nothing left to pack anything in, even if I did get up the guts to go back home. They sleep in my bed and take my watch that I got for graduation from the eighth grade. I didn't graduate the high school. I came to New York for another queen contest, but I didn't win that one. Why do I give money away? I need money. Miss Copper Queen — 1949.

CRISSIE

I'm glad I don't have to worry about money any more. Terrible responsibility! B.A. is a good business woman. I had lots of money once, and all the machines they bought, those machines had me and they told me they wanted more and more and I fed them until I just ran out of feed.

B.A.

(*disgusted*) You don't have any money, eh?

COPPER QUEEN

'Course I got money. They wouldn't let me starve.

CRISSIE

They wouldn't let you starve, and neither would we.

COPPER QUEEN

They send me lots of money. And I need it. I got a hell of a habit to support. Where is he? Oh, but this is good. I work, too. I work as hard as you two do, that's what hung me about you two, seeing you prospect like a couple of Mountain Men looking through those litter baskets and garbage pans, placer miners, panning a rich stream.

B.A.

Send you money, eh? What is it? They pay you to *stay* away?

COPPER QUEEN

They's generous. They don't want me to come home like this. They don't want him to see me like this. Yeah, you need money in this town. Hell, the pioneers had it easy. I got a hundred from hustling and I picked up fifty for posing in m'birthday suit. And I got my month's allowance from Mom.

B.A.

Who'd give you an allowance? You don't even have a mailbox.

COPPER QUEEN

Hell, I don't want to be like this. But you want to know a secret?

CRISSIE

Yes, yes.

COPPER QUEEN

(*to B.A.*) And do you want to know a secret? (*B.A. nods*) I'm a pushover. I guess I like it. I like to be dominated. I . . CRAVE . . being . . dominated!

B.A.

You poor little girl. You better let me keep your money for you; somebody would rob it from you the state you're in.

COPPER QUEEN

It's in this here bag. You keep it for a while. I wouldn't have it all in one place like that. It's bad. (*angry*) You give some of the money to her to hold. (*gestures toward Crissie, and B.A. gives Crissie some money*)

CRISSIE

Now it's safe, dear. It's in two places.

EX-MISS COPPER QUEEN ON A SET OF PILLS

COPPER QUEEN

Yes. I'll tell you something, if you'll bring me the baby to hold . .

B.A.

You tell first.

COPPER QUEEN

It's something you won't believe; it's stranger than anything. I loved him since I loved anyone. No matter wherever I am . . that boy knows . . before I do. Do you know that he can find me within five minutes when I hit that Butte town. No more'n five minutes, and he knows where. I look around, I just might turn around, and there he is . . But you can't take a pimp home to yer father and mother. Don't never try it.

B.A.

What a mess.

COPPER QUEEN

Can you imagine how I could take him home? But that tender boy, he can find me no matter what day or hour or where, when I roll into Butte. We find each other. I've loved him for ten years, and he's loved me. Yes, he has!

B.A.

Your people, do they know where you are?

COPPER QUEEN

They think they know. But they don't know, really. Fact is, they have never even been able to find me. You know why?

CRISSIE

Why?

COPPER QUEEN

Because they don't know how to look! (*laughs*)

B.A.

Where do you live, girl?

COPPER QUEEN

Butte, Montana.

B.A.

I mean in New York.

COPPER QUEEN

I live here and there, mostly there. (*giggles*) I'm a transient. (*looks at Crissie*) You know, you have 'em in Cal. Them transient workers that follow the harvests and live in tents, like the Okies used to be. I'm a Montana Okie. But damnit I can still work — if I could just walk.

B.A.

You work every day?

COPPER QUEEN

I always work, no matter how stoned or hung up I am. I come from a long line of workers. Don't matter how much bread you store in the box, everybody works in the West. You couldn'ta stayed alive in the West in the old days if you didn't work . . Do you work?

B.A.

Of course, you just seen us. We don't even take Sundays off. We start work while it's still dark to beat the Bowery bums to the pickings. However, we're better organized; we're business women, and we have a warm place to sleep.

COPPER QUEEN

I need that . . warm place . . a warm place . . to sleep.

CRISSIE

Let's take her home with us, B.A., the lonely little thing.

B.A.

No room.

CRISSIE

Please, B.A. We could have at last someone to talk to, she and I.

B.A.

Her people would have us picked up for kidnapping.

CRISSIE

Why, she's a grown woman, and besides, they don't know our address. We're unlisted!

B.A.

Definitely we cannot take her.

CRISSIE

But someone to talk to — you don't know what that means!

B.A.

I talk to you, don't I? Who pulls out the plugs — who beats up the mix-master — who holds you in the night when the brocade starts to fly?

CRISSIE

Oh, B.A., I'm sorry. I didn't mean to say it that way. I didn't mean to hurt you . . I . .

B.A.

(*indignant*) I resent that! I've never been hurt in my life.

CRISSIE

She needs rest, poor thing. Look at the circles under her eyes. Please let's take her to our basement and put her to bed, and then finish our picking. I'll work twice as fast. I promise.

EX-MISS COPPER QUEEN ON A SET OF PILLS

B.A.

She probably can't move. We can't afford any unmovable items taking space. Be months to get her into a decent salable condition.

COPPER QUEEN

Think and see if you could know and maybe you could tell me why my mother just sat there on her needlepoint chair with her eyelids heavy like the Virgin Mary? She knew I was drunk? Didn't she! I tell you she knew it! She saw me all sloppy and come staggering in higher than anyone can be, and she just sat there and pretended nothing was wrong.

CRISSIE

Our sitting room had needlepoint chairs.

COPPER QUEEN

How could she do that? She sat there so holy and looking like an innocent lamb, looking with her eyes from one side of the room to the other like she didn't see me. She thought I was the wall . . and the stairs going up. But it was me all right! I crawled past that wall. I was drunk; I *knew* I was drunk . . and I called to her . . and I couldn't see . . but she wouldn't touch me . . I just wanted to go upstairs and talk to my baby before he went to sleep. But she took him, and called him "Brother." It ain't legal. He's *my* son!

CRISSIE

Don't you worry. We'll find you a baby again. We find new things every day. Don't we, B.A.? You can push the carriage all the way home if you want to. (*Copper Queen nods and takes Crissie's hands*)

COPPER QUEEN

They were so good to me. We went down to Arizona to have the baby in a nice resort home. The best in the Southwest. Daddy came, too. It was the first vacation we'd ever had, all of us together. Then they said I could come to New York and stay as long as I wanted. Forever, even . . and not have to live in a dumb small town . . they're raising him like their own son . . they're so good to him . . and they send me my money every month . . every liver-squeezing month . . She just sat there the whole time like the Virgin Mary . . She thinks he came straight to her from God . . She pretended I had nothing to do with it . . just between her and God . . Is ten years a long time to love someone . . ?

B.A.

No time — hardly a turn in the litter basket. We have to go back to work now. Thank you for the wine. It was clean and good. (*pockets the money*)

COPPER QUEEN

Help me up now. I get to see that baby.

CRISSIE

(*pleading*) B.A. . .

B.A.

Some other time. We got a schedule to meet.

COPPER QUEEN

You drank my wine. You promised . . you promised I could see that boy!

B.A.

And you can, too. Just as soon as we get back here. Tomorrow morning at the same time.

COPPER QUEEN

(*struggling to her feet*) I've got to see that boy. (*lurches — but regains her balance*)

B.A.

Tomorrow, it's too late now.

CRISSIE

(*can't bear to see Copper Queen disappointed*) Stop her, B.A.

COPPER QUEEN

(*staggers to the carriage, looks in, sees her own child there among the rags*) Oh . . yeah . . O yeah . . baby. Hi lover! Hi fat boy! God you've grown so. Me — I've shrunk . . You don't have enough covers . . She should cover you more . . God knows she's got money to do it with . . (*She takes off her fur coat and painfully manages to get the coat tucked around the carriage. B.A. casts a satisfied glance toward Crissie. The coat is an unexpected bonus.*) Here, my honey boy. It's cold in this city. That's better, huh. Don't look at me like that. Take me back. You know me? You want me? Take me back. You're new enough to give me another chance. I'll be good. I'll go straight. I'll be such a good Mommie. See how I love you — see . .

B.A.

(*coming over to the carriage*) He's a fine-looking boy.

COPPER QUEEN

Baby baby boy. Pretty baby boy . . nobody could have talked me out of having you. (*shudders; the pills are wearing off*)

B.A.

Crissie. It's nearly six A.M. Get her away. Talk her back to the stoop. We have to get down to the next street. The bloody Bowery bums will beat us to it.

CRISSIE

But she's found her baby, B.A., and we've found this — (*holds her share of money*)

COPPER QUEEN

(*rocking the carriage*) Rock that boy, boy, rock-a-bye boy and a rock, and a rock, and a rickity boy rock . .

B.A.

(*taking Copper Queen by the arm*) I have an idea. It's an orderly one, and fits in with the morning program. You station yourself here, while we run down to pick Avenue D. When we finish at six-thirteen we'll hurry back and pick you up. And then you know what?

COPPER QUEEN

No. What?

B.A.

When we get back here, we'll let *you* wheel the buggy all the way down to Avenue B.

COPPER QUEEN

Me? You would trust me? You would trust me to do that? And you don't even know me?

B.A.

(*solemnly*) I would trust you.

COPPER QUEEN

Much obliged. I sure do thank you.

CRISSIE

(*wanting to believe B.A.*) And when we get all finished with work, maybe you and I could sit in the East River Park and just talk . . and take the baby for some river air . . and just do as we please . .

COPPER QUEEN

I'd like that. Oh, I would like that, little lady.

CRISSIE

I'll work fast. So fast. I can hardly wait.

B.A.

Come on, Crissie. If we march, we'll just make the next stoplight.

COPPER QUEEN

You swear now, you'll meet me right here! Right here! You like me, right? I never took anything in my life. I give it away. I gave the clothes off my back and the skin off my face.

103

B.A.

(*pulling the carriage away from Copper Queen*) Come on. We've got to make the light. They've just finished putting out the cans on the next street.

COPPER QUEEN

(*without the carriage to support her, she falls back toward the stairs*) And then you'll meet me?

CRISSIE

(*catching Copper Queen*) We can't leave her!

B.A.

(*grabbing Crissie by the arm*) Come on, Crissie, or I'll turn the electric current back on.

CRISSIE

(*quickly*) Good-bye, Miss Copper Queen. Remember, I meant what I said — if you ever come out to San Francisco . .

B.A.

(*almost offstage, pushing the buggy before her*) Crissie!

CRISSIE

I'm coming . . thank you Miss Queen . . for thinking me pretty . . (*they're gone*)

COPPER QUEEN

(*waving after them with all her strength*) I'll wait here, little lady. I be right here till you come pick me up. I get to wheel him all the way down to Avenue B . . you said! All the way home to . . Avenue . . B . . Avenue . . B . . All the way . .

> As the lights go down the curtain closes slowly. Copper Queen sings as she lies back down on the stoop:

Ty yi yo git along little girlies
You knew that Montana was yer old home —

You walked and you talked and you
Showed off yer asses

Now you got to find you a
New — old home —

And we'll take the fat baby
To Avenue B —
And take my baby to
Avenue B —

EX-MISS COPPER QUEEN ON A SET OF PILLS

All the way down to —
All the way —
All the way down to Avenue B —

B . . B . . B . .

Her voice fades out and she is rigid.

CURTAIN

ELIZABETH JOHNSON

A Bad Play for an Old Lady

A Bad Play for an Old Lady by Elizabeth Johnson was first presented on September 20 and 24, 1964, at the Tyrone Guthrie Theatre, Minneapolis. It was directed by Edward Payson Call.

Cast of Characters

FLOWERMAN	Michael Levin
CHARLIE	Sandy McCallum
MARY	Yvonne McElroy

PLAYWRIGHT'S PREFACE

I LIKE to go to the movies, Mother," and I go to the movies all the time. One night I attack the Bastille and the next night sleep with Richard Burton and later in the week eat soup with Anthony Quinn after playing my sad trumpet song. And I break my watch and die in the grass — the most famous tightrope-walker of all time.

Occasionally (like reading the *Congressional Record*) I attend the theatre. What a dreadful bore! There I sit all dressed up eating Rolaids and making plans for being depressed the rest of the evening. Oh, there have been a few exceptions, such as *The Connection* and the first act of *Square in the Eye* and *Virginia Woolf* and the *last* act of *After the Fall*; but about those "roses" and "pigs" and the dirty homecoming skits being done in the Village . . The latter might become a great new parlor game — that's all; but the former, like the majority of the so-called "new plays by new playwrights," are no more than peekhole playlets. Peek into the bedroom, the bathroom, the kitchen to see the nasties going on. If they were done on film I might get involved in the nasties but these playlets cannot be done in the theatre without climbing back into Ibsen's sandbox and using his pail and shovel for playing the game. Peekhole drama in the theatre is about as dreadful as old Lady Wishfort doing the Frug. The old girl just can't dance that way without being awkward and dull and embarrassing. So the boys can keep on piling up the statistics about the failure of "straight drama" and berate the public for having no taste. We'll still go to the movies.

That is, until theatre realizes it has the only magic left in this sweet land. And oh Mother, it has more magic than the movies or "a whole string of cat-houses in the valley" ever dreamed of having, for it is the one corner in the land where the immense meaning of "freedom" can still be played with — above, within, and beyond — reality. I am saying all of this only to set the scene for the "Flowerman" who is the key to *Bad Play*.

Theatre is some walls set up to form an enclosure, in which anything, a thing not yet named, past murder, past mirth, past pain, past pleasure, can "happen." Happen in a "place" that has never been seen before, or dreamed of; in a time that is neither dawn nor day nor springtime nor wintertime, in the middle of the nighttime, in another time, a secret time, an unheard-of time — a time that has no time — except for those particular hours in the theatre. And playing this new action, in this new time, can be strange creatures in strange costumes, or only the essence of these creatures, or the soul of a soul that only dreams it is a soul; and these nameless players can play any game — so long as it is a game of courtship, and all games are, whether they take place on Wall Street or in Vietnam or in a whorehouse in Sculley Square. This game of courtship (in the theatre) uses a strange language and strange gestures to court the silent players (the audience) into an act of love, using those rhythms of love so there can be birth. The birth of dreaming — or waking from the dreaming. The creating and breaking of reality — lest it be taken too seriously.

All of this may sound merely like madness — but it is a madness that resembles the unconscious mind. Freud said that art is an assault of the unconscious on the conscious but differs from dreaming in that it uses "a form" to make the assault palatable, pleasurable, and bearable. And now enter the Flowerman, for he is what gives form to the madness and reality (his reality) to the dreaming, for he is an artist as well as a dreamer. And he is a genius in that he possesses original ideas (as all lunatics do) but is able to embody the idea in a concrete and articulate form. (Sir Cyril Burt defined a genius as a "sleepwalker" whose dreams have hit upon the truth.)

Nothing much needs to be said about Charlie and Mary, the other two characters in this play, for I simply took them off the sidewalk — or rather they own a little house "on the corner of Fourth and Lake." But for this particular incident, happening, action, the Flowerman decides to play with them.

Only a few of the Flowerman's strange gestures are used in this play — those which he feels will best fascinate and entice and court Mary and Charlie and their audience. The Flowerman controls the lighting, controls the "sense of place," controls the "actions played" — all of which need bear no relation to the outside world, so careful and complete is the reality he creates, the better to fascinate and bewilder into seeking. He does not do this with the magician's sleight of hand (this would be condescending to our need to hinge our imagination and dreaming firmly to a television "Addams Family" kind of magic); rather he controls by using the potential of the theatre to be anyplace, anytime, where anything can happen. He does not harangue the pigeon feeders in Washington Square Park or "sit-in" or "teach-in" or picket the Capitol. Like Chekhov he wants to say "you ought to be ashamed at how badly you live" but then who doesn't already know that. Within minutes of his meeting Mary she fans the sweat between her breasts sighing "It's all so damned dull." Using this awareness of the dullness, he forces the players to play harder, to be better actors and, if they are strong like Mary, still have some juice left — they come out having dignity. And when he leaves the theatre to "chalk 'Merde' on the walls of the city," to "hang out in alleys and look over the leftovers" he is looking again for those clues to keep lives from being laid "as cheaply and easily" as "some bony whore."

Now you might say all of this can be done on television but it can't. That little screen so good for peeking just doesn't allow "bigness," and while the film can give Lawrence of Arabia his whole dry desert and ten million dry camels, it can't trap Mary and Charlie into a place where they can be watched — first to squirm, grabbing everything that is familiar, and when the familiar is removed attempt to break out revealing a panic that would smash down walls if it could, and since it can't at least wants the walls down and threatens that they will come down. (Check the subways, Central Park in the dark, the streets of any city at night — it's already happening.) There's panic in the land.

It is exciting to me that the Flowerman doesn't stop or end, is not contained within the play. We need Flowerman more than we need poverty-program coordinators. The only inhibition is that he must play in the theatre — he would be laughed at on the sidewalks, banned from the U.N. building, be unemployable in any American city, and the secret

111

service men wouldn't allow him to watch a Lyndon-Ladybird parade, for he has strange gestures and strange customs — and he whispers "you are unique," a dangerous message in this age of the Great Society of terpin-hydrate-takers and glue-sniffers and tranquil eaters. Without the Flower-man, Charlie and Mary would have a little glass of Mogen David, watch television, and go to bed early.

The reason I am going to such lengths in describing the Flowerman is that I can't get this play on paper — I don't know how to "write" it. (I wonder if anyone has ever written a "play.") In asking you to imagine the limitless limitations of the Flowerman I ask your own imagination to "move out." *The play isn't in the dialogue.* In fact if you are going to read the script quickly I would rather you skip the dialogue and try to visualize the stage directions.

The play takes place (the Flowerman completes his action) in some ten "beats." In each beat the scene changes, the action is different, the panic increases — as time is running out, something must happen. So much is accomplished in such a short time because the Flowerman uses our most powerful memory of action, the action of childhood, when our bodies were free and were used to express ourselves instead of just carrying around our heads and neuroses. He wakes up a sense of play, of games, thus courting Mary and Charlie and the audience into actions that contrast with the dull tightness of their unlived bodies. The bodies react and so does the mind. And because there is a universal memory of childhood games and rhythms the audience feels an empathy greater than when they see actors simply sitting on the sofa or sipping tea, or watch Doris in bed with her duck. The action frees and involves at the same time. I saw this kind of empathy in the Guthrie Theatre production of this play when the beautiful audience vocally responded to the jumping rope business — a spontaneous response because suddenly (in this context) the action looks strange but it is an action vaguely remembered by the mind, well remembered by the body. Thus the dialogue of the play can be denied and escaped — the action cannot. And because it cannot the theatre is again a powerful place, not to peek, but to play, and the Flowerman is allowed his power of vision. Which more or less amounts to saying that given a better play (in real life) Mary would be beautiful and we all would know this — not just the Flowerman.

PLAYWRIGHT'S PREFACE

In closing I would like to say thank you to the Office for Advanced Drama Research for several reasons: First, there is something delicious and healthy about thanking an institution when all of my writing attacks institutions. Second, this project allowed me freedom to work with an "idea of theatre" which was far more important to me than simply having a play done. Also the project (its power and money) opened the doors of the temple. And a play which says that temples have become bigger and more important than people should be done in a beautiful temple — which the Guthrie Theatre is.

In his Introduction to this volume Dr. Ballet says the playwright in modern America works in a vacuum. I have found it necessary to people my vacuum with actors, and even if they don't want to come to "my party" in person, their talent attends my typewriter so my characters leave the attic of my brain and get on the stage. Thus I am able to work with the finest talent available in the American theatre — among whom I include Evie McElroy and Michael Levin, the two actors I borrow most often to inhabit and uninhibit my "fictions."

When she is on stage you are sure that Miss McElroy has body odor, that she "meant to fix her hair before she came," that she is right off a stool from Johnny's bar, and you wonder a little "how in hell she got into the theatre," but she could sit on stage and do nothing but rummage through her purse for an hour and keep the audience hypnotized — they would somehow become totally involved in the search through her purse. This quality I pumped into the creation of Mary, and knowing that such an actress as Miss McElroy exists made creating the character an exciting and a more real experience.

Mr. Levin is an alley cat on stage, violently male, who always seems a little angry that he has to be on stage at all but the sidewalk at present is too dull. He has a stage presence I have seen in few actors — you are unable to define him, or see his face, and always there is an anticipation of the unexpected. Most powerfully he is able to give a sense of love, of caring, toward the other characters in the play — which in turn makes the audience care. There is a sense of humanity about him and for this reason the Flowerman takes Mary's homely crying face in his hands and tells her that "she is beautiful." The actor taught me by his acting.

ELIZABETH JOHNSON

And so, finally, I thank the project for making it possible for this actor and actress to re-create the roles of the Flowerman and Mary, which they did powerfully and brilliantly, roles which were created for them — in a vacuum.

ELIZABETH JOHNSON

St. Paul, Minnesota
July 1965

THE PLAY

Cast of Characters

FLOWERMAN
CHARLIE
MARY

A BAD PLAY FOR AN OLD LADY

The stage is open and while the audience is being seated the Flowerman is sleeping on the top platform with a newspaper over his face. He resembles only a pile of old rags. The house lights go out and very gradually a small pinlight comes up on the Flowerman. He stirs, brushes aside the newspaper, stretches as though waking from his personal sleep — i.e., not yet aware that he is a character in a play.

FLOWERMAN
A little coolness, please?
Let the darkness be . .
Some water?
A kiss . .
Sweet tenderness.
A bottle of wine . .
Sees that the light is neither sun nor moon. Raises on his hands and knees, animal position, head down.
Ahhhhh, I forgot . .
Shakes off the sleep. Suddenly remembers or knows.
Then is it time?
To play this play?
He listens; there is only silence. Checks out his strange costume, his flower hands, with some surprise, almost revulsion. To himself:
It seems I am the product of some demented doll-maker . .
Laughs, looks at the audience.
And who in hell dreamed up you? And was he feebleminded too?

Swings his legs over the side of the platform, eats a bunch of grapes, chatting — at first — with the audience.

We might chase beauty down the streets.

She has long legs and runs well . .

Ack, you have little taste for that.

YOU LIMIT ME . .

(*quick check on anger*) Or rather I am limited. In such a form I am reduced to absurdity and must stay within the house . . (*wheels, his eyes setting the limits of the enclosure, i.e., the theatre*) and play with souls all warm in fat to see what can be done about our obsession with tissue paper. (*dancelike marionette movement*) I'm to play a play and so it's said that when it's done . .

I DROP DEAD.

(*picks up the newspaper used while sleeping*) Oh, and I must spread newspapers for Charlie's death. Being more natural, in fact much like you, he will bleed. We'll lay him there. (*slightly curious, playful*) I wonder how long your plays are going to last, ere the rain drips through your nude skeletons grinning in the earth, beneath the stage on which you played . .

Your own "bad" plays.

(*deep bow*) I wish you all the "best" of roles. And may you learn to walk without a crutch and learn to speak (*pause*) so that it does not resemble eating (*pause*) each other.

The Flowerman now leaves the top platform, snaps his fingers for a pool of light on the second platform, signals for the pinlight to go off. This top platform is his only private domain, the place from which he watches the playing of Mary and Charlie, where he keeps his props, such as the pigeon suit and the makeup for Mary. Only when Charlie decides to be a pigeon and Mary a whore is this area used as an acting area for other than the Flowerman. As the Flowerman moves into the second area, Charlie begins his slow entrance through the audience. There is simple narration from the Flowerman as Charlie, intent on his own thoughts, comes slowly down the aisle:

At night there are lonely puzzled men who crawl out of corners and walk the sidewalks of your city. Ragpickers who smell of wine, for wine makes magic. And the demented, and deformed and aged whores walk then — in your clean city — for the darkness is kind to their ugliness. And kind to their darkling dreams that reality suffocates within its walls.

And Charlie walks.

And why does Charlie walk? This simple dull man who is neither outlaw
   nor poet?
Perhaps someone whispered in his ear that he was alive?
And he wonders how to make it not a lie.
Or maybe only to leave animal tracks behind him in the snow.
   Very softly calling:
Come, Charlie.
   He spreads out the newspapers.
The scene is set.
   *He freezes in position. Charlie walks on stage, still not aware of any
   direction. Stops. Looks around him confused about what the place
   is — like our attitude toward "place" in a dream. Charlie looks at the
   Flowerman and carefully and stiffly begins to walk away. The Flower-
   man takes a few steps and calls softly:*
Charlie.
   *Charlie stops and without turning reaches his hand behind him. We
   see the Flowerman take it with his flower fingers.*
   CHARLIE
(*softly — smothered*) Aggggggggghhhhhhhhhh. I'm not afraid, you're not
real, live or anything. A funny sound or just the way things feel in the
night, limb of a tree or a cobweb. I can brush you away . .
   FLOWERMAN
One of the "things" that wait in the shadows?
   CHARLIE
Like the sandman . .
   FLOWERMAN
Sandle man, candle boy, beggarman . .
   CHARLIE
"Go to sleep Charlie," my mother used to say, "or the sandman'll get
you." An' we all know what he did to the little boy next door. (*apologizing
for his reaction of fear*) I'm afraid sometimes . .
   FLOWERMAN
Of what?
   CHARLIE
The "things" standing just outside the door. (*apprehensive*) Or behind
me in the dark. At the water cooler I let everyone go first. Those "things"
are waiting. They wait, always waiting . . (*rush of words*) I lost my keys
today. I'm usually very careful about things like that. One must not lose
their keys or identification cards or . .

119

ELIZABETH JOHNSON

FLOWERMAN

Why?

CHARLIE

Why? Why then no one would believe who we are . .

FLOWERMAN

You could always show them your navel . .

CHARLIE

My navel . .

FLOWERMAN

It proves you had a mother.

CHARLIE

I did. She was a very strict Lutheran . .

FLOWERMAN

I'm sorry.

CHARLIE

(*confused, he rushes on*) I lost my keys, dropped them in the park, had some popcorn in my pockets — for the pigeons — an' I, well I (*slow*) lost the keys to my house. An' tonight while I was going to sleep I could hear the front door (*slow*) opening very slowly — am I dreaming?

FLOWERMAN

Aren't we all, all the time?

CHARLIE

Then I want to wake up . .

FLOWERMAN

What a brave little man you are. Operate then, on the cataracts in your
  brain.
Best we only dream we are awake.
Blind men dreaming of seeing and dead men dreaming of Being.
Perhaps the world's only a trick done with mirrors, Charlie,
And we are simply figments of someone's imagination.

CHARLIE

Whose?

FLOWERMAN

Obviously someone who wanted the trout streams polluted
And the wild flowers picked
And the Indians wiped out.

CHARLIE

It was a— a— a fine imagination.

FLOWERMAN

I saw a man today puking in a paper bag.

120

CHARLIE

That was his own fault. I don't want to talk to you — go away. You're making me nervous.

FLOWERMAN

Why?

CHARLIE

Well, a man's got to know where he stands an' — an' who he is!

FLOWERMAN

Why?

CHARLIE

Go away, you — you're just a — a . .

FLOWERMAN

Product of a dream?

By-product of insanity or a nightmare?

And what are you?

CHARLIE

I know. A man's got to know. I know I'm a man — my name's Charlie. I live on the corner of Fourth an' Lake . . (*the Flowerman dances away from him, runs up the aisle to sit in the audience, leaving Charlie alone on the stage*)

FLOWERMAN

Where is that in relation to the Pacific Ocean?

CHARLIE

Due south.

FLOWERMAN

To the stars?

CHARLIE

Directly under.

FLOWERMAN

Planet Mars?

CHARLIE

A — a — a — a little to the left of a straight line. (*hesitates*) Where are you? I don't want to be left alone.

FLOWERMAN

You're not. (*claps his hands and the houselights come up to half on the audience*)

CHARLIE

(*looks around him, grins, relieved*) Yeahhh. Well see, me an' them — we all . .

FLOWERMAN

Got navels. Every single one.

CHARLIE

Sure, an' we got names an' we do things an' . .

He speaks as though introducing himself to the audience in hopes of being friends, gaining acceptance, etc. Their silence finally unnerves him.

Myself, I work in a toy factory.

Put dead soldiers, toy ones that is, in enemy tanks.

Get off work at four.

Got a little problem with asthma

An' I got a wife.

You — you'll like Mary.

Well.

Yeah.

Pause.

They're all just sitting and waiting.

FLOWERMAN

For what?

CHARLIE

I don't know.

FLOWERMAN

What do they want?

CHARLIE

I don't know. Do they? (*hesitantly to the audience*) Do you know what you want? From me?

FLOWERMAN

Dances out along the step of stage.

Do you? Do you? Do you?

Stops abruptly, turns to Charlie.

They only know one fact.

That you will die, Charlie — and so they're waiting for that.

For the details of your death.

There's something in all of us that hungers for a Gothic tale.

To the audience:

That isn't a very nice thing to do to Charlie, is it?

With new energy:

Come, Charlie, you must forget them now.

Charlie moves toward the Flowerman, looking backwards over his shoulder.

Char-lie, you can't play with life if you're afraid.

Forget them — and what they're waiting for — come "play" with me.

CHARLIE

(*sits on the stage, tired, nervously looks around him*) What kind of night is it?

FLOWERMAN

A night after another carefully dull day.

It's a night of terror, of course.

Charlie starts toward him. The Flowerman lays his finger on Charlie's lips.

Sh-h-h-h-h-h-h-h.

Cups Charlie's face in his hands.

And you have a dull face.

But there's a fragment of hell in your brain.

And a piece of lace

Draws out the piece of lace.

In your pocket.

CHARLIE

(*laughs nervously*) From a girl — a girl named Nellie. (*tries to grab the lace back as the Flowerman dances away*)

FLOWERMAN

Do you snivel in your piece of lace?

And weep for Nellie?

Quite kindly:

Weep for her.

Weep for all the Nellies

With dark eyes.

Dream of their thighs.

Wax-like stamen dusty with pollen.

And their dark lips.

The silks they wore.

The Nellies.

Laughs.

All the Nellies you never touched.

CHARLIE

I don't want any dirty dreams . .

FLOWERMAN

Why?

CHARLIE

Got enough problems. You know — it says, thou shalt not covet thy

neighbor's wife. Yeah, well I do. Covet my neighbor's wife. Very much.
An' his goods too. (*nervously looks around, arms and hands jerk*)

FLOWERMAN

Little toy man . .

CHARLIE

No'm not. I'm a man . .

FLOWERMAN

That resembles (*writes*) an insect pinned to a board.

CHARLIE

What're you doing?

FLOWERMAN

This is my guest book.
Where is the fat woman?

CHARLIE

You're MY guest. This is my dream — an' you get out of it.

FLOWERMAN

I deal in dreams . .

CHARLIE

You belong to some kind of union?

FLOWERMAN

No, the flowermen haven't organized yet.
I'm only here to help. That's all.
  Blows smoke through his flower fingers.
To help you with your pain.
And to tell your lies and to dance with you.
The lady's late.

CHARLIE

(*backs away from him*) Mary Mary MARY MARY!
  As Charlie yells, the Flowerman twists and turns him while singing the
  name Mary. Charlie points to the top exit door that is opening.
  Mary comes in, looks around, sniffs. For some reason the place pleases
  her and she laughs softly — increases to hearty laughter. She's carry-
  ing three shopping bags; hanging out of one is a naked chicken.

MARY

Charlieeeeeeeee. (*calls softly*) Hey, Charlieeeeee. (*waits*) Ollllllliiiiiiieeeee
Ollliiieee Xan freeeeeeeeeooooooooo.

FLOWERMAN

Whoever won't come will be iteeeeeeooooooo.

MARY

(*laughs again*) Hey, Charlie, you dried-up bastard, where are you?

CHARLIE

Down here. I — I'm not doing anything, didn't expect you . .

MARY

That's a lie. Why go around offending strangers when you and me got it down to an art.

CHARLIE

You gonna be offensive?

MARY

Hell, honey, I haven't got any choice. Say, a pimply-faced boy out in the hall tried to stop me from coming in. (*yells with joy*) Seems it's a place for kings down there, Charlie. And saints. Couple times a week they burn one in the basement. I promised to make me a little crown out of newspapers next time. It must be a storeroom. An old storeroom.

CHARLIE

I don't think so.

MARY

You're not sure? (*all of the following as she is coming down the stairs*)

CHARLIE

No. It feels different. There's rats here but . .

MARY

Club 'em over the back with a stick, boy.

CHARLIE

Can't see 'em. Place is clean, but the air — air smells dirty.

MARY

Aghh, it's the same all over. Air's got a couple hundred years of decayed dreaming in it.

CHARLIE

This place has got that all right.

MARY

Lick your finger and lift it in the wind.

CHARLIE

No wind.

MARY

Rip a little paper off the windows . .

CHARLIE

Ain't no windows.

MARY

Yeah. Well, what's it seem like? How do the walls feel? That's the way you always tell, you feel of the walls. If they got that earthy smell about them and are a bit crumbly — you've had it. Gonna be cramped for space for all eternity.

FLOWERMAN

There are no walls, Mary.

MARY

That's bad. We're a hell of a lot dirtier in public than we ever thought of being in private.

CHARLIE

It's — it's a place to play . .

MARY

Have a little . .

FLOWERMAN

Wandering in the shadows backstage.

Orgy?

Funland?

Playlet?

A play in which we play ourselves?

A dream?

Daydream?

A scream in the evening?

After the carnival —

Instead of the circus . .

MARY

(*answers the voice — calls out*) 'Cause we didn't get asked to the party.

CHARLIE

Which party?

MARY

The one where you laugh a lot. (*steps onstage, looks around*) Maybe we should have had our little purging out on the sidewalk. Or in the park. The park's pretty. 'Cept in the dark you could get murdered by some duck lover. Wish some nice young man would rape me. So who's all coming? (*Charlie numbly shakes his head*) I can't imagine having an orgy with just you, Charlie. (*Charlie is nervously aware the Flowerman is watching from the top platform*)

CHARLIE

I think I'm having a nnnnightmare.

MARY

Do you good, baby. Don't just sit there, Charlie. How you gonna have a nightmare if you just sit there . .

126

A BAD PLAY FOR AN OLD LADY

CHARLIE

It's easy . .

MARY

Yeah? (*climbs into the empty chair the Flowerman has placed beside Charlie: they are now seated like spectators facing the spectators*) 'Nuff people out to have one of those old-fashioned fertility festivals — like them ancient Greeks, dirty devils. Agh, we'd just get the birth-control ladies on our backs. (*turns to play with Charlie*) Charlie, we can't just sit here. Gotta move it, honey, swing loose. (*She rummages in her shopping bags, busily sets the scene for a picnic in the alley — spreads a blanket, etc. Charlie likes these preparations since they don't seem to be so much at the mercy of the Flowerman. Thinks maybe Mary can carry the whole thing off — i.e., they'll have a good time in this strange place and just go home.*) Little Mogen David — got it especially for you, to celebrate your citation from the toy factory, forty-seven years without an accident. Knew you could do it, Charlie. And I brought along some decorations . . (*hands Charlie a couple of candles stuck in Chianti bottles*) so our picnic in the alley can be grandly lighted. Here, Charlie . . (*shoves a party horn in his mouth*) blow it! Fun, huh? Ain't this the damndest fun, Charlie? And some olives — eat 'em . . (*shoves them in his mouth*) eat 'em up. Olives make you passionate. Here eat the whole damn bottle. (*they drink wine, eat olives, Charlie blows his horn, etc.*) Wish I had on my red silk dress. Imagine all this fat in red silk. Overwhelming. Ah, it's all so damned dull. Doomed to solitary confinement in a pile of fat. But then what the hell — it's better'n bein' one of them plastic girls — saw some out on the sidewalk and they can walk and talk and everything, all made all nice out of plastic, more genteel parts are foam rubber. Charlie, they can even have babies. Scary, ain't it? That's after they connect with the men, the ones that got the little keys in their backs. At some circumcision ceremony they get keys *jammed* in their backs. Charlie, we are living in a bad dream.

CHARLIE

Don't say that. (*frightened again*)

MARY

What's your problem, honey? Your little key hurting you . .

CHARLIE

A man's got to know who he is — an' . .

MARY

(*bored with the picnic*) You like candles in Chianti bottles, Charlie? You like not having an accident for forty-seven years?

127

CHARLIE

A man's got to be careful . .

MARY

That's pretty damn careful. You like Mogen David? They get all these limp grapes and then unwashed monks sit on 'em. You like — you like four different colors in toilet paper? Yup, we got that and we got that ice-cool deodorant that can't get sticky or gluey, even if you smear it all over the windows like they do on television. I got a jarful under each arm. Jesus — I can hardly stand it — this is so exciting. Charlie?

CHARLIE

What?

MARY

Charlie, what would you say about me getting dope addicted?

CHARLIE

I don't know, you being Catholic an' all . .

MARY

Ah hell, baby, Catholics are great on hallucinations. Nuts about 'em. That's okay, Charlie. Here — just put your head in my lap and imagine that I'm the goddess of love and maybe we can get something going. Comfortable?

CHARLIE

A little embarrassed.

MARY

(suddenly tender with Charlie) Can't kick it though, can we? The bad dream. I mean like we still — we still get to use the public john on Forty-Second Street and smell the lilacs and — Charlie, what are we doing here?

CHARLIE

I don't know.

MARY

Hey, meeting here in this place and all, maybe we get to hop it up a little.

CHARLIE

Why'd you come?

MARY

    Evenly — a threat:

'Cause I couldn't sleep, Charlie.

Not all day —

And all night —

Not every day — I can't sleep, Charlie!

Kinda like magic, you and me being here —

In the heart of the temple.

128

Right in the middle of town.

In the morning we'll have our bowls of exciting cereal and —

But tonight —

We . .

FLOWERMAN

Are players.

They have stood up to move and now freeze in their positions —
seeing nothing.

CHARLIE

Are we only . .

MARY

Players?

The Flowerman walks around them, looking them over.

FLOWERMAN

So we are. Are all players.

Mary, your top lip is sweating and, Charlie, your breath smells of you . .

Puts out his hands to hold the silence, includes the audience.

And we all breathe out and in and out and in — like soft hands opening
and closing.

As we play these moments that have n'er been played before by anyone.

They are ours to use.

Short command to Mary and Charlie:

Use them well.

He snaps his fingers at the clutter on stage and Mary and Charlie hast-
ily shove the blanket and bottles, etc., back into her shopping bags
as the Flowerman goes on talking in simple narration.

It must be kept in mind that no one here is as dependable as this stool or
the wooden platform on which we stand. And so there is no assurance
that a lie cannot be told — or a truth revealed bearing confession to that
sickly repulsive child that lives in all of us. Or someone out there suddenly go mad and crawl the walls. Or scream. Or laugh. Cry. We are not
Masters of such things. *Yet.* (*turns Mary and Charlie into him*) This very
light is diseased, unreal, and watching us are worn and nervous men.
(*withdraws his hands, and leaves them — without their picnic, their*
props, alone — having nothing to do: they have been told what the "place"
is like)

MARY

Charlie, who is he? (*Charlie only stares at the Flowerman*) *Charlie?*

CHARLIE

I think (*pause*) I (*pause*) like (*pause*) him. He said I resemble an insect.

129

MARY

That wasn't a compliment, Charlie.

CHARLIE

Didn't say *I* was an insect — said I was a man who resembles an insect. I think he's fascinated with it. I like his fascination . . (*hesitantly*) I — I might perform for you, Mr. Flowerman . .

MARY

Oh no, you're not. Taken up with trash . .

CHARLIE

(*ignoring her — still to the Flowerman*) If you got anything in mind — for the well-trained insect man, domesticated. Tricks of derring-do? (*Charlie laughs at this in self-deprecation*)

MARY

(*calling to the Flowerman*) Hey, you, don't pay no mind to Charlie. Last week he thought of joining the masons so he could be in the circus. Charlie, you're small enough the way you are. Now, Mr. Flowerhead, if you just want to move on, go recruit someplace else . .

FLOWERMAN

The "scene" is here . .

MARY

Look, if we're trespassing . .

FLOWERMAN

(*laughs*) When aren't you? Did you inherit . .

MARY

Charlie and I bought a little piece of property — corner of Fourth and Lake . .

FLOWERMAN

I am the owner of a dream . .

MARY

Yeah? Where you keep it?

FLOWERMAN

Here. And I watch it work.

MARY

You're like a night watchman?

FLOWERMAN

Yes.

MARY

Who needs you?

FLOWERMAN

You.

MARY

I'm a free kind of woman. Don't need . .

FLOWERMAN

Then why did you prostitute yourself to a toy man?

MARY

Look, you got a dirty mouth . .

FLOWERMAN

Because he was the only thing the earth would allow you to possess.
Squuueeeezzze him, Mary.

MARY

I'm not going to play with . .

FLOWERMAN

You are already . .

MARY

I believe in . .

FLOWERMAN

In what?

MARY

In keepin' my corner clean . .

FLOWERMAN

Inside?

MARY

Naw, inside I'm a regular pigsty.

FLOWERMAN

I'm the hero of . .

MARY

You'll never get that kind of role in the movies. I can tell you that . .

FLOWERMAN

The hero of unreality.
Of that pigsty.

MARY

What do you do? All spooked up like that?

FLOWERMAN

I chalk the word "Merde" on the walls of the city.
I hang out in alleys and look over the leftovers.

MARY

You eat 'em.

FLOWERMAN

No, I dress them up in pretty costumes and teach them to dance.

MARY

Dancing teacher?

FLOWERMAN

Yes.

MARY

I'd like to dance.

FLOWERMAN

I'll let you.

Mary and Charlie stare at him silently.

"Play."

MARY

At what?

FLOWERMAN

Tosses them sword props from stage.

At murder if you want.

At mirth.

Act out your pain, your pleasure . .

MARY

So who put you in charge?

FLOWERMAN

This isn't the night for home movies, Mary. That you lead dull lives is of little importance; why bring the plays that we play daily here. (*begging them, for them to have dignity*) Permit me to love your mystery — it still exists, despite the lack of newspaper coverage. (*stares at them for a moment, gives in to anger*) Ahhh, I am old and I am tired. And ugly. (*moves quickly to the platform, his back to them*)

MARY

So what have you got to offer?

FLOWERMAN

A form without an end. (*with his foot rolls a ball toward them*) Here's a red ball for you to play with. (*walks out of their sight but audience can see him watching them*)

CHARLIE

What're we doing?

MARY

Playing. With this red ball. (*they sit on the stage like two children, legs spread out, rolling the ball to one another, using it for emphasis, etc., at times*)

CHARLIE

Why?

MARY

We must want something, Charlie, or we wouldn't stay here.

CHARLIE

Want what?

MARY

Just want. Can't put my finger on it, but like hell, Charlie, maybe we need some new games. Charlie, I — I feel like I'm gonna blow up. It's not enough to hate John Birch and the Communists and Clare Boothe Luce.

CHARLIE

Clare Boothe Luce?

MARY

Yeah, I hate her.

CHARLIE

Why?

MARY

We don't have to know that, Charlie. Just hate her. Don't you hate the Communists, Charlie? (*Mary is not talking for message — she is only emptying herself out, trying to find what it is that is bothering her; her playing is much intensified over the picnic scene*)

CHARLIE

Yeah, I hate 'em.

MARY

Well, you better. That's the going symbol. If you don't you better get out, go on their side, and hate us. See, stuff like that keeps us from flagellating ourselves in the alley. You start flagellating, Charlie, and stop hating and they'll send you to the clinic to get mentally healthy. (*pause*) I want — I want . . (*starts to rise, looking up at the Flowerman; he in turn moves toward her*)

CHARLIE

Mary, you stay away from him. (*now to keep her from going along with the Flowerman in whatever game it is he wants to play, Charlie uses whatever props are available to entertain Mary as she goes on talking*) Everything's all right.

MARY

Like sure, who needs a bad poet? Just that I'm starting to get glad for the damndest things. Doctor took a cancer test of me and said it wasn't typical. I said I was glad — for once I could belong to one of them nice minority groups like the Negroes. So I came out of the doctor's office all proud and sat down on a bench waiting for the bus and the lady next to me said her daughter was a multiple sclerosis. Topped me just like that. Hell, I told her I had a daughter that was a fifty-seven-year-old waterhead. We just sat there waiting for the bus knowing we weren't typical. Charlie, maybe you and I should take to madness instead of trying to fight this thing out alone.

CHARLIE

I don't know. I — I'm too tired. He's here . .

MARY

I won't let him get you. He wants to take your pin out. I won't let him turn you on. Sometimes I think you should be just turned off and die, Charlie. I don't know why I think that. 'Spose it's easier. My sister took to madness.

CHARLIE

I know. I find her unpleasant, rather nasty.

MARY

I got to hand it to her. She's having herself a ball.

CHARLIE

She lifts her dress up over her head an' dances in the backyard.

MARY

I sat with her the afternoon and I thought what the hell. We both filled our mouths full of radishes, plugged up our ears with 'em, dropped bunches down our necks — now if the folks out there wanted radishes consumed instead of refrigerators she'd be a damn good citizen to have around. A real eater. You ever think of taking to madness, Charlie?

CHARLIE

No.

MARY

You ever do anything, Charlie?

CHARLIE

I dream about them rats . .

MARY

(calls out her line with her eyes on the Flowerman, who takes this as his cue to move in on Charlie with her) Forty-two years dreaming about the rats.

CHARLIE

The way they feel running over your feet when you're sleeping and down the center of your back. The way they skitter around corners . .

MARY

Forty-two years dreaming about them rats and you never seen one . .

134

CHARLIE

Floating in the river . .

FLOWERMAN

But in the trenches during the war you never saw any and that's where you wanted the rats. You handed out horse blankets, that's what you did.

CHARLIE

(*yells in frustrated anger*) I KNOW ALL THAT! (*the Flowerman switches off the lights; there are only candles on the stage*)

MARY

Ahhhhhhhh. Hey, Charlie, stand up! Wave your arms. You gotta great big shadow. Makes me water up and want to cry. How come you made love to me for twenty-five years like you were apologizing for it? Being a Protestant has been part of your problem, Charlie. Can't your shadow do something?

CHARLIE

I can make barking dogs. (*does so*)

MARY

And I can make ducks eating their fingers. (*they squat like two children with their shadow play; the Flowerman comes behind them and lays his hands on their shoulders*) That's not enough is it, bad poet?

CHARLIE

It's fun making shadows.

FLOWERMAN

Make them laugh then. Let your shadows scream for you . .

MARY

I ain't got no screams inside of me . .

FLOWERMAN

You lie. Strangle your shadows on the walls.

CHARLIE

I don't want to do that. I'd rather just hate Clare Boothe Luce, 'long with Mary. Sometimes . .

FLOWERMAN

Yes.

CHARLIE

When I dream I hate Mary . .

MARY

Along with the rats he dreams about them girlie pitchers hung inside the closet door. What do you think about when you look at them pitchers, Charlie?

135

FLOWERMAN
Send your shadows out to play.

CHARLIE
Maybe mine would strangle little girls . .

FLOWERMAN
Afraid again?

CHARLIE
I have to be careful. It'd disappoint my mother.

MARY
Wish they could do something. Sometimes I feel this big. (*strides toward her shadow, watching it grow*) Like I got my powers. Instead of — of being a — a . .

FLOWERMAN
A big beetle that someone's tipped over on its back.
Writes this down.
Your arms and legs clawing away at the air, running motionless.

CHARLIE
(*moves aside to the Flowerman*) Did you write that down?

FLOWERMAN
In my guest book.

CHARLIE
What're you going to do with it?

FLOWERMAN
It's a record of subtle crimes.

MARY
(*ignoring all this and watching her shadow*) Charlie, you think it's enough? You making barking dogs and me making ducks eating their fingers? And then every Saturday night we go down to your brother's place and play Ping-Pong. I get so damned sick of Ping-Pong. I'd like to kill that little ball, maul it to death. And once a year we get to sit in the sand and watch the fireworks in the sky. And every day lick stamps.

CHARLIE
You don't have to lick 'em.

MARY
Every night lick stamps to get matching lamps for each end of the sofa. It takes 93,000 stamps to get good matching lamps. Just think of licking 93,000 stamps.

CHARLIE
You don't have to lick 'em. You can wipe 'em with a rag. (*pause*) I want you to be good now, Mary, be a good woman . .

A BAD PLAY FOR AN OLD LADY

MARY

It all don't seem to be enough, when I feel like this, when I got my powers.

CHARLIE

I always wanted to do something for you, Mary. I — I ran for alderman.

MARY

Yeah, you did that.

CHARLIE

I'd come home dead tired.

MARY

You'd come home dead tired.

CHARLIE

An' I'd get the sign out of the garage an' put it on the back of the car.

MARY

You'd get the sign out of the garage and put it on the back of the car.

CHARLIE

An' then I'd drive all over town.

MARY

Drive all over town.

CHARLIE

Naming myself for alderman. (*like a battle cry*) Charles Schwartz for alderman.

MARY

(*picks up cry*) Charles Schwartz for alderman.

FLOWERMAN

(*grabs their hands and waves them*) Charles Schwartz for alderman!

MARY

(*waving the naked chicken, yells*) C'mon, Flowerman, lead on!

ALL THREE

To the tune of "Hi-Ho, Hi-Ho, It's Off to Work We Go," they march up and down the stage singing, with the Flowerman leading them.
Charles Schwartz, Charles Schwartz, Charles Schwartz for alderman, Charles Schwartz, Charles Schwartz, Charles Schwartz . .
They build to a wild tempo and go into a locomotive cheer, spelling out "C-h-a-r-l-i-e Schwartz, Schwartz." Charlie, waving his hand like a campaigning politician, gradually runs down, smiling happily. He walks away from them humming the song and lies down on an old trunk. Mary looks at him sadly, takes the blanket used for the picnic and spreads it over him. The Flowerman motions for the lights to soften.

137

MARY

You just go to sleep now, Charlie, and dream about them rats.

CHARLIE

An' when the votes came in . .

MARY

Go to sleep, Charlie, you got the rats . .

CHARLIE

(*growing very sleepy*) I only got three votes. (*pause*) Yours (*pause*) and mine (*pause*) and someone else's. (*long pause*) I always wondered about that one. Could we just . . (*rises and freezes in position about to leave the stage*)

MARY

Go home? (*freezes halfway between Charlie and the Flowerman*)

CHARLIE

An' sleep?

MARY

In our corner?

CHARLIE

The walls . .

MARY

Pasted shut with yellowed wallpaper.

FLOWERMAN

To die.
Silently —
So quietly.
So quietly.

CHARLIE

Good night.

MARY

Good night.

> *Charlie is dragging his blanket. They look like a little, dowdy couple leaving the stage for their dull corner in the city. They turn on the good-byes and freeze again.*

CHARLIE

We'll walk . .

MARY

Together on the sidewalks.

CHARLIE

Stay outta . .

A BAD PLAY FOR AN OLD LADY

MARY

The shadows of the buildings.

CHARLIE

And sleep.

MARY

And rot.

FLOWERMAN

And whine softly in your walls of yellowed wallpaper.

Turns them like dolls toward him.

Stay and "play"!

I'll feed you sweetmeats —

And serve you tea —

And I have a little chloroform rag to hold under your nose in case you want to scream.

The scratching of a man against the walls of his cell grows feebler and feebler and he dies with a little of the wall under his fingernails.

I would set you free —

But I have no means.

You still have energy —

I'll play with that.

Stay and "play."

MARY

C'mon, Charlie, let's "play."

CHARLIE

At what?

Now the Flowerman leads them in games — follow the leader, hop-scotch, etc. — timed with Mary's speech.

MARY

Play ring-around-rosy

And all drop dead.

Play at panic, Charlie, and find who's the boogie in the corner.

Play like we're people, baby,

In the land of the free.

Play with progress, honey, 'cause it's made us all so happy!

Play with costumes — 'cause naked we don't belong to any organization
— except man — and he's so dirty.

Hell, play 'cause we're the only animals who can laugh.

FLOWERMAN

Animals are put in cages.

MARY

Animals are put in cages.
Wild ones in the madhouse
And tame ones in the bank.
Weaker ones they domesticate and let them become keepers and feeders
of machines. Real-refined and you get to work for I.B.M.
I know all about the care and feeding of the animals . .

FLOWERMAN

Runs with the ball.
You must behave for your bread.
And learn a trick to perform for coins.

MARY

Not tonight.

FLOWERMAN

That's right.

MARY

Tonight I battle with my enemy . .

CHARLIE

It's not me. I never did nothing to you.

MARY

That's right, Charlie, you sure never did. Why you'd qualify as one of
them poverty pockets, honey. I say Yipppeee for them folks down in
Harlem, at least they think they know who their enemy is — wish to
hell I knew mine . . (*looks around her*)

FLOWERMAN

(*ties a towel around Mary's eyes and spins her for blindman's buff*)
Blindman's buff . .

MARY

(*runs groping in the dark as the Flowerman blindfolds Charlie*) I can't
find anyone . . (*pause*) it's like no one's here . . (*pause*) who's all
playing?

FLOWERMAN

No one.

MARY

You mean I . .

FLOWERMAN

What?

MARY

All this stumbling . . (*pause*) It's all dark and . .

140

FLOWERMAN
Mary Mary.

CHARLIE
Mary Mary.

FLOWERMAN
Mary.

MARY
I stumble against objects. That's all there is. (*the Flowerman grabs her hand, puts a donkey tail in it with a pin*)

FLOWERMAN
New game — pin the tail on the donkey . . (*Mary lurches in several directions*)

MARY
Where's the wall?

FLOWERMAN
What wall?

CHARLIE
The wall with the donkey?

MARY
Where's the donkey?

FLOWERMAN
There isn't one.

MARY
How do we win?

FLOWERMAN
Jump rope and I'll show you . . (*lashes the floor with a jump rope and standing against each other they jump*)

MARY AND CHARLIE
One two buckle your shoe
Three four shut the door
Five six pick up sticks
Seven eight lay them straight . .
Jump
Jump
Jump
Jump

The rope is beating so fast now they can only jump.

FLOWERMAN
(*runs around them as they continue jumping, and ties them together with*

the jump rope) Next we'll play ball and jacks without a ball. And Ping-Pong without a paddle . .

MARY

What are you doing? (*they huddle together, begin to panic*) You've trapped us.

FLOWERMAN

You let me — why? (*they stand silently*)

CHARLIE

What are you going to do to us?

FLOWERMAN

(*puzzled*) What do you think?

CHARLIE

There's witnesses — out there, if you're gonna . .

FLOWERMAN

I wanted you alive —
What did you want?
WHAT DID YOU WANT?
Just games, little games to play, games to win at, win what?

MARY

You said you'd set us free.

FLOWERMAN

Is that what you wanted?

CHARLIE

Yes.

FLOWERMAN

I don't know you at all.
Free from what? How could you want freedom and end up like this?

MARY

We wanted freedom from time. From time. There's all that time . .

CHARLIE

There's hours an' weeks an' months an' years . .

FLOWERMAN

(*holding the end of the rope, runs to the top of the platform*) But you have so little time.

CHARLIE

No.

MARY

(*the two are struggling insanely against each other and the rope*) We have forever. (*pause*) And there's got to be something to do. We always have

142

to find something to do. There's energy, that wants to act, has got to do
something — with all that time.

FLOWERMAN

Not free from time. Free *in* time. Not freedom from — but freedom to . .

MARY

To do WHAT?

FLOWERMAN

(*lashes the rope, and they fall down, rolling over on top of each other and
across the stage out of the rope*) YOU FIND THAT OUT. (*they pull off their
blindfolds and stare at him*) You're not the victims of some crime. You're
the criminals . .

MARY

How do we get out of here?

FLOWERMAN

It's not going to be easy.
This play is not some bony whore that can be laid as cheaply and easily
    as you've laid your lives.
LET IT BE HARD TO ACT!

MARY

Dance with me, Flowerman. I'm ready.
I got on my old lace step-ins and I dance with an ancient lover.
Crank the victrola, Charlie . .

   Charlie cranks an imaginary victrola.

FLOWERMAN

I've saved two Indianhead pennies for your eyes.
When they turn green I'll . .

MARY

No, not me — I didn't like the dark and I didn't like my hands tied. It's
him, save him — help him. (*with the Flowerman begins doing the minuet,
twisting her neck around to talk*) He gets up in the morning to go put
them dead soldiers in toy tanks. I get so I can't stand him. I look at him
when he comes in the door and he's a little toy man. He doesn't eat much
anymore. Just tea with a lot of sugar and some day-old biscuits, he doesn't
eat the fresh ones 'cause the old ones might go to waste. And — and I
get stingy on the food with him. I put smaller and smaller amounts on
his plate. So he's weaker in the morning and then it's easier for him to
stand there all day, all these good days in April, and put little men in —
come, Charlie, and dance with us.

143

ELIZABETH JOHNSON

FLOWERMAN

Do you want to? (*Charlie nods his head and he and Mary take their places for the minuet*)

MARY

Have a ball, Charlie, a grand ball.
I'm Scarlett O'Hara who ain't never been hungry again.

CHARLIE

I always thought of myself a little like Ashley Wilkes.

MARY

Did you, baby?

CHARLIE

Bowing to Mary in the dance.
You ever been unfaithful to me, Mary?

MARY

Yeah, that time down to your brother's place . .

FLOWERMAN

Left foot, Charlie, tap, tap, tap, follow the music.

MARY

You love me, Charlie?
All three move beautifully and precisely with perfect form within the minuet, a very contained dance.

CHARLIE

No, no, I don't. I feel kindly toward you.
Tap. Tap. Tap.
But for a long time you've been smelling like a rotten lemon.
And sometimes you remind me of a big squash bug.
Their voices are modulated, dreamlike.

FLOWERMAN

When did you first become monsters?
Curtsy now and bow.

MARY

And bow.

CHARLIE

And bow.
I've spent my life feeding a large squash . .

MARY

Because you couldn't bear to be without its tangling vines.
Move in close and kiss
And duck.
I crippled you . .

144

CHARLIE

The pain was sweet.

MARY

Your dirty linen . .

CHARLIE

Your love of candy . .

MARY

On our wedding night we wore Halloween masks . .

CHARLIE

Paper bags over our faces.
I was scared.

MARY

You were good to me, Charlie.
Circle slowly —
Circle slowly . .

FLOWERMAN

Dip and nod.

MARY

We are dying, Charlie.

CHARLIE

We are dancing.
Ashley Wilkes at the carnival with bad teeth.

MARY

Scarlett O'Hara with a mouth disease . .

FLOWERMAN

Circle left and circle right —
Curtsy left and
Dip and nod.

MARY

Circle faster.

CHARLIE

Circle faster.

FLOWERMAN

Circle left and circle right
And . .

MARY

Wilder music —
Could we have wilder music . .

*As they ask for it the music goes faster, but they can no longer move
in the minuet at this pace and by the end of their speeches they are*

*jerking helplessly with the music, rising up and down on their toes like
mechanical dolls.*

CHARLIE

The dance is strangling me. Could we have some wine?
How about a little wine?

MARY

I can't breathe —
I'm an old whore — that prostituted herself to a toy man.

CHARLIE

It ain't who I am —
What I'm wearing and
Moving like this . .

FLOWERMAN

Dip and nod . .

MARY

Circle right . .

CHARLIE

I'm someone else.
When I look in a mirror
I don't know that person — it isn't me.
I don't feel like that.
I got sparkling warm eyes
And red lips.
I don't wear wrinkles and mouse hair.
I got mouse hair.

FLOWERMAN

These are our costumes.

MARY

Mine's pretty ratty —
For a passionate woman like me.

CHARLIE

I don't like this dancing. I can't hear the music.

FLOWERMAN

You can have different costumes. I only dream I am a flowerman.

MARY

Who are you?

FLOWERMAN

A saint without any good lines to say.
He laughs, they laugh with him.

MARY

Me, I'm actually a Parisian whore without the face for it.

FLOWERMAN

And what are you, Charlie?

CHARLIE

I'm a pigeon. That's what I am, a pigeon.

MARY

Goddamnit, Charlie, you do have some imagination left.
The Flowerman takes the bird suit out of the trunk.

FLOWERMAN

You like their eyes don't you, Charlie?

CHARLIE

Yeah. They're warm and sparkling.

FLOWERMAN

And the way they dip and nod their heads.

MARY

A bird, Charlie? I thought you always dreamed about them rats.

CHARLIE

No, I . .

FLOWERMAN

Pigeons get to sleep in the sun, and their nests are colored by stained
glass windows.
They beat their wings when the big bell rings —
And walk along the ledges of the church spires.

CHARLIE

That's better'n being a man — who works in a toy factory. When I was a
boy I thought of being a monk, their obedience never seemed so bad. To
me. (*getting into the pigeon suit*) The guy who owns the toy factory, his
name is Mr. Poophard and he smells like he's got a rotten potato hidden
in his parts. It always makes me feel silly being obedient to a man named
Mr. Poophard who smells like . . After a while I learned to . .

FLOWERMAN

Numb out. Be numb out, Charlie.

CHARLIE

I'm going to be a pigeon —
And I'm going out in the park.

FLOWERMAN

Will you be afraid?

CHARLIE
There's just a lot of Charlies out there.
You know, insects pinned to boards —
They sit and want . .

MARY
Helps Charlie pull up the suit.
Go on. Get into your war feathers, Charlie.

CHARLIE
It fits. I think it fits.

MARY
Turns to dig a wig out of the trunk.
And I got red curls to wear.
You like 'em.
We're gonna show 'em that Charlie and Mary got passions.

CHARLIE
You like my wings.
You sure they look all right?

MARY
Well, hell yes.
The Flowerman hands her a large rouge pad.
The rouge!
Give it to him.
Smear it on me, Charlie.
Great red cheeks that'll shine on the boulevard like roses.

CHARLIE
No.

MARY
Please, Charlie.
Do it!

FLOWERMAN
He wants to but he can't.
Let me.
The Flowerman tilts her head back.

CHARLIE
My arms, they're my wings.
Inside here.
He flaps them.

MARY
Get loose. Swing loose.
She twists and the Flowerman rouges her cheeks. Charlie panics.

CHARLIE

Don't do (*pause*) *that.*

Your hands.

Don't do that to her.

He runs, butts up against the Flowerman. She swings her face, red-rouged cheeks, red curls.

Cover my head.

The Flowerman pulls the hood of the pigeon costume over Charlie's face.

MARY

A pigeon. A great fat pigeon.

Take it off.

She moves toward him. Frightened, he pulls back.

CHARLIE

I'm going out in the sunshine now.

MARY

I know your goodness, Charlie.

CHARLIE

I can't hear you.

Indicates the hood.

MARY

It's all right, Charlie, to be gentle.

To be tender.

CHARLIE

I like the sunshine in the park.

I never ever had much time in the sunshine.

And I like popcorn.

MARY

He's an awfully big pigeon —

Isn't he?

Charlie.

CHARLIE

I feel good.

Well 'bye —

'Bye now.

MARY

You gonna come back?

It's all getting funny —

Turns to the Flowerman.

149

I don't know who he is —
And he can't hear me talking.
>FLOWERMAN

What did you want to say?
>MARY

I can't think of a damned thing. Hope there's lots of popcorn or something — have fun with the birds or something. I wonder if we ever said
anything? But him being a bird sure makes it a hell of a lot harder. And
he could have showed a little respect for me being a Parisian whore. I got
to pick up some social graces for this getup before I hit the promenade.
>FLOWERMAN

Pick it up, Mary.
>*Begins to snap his fingers.*
Oh, you are so lovely.
You want music?
>MARY

Gimme some balloons.
Lotsa red balloons.
>*Grabs them. Music is playing.*
And blue lights.
I want the blue lights.
>*The Flowerman snaps his fingers for the lights.*
Yeah ha. I am so ripe.
I'm moving out.
>FLOWERMAN

It's funland, Mary.
No thieves of your pleasure . .
>MARY

No man.
>FLOWERMAN

No beggars for your pain.
>MARY

Pain's obsolete.
>FLOWERMAN

No need to know.
>MARY

Smells good
And tastes good.
I wanta throw open that door
And this door

And swim out.
Lemme go.
She lets out a wild yell.
Flog the world with a naked chicken . .
FLOWERMAN
No.
MARY
Fill up my old douche with kerosene and burn down the city . .
FLOWERMAN
No.
MARY
Violence . .
FLOWERMAN
That's cheap . .
MARY
Something filthy . .
FLOWERMAN
That's too easy.
MARY
There are walls . .
FLOWERMAN
No.
MARY
There are doors I can't open . .
FLOWERMAN
No.
MARY
Do you lie?
FLOWERMAN
No?
MARY
Grabs him.
Do you lie?
FLOWERMAN
I have hyacinth feet.
And larkspur fingers.
You have sweet flesh —
It can tell no lies —
It feels the sun
And wills to run.

Dancing behind her, he looks down the tunnel. Then like a song director he moves in front of her. There is a sense of urgency about him.

And now there's a little song for you to sing.

My country, 'tis of thee —

Sing, Mary . .

    MARY AND FLOWERMAN

Robust patriotism.

My country, 'tis of thee,

Sweet land of liberty,

Of thee I sing.

    The Flowerman stands in front of Mary, directing her in the song. Slowly he backs away from her down the tunnel, still directing her to sing.

    MARY

My country, 'tis of thee.

    FLOWERMAN

Calls from the tunnel.

Sing, Mary,

Keep singing . .

    MARY

Sweet land of liberty,

Sings more hesitantly, peering down the tunnel to see what is happening.

Of thee I sing.

My country, 'tis of thee.

    FLOWERMAN

Calls to her while she keeps on singing.

Mary.

All pigeons have to be registered with the park commissioner.

    MARY

Sweet land of liberty.

    FLOWERMAN

And the good citizens got scared of a bird that big.

    MARY

Of thee I sing.

It was just a costume.

When Charlie's naked he ain't so scary.

    FLOWERMAN

The park commissioner was wearing a costume too.

And the good citizens that shot him.
Don't we all wear costumes, Mary?

    MARY

Yeah, I guess so.
Shouldn'a taken the pin out —
Just left him wigglin' . .

    FLOWERMAN

Until dead?

    MARY

No.
Maybe he got to scratch a little something out there.
Hey, baby —
You — you shoulda watched out for them Charlies.
They got the scaries —
Want the insects pinned —
Got no way to let out their nasties —

    Mary has him in her arms.

It's a dirty rotten shame.
He coulda had a little fun —
There's sunshine in the park.

    FLOWERMAN

Lay him down
On these old newspapers.
We'll cover him with Nellie's lace.

    The Flowerman draws the lace out of his pocket.

    MARY

Here.

    Unpins her feather boa.

I don't feel up to being a Parisian whore.
What with Charlie dead and all.

    Dumps the gaudy feathers on him.

Oughta make out a little sign.
Here lies Charlie — who ran for alderman.

    FLOWERMAN

And dreamed of Nellie.

    MARY

Apologized for makin' love —
For twenty-five years.
I'm a little sorry too, Charlie.

Makin' love —
Shoulda made a man.
    FLOWERMAN
It's time . .
    MARY
    Slowly raises her head.
No.
    FLOWERMAN
Time to go now —
All plays have limits and this one's done.
    MARY
No no no no.
A couple more pages —
One more scene —
Bring in some more people.
    FLOWERMAN
Too late for new characters. We would cheapen the form our imitations
    take.
    MARY
Something to do. Gimme something to do.
I — I could raise tulips.
    FLOWERMAN
There's no earth here.
The world's turning to construction.
We make our own flowers — out of plastic.
    Unpins his flower hands.
Fair copies, don't you think?
    MARY
Hey look, hey, Mr. Flowerman —
Mr. Flowerman —
MISTER FLOWERMAN, YOU KNOW, THAT'S LIKE NOTHING, YOU KNOW.
    FLOWERMAN
I know.
    His back to her, he peels off his costume, throws it in the trunk.
Only scraps and bits and pieces, torn lace and salvaged fog.
    Rubs off his flowerman eyes, makeup.
It's hardly a fact.
Stays in the shadows, plays with the dark —
And has a love for red.
    Stands looking at her, a simple man.

There are worse roles to play.

MARY

Who are you?

FLOWERMAN

A hired actor.

MARY

Hired by . .

FLOWERMAN

By whoever hired you — and said you had to act.

MARY

So you got anything else to tell me, Bad Poet?

FLOWERMAN

Sets the shopping bags she brought on the stage beside her, puts her hat on her head.

Tell you . .

MARY

What?

FLOWERMAN

Holds her crying homely face in his hands.

I tell you — that your face is beautiful.

Starts up the aisle.

MARY

Please . .

The Flowerman turns for a moment, motions for the lights to come down onstage — only a small light on her remains — then he continues up the aisle whistling "Playmate, Come out and Play with Me."

How shall I play? It's getting dark and there are only objects to stumble
    against. My old games feel dirty.

Sees he is about to go out the back door.

Ad lib it —

Go it on your own.

FLOWERMAN

Exact echo of her words.

Ad lib it —

Go it on your own.

Exits.

MARY

(*as if talking to the corners, the shadows of the theatre, the remnants of the Flowerman*) Give me some poetry to say. I am capable of poetry if you just give me some to say. I'd like to talk pretty. Give me a few good

lines. One grand speech so I could knock 'em dead in the aisles. So you could pick me out of the mess on the sidewalks. Let me through . . (*pause*) Let me through . . (*pushes imaginary people out of her way, looks around her, and sees there's no one and she's done nothing*)
They said this was a place for kings and saints. Well, here's my
Halo made out of newspapers, my newspaper crown —
My collar, the rope around my neck made out of newspapers.
Let me be a queen — but I gotta have a costume . .
She digs the things out of the trunk, throws them.
IS THIS ALL?
Grabs the remnants of the Flowerman.
You got to say about me. Look I could knock the sides out of this place.
I got my powers.
I don't want to go home and lick stamps and buy cookies for the girl
    scouts and support cancer and weep for a dead bird.
I'm all hopped up on living — I'm so high I can't come down.
Her speech is not *directed at the audience; rather she begs something, someone else to help.*
Turn me on and let me fly . .
I COULD SING.
But this bad dream — ain't got no good tunes in it.
I DECLARE WAR ON THE PEACE OF LIARS.
I don't want to drive carefully and be socially secure — if that's all there
    is —
'Cause I'm alive —
And I know I'm alive 'cause —
Because I . .
(*gropes, feels in the air for words*) Give me some lines — goddamnit, give me some lines. (*as if they come one by one*)
'Cause I can still smell the lilacs and use the public john on Forty-Second
    Street,
And when it rains the hot concrete stinks.
I'm alive
And I'm scared of the good citizens who never saw a bird that big.
So they shot Cock Robin. Smaller birds are still eating their popcorn.
And I'm scared of the plastic people and those men with the little keys
    in their backs —
They better not think they know me.
I'm — I'm an animal who laughs.
Helplessly she beats her fists on the floor laughing. Her laughter be-

comes almost insane and there is crying mixed in it — an angry kind of
crying.

So how come I gotta be so serious about the temples.

Build 'em high and white

Raises her hand to the temples, shields her eyes — against their huge-
ness.

And all shining in the sun, and then when you tell me that I gotta behave
in those temples, not put dirty hand marks on the walls —

When the temples leave me all lonely down here —

She huddles in the small spot of light.

Then I want the temples to all come tumbling down

A threat:

So we animals who laugh can get out our wheelbarrows and clean the
rubble out of the streets . .

She gropes, trying for words, for sound — an animal. Almost in the
dark she whispers:

They said — my face was beautiful.

THE END

TERRENCE McNALLY

And Things That Go Bump
in the Night

for my father and mother

"From ghoulies and ghosties
Long leggitie beasties
And things that go bump in the night
Good Lord deliver us!"

— *14th Century Scottish folk prayer*

And Things That Go Bump in the Night by Terrence Mc-
Nally was performed on February 4, 5, 6, 7, 1964, at the
Tyrone Guthrie Theatre, Minneapolis. It was directed by
Lawrence Kornfeld. Set by Dahl Delu. Costumes by Sally-
Ross Dinsmore. Lighting by Richard Borgen.

Cast of Characters

FA	Alvah Stanley
GRANDFA	Ferdi Hoffman
SIGFRID	Robert Drivas
LAKME	Lois Unger
RUBY	Leueen McGrath
CLARENCE	Joseph Chaikin

The Broadway production presented by Theodore Mann
and Joseph E. Levine in association with Katzka-Berne
Productions opened on April 26, 1965, at the Royale Theatre, New York City. It was directed by Michael Cacoyannis. Set by Ed Wittstein. Costumes by Noel Taylor. Lighting by Jules Fisher.

Cast of Characters

FA	Clifton James
GRANDFA	Ferdi Hoffman
SIGFRID	Robert Drivas
LAKME	Susan Anspach
RUBY	Eileen Heckart
CLARENCE	Marco St. John

PLAYWRIGHT'S PREFACE

At the time *And Things That Go Bump in the Night* was first performed, at Actors' Studio in New York City in December 1962, the play was called *There Is Something Out There* and was in one act. I had written it the summer before. The cast for this production included Madeline Sherwood, Ben Piazza, Hal England, and Barbara Dana. The director was John Stix.

The response was violent. The play and its author were scorned, reviled, rebuked, and generally crucified. One young lady came perilously close to a nervous breakdown in her hysterical tirade against the play. She was dressed entirely in black — the big floppy hat, the dress, the stockings, the high boots, everything black — and her voice was very loud. She made an indelible impression on all present, especially the author. She was the first in a long line of Ladies in Black howling their outrage at his play.

Others that afternoon were equally violent in their approval of the work. It would be nice to say they were dressed entirely in white. They weren't. They were a motley lot and their opinions ranged from qualified affirmatives to one or two really spectacular outbursts of enthusiasm. It was a heated discussion all the way, with the Ladies in Black snorting off in triumph and a few of the Mottled lingering behind just long enough to whisper encouragements.

The play was put into three acts and retitled the following summer, the summer of 1963. A few weeks later I received a letter from Arthur Ballet of the Office for Advanced Drama Research at the University of Minnesota explaining the Rockefeller grant and asking if I would be interested in participating. My name had been suggested by Alan Schneider, the director, who had seen the play in its one-act version at Actors' Studio. I met Dr. Ballet a week or two later, gave him the play to read, and by early fall we had made final plans for the play's production in Minneapolis at the Tyrone Guthrie Theatre.

The choice of cast and director was left entirely up to me. I had admired Lawrence Kornfeld's direction at the Judson Poets' Theatre and was delighted when he accepted my invitation to direct. We arrived in Minneapolis early in January and began to rehearse. Rex Partington and Yvonne McElroy, our stage managers, showed us every possible courtesy and enthusiasm. So did everyone else in Minneapolis involved with the production. Five weeks later the audiences who came to the Guthrie saw an excellent performance of *And Things That Go Bump in the Night*. What they thought of the play itself I leave up to them. Once again the Ladies in Black were present and from the results of a poll taken by the University it would seem that this time *les dames en noir* were persons of forty plus years in the upper middle and over income brackets of either the Episcopalian or Presbyterian persuasions. The people who "liked" the play seemed to be poor, young, and Jewish. The score of this poll was slightly, but ever so, in our favor.

The Minneapolis experience was memorable on every level. Leueen MacGrath played Ruby with a malevolent intelligence, a passionate respect for evil, and a gallant bravery in the face of the inevitable that was light years beyond this poor attempt to describe it. Ruby is not a sympathetic part but Miss MacGrath was not afraid. That she moved the audience in her final moments is a matter of record. That she had the guts to wait till then, her very last speech, for the audience to "go" with her is an example of acting courage I have seen too seldom in our Freudian, Method, "Oh, God, isn't it sad I'm such an awful person? but you see, when I was five . ." oriented theatre. It was a noble, uncompromising performance. Robert Drivas not only played the part of Sigfrid, he extended it. I learned from his performance. I learned more about the character himself, more about the play as a totality, more about that thin line which separates creative acting from routine. His was a passionate, luscious interpretation. Incredibly disciplined, the storm clouds building from within, and then, in the final act, the bursting. Again a part was played as I had written it. And then some. Joseph Chaikin was enormously moving as Clarence, Ferdi Hoffman was Grandfa incarnate, and Lois Unger a delightful Lakme.

I go on about the actors not to flatter but to thank them. From them the play took its life, its shape, and its rhythm. The greatest value of the Minneapolis experiment was this bringing together of actors and author. I saw the play and heard it, many times in rehearsal, four times with an audience. My only regret is that the experience was so abrupt. We were flown from New York, we rehearsed five weeks, gave four performances and were flown back the very next day. We would have liked to stay longer, put the play aside for a while, prowled about some, gone back to work, maybe worked on something else for a time, performed, rehearsed some more, performed again. We had a taste of working in a way not possible in the commercial theatre with its limited rehearsal period and attendant hysteria and we have since grown greedy for more of it.

I returned to New York, optioned the play to Kermit Bloomgarden (a venerable patriarch of the Broadway theatre who professed to like the play although he is neither young nor poor albeit Jewish) and set about cutting and revising. The play had been enormously long in Minneapolis, too long, in fact, but I had left it uncut since the performances there seemed the ideal opportunity to hear all of it first and then, at leisure, whittle at the dead spots. The revisions were primarily in the third act, which struck the Minneapolis audiences as static. I agreed with them.

We were planning an early fall production. The summer passed; Bloomgarden dragged his feet. It was fall; Bloomgarden was imbedded in cement. I sent the play to Michael Cacoyannis. He liked it and gave it to Ted Mann, who proved to be a veritable twinkletoes of a producer and a wonderful gentleman to boot. By Christmas it was settled that we would go into rehearsal in late February, as soon as Cacoyannis returned from a Paris commitment.

We opened in April. This time the Ladies in Black turned out to be the daily critics. Their performance made the original's back at Actors' Studio look tame. Two of them went so far as to demand that I be electrocuted on that fence in the second act. The others contented themselves with rock throwing and name calling. People asked me how I felt. I told them. Others treated me as if my entire family had been exterminated by one grisly blow of fate. I accepted their condolences. My younger brother, Peter, who had come from Texas fully expecting to see his big brother carried through the streets of New York in Roman triumph, said un-flinchingly, "Well, there's no place to go but up." He was right, too.

Is the play, then, "bad"? I think not. Broadway is glutted with "bad" plays, yet none of them are greeted with the vehemence the critics lavished on this one. Over twenty thousand people saw the play in New York. I don't know who they were or where they came from. I don't even know if they were Jewish. But they came and they were there of their own vo-lition. They were aroused and making it felt. Some even demonstrated in front of the theatre, urging passersbys to attend. The play had found an audience, our producer lowered the prices, and the remaining perform-ances were sold out. It was deeply gratifying to all of us.

And now the play is being published. The present text is the one we went into rehearsal with for the New York production. It is not the text we opened with. The cuts made during production were voluminous and, I fear, detrimental. They were made for a variety of reasons, none of them sound, and it is good to have them restored.

The play is about fear and negation. Ruby is its hero, Sigfrid and Grandfa its conscience, Clarence and Lakme its victims. It is also a play about choice: the choice of evil, which is a constant, over chaos, which is not necessarily a good. It is a tragedy of intelligence. Ruby perceives too clearly many truths but does not see the basic one: we cannot destroy everything without destroying ourselves. Her error is her negation of all links with mankind. Her way of life must end as it does, in a colossal suicide. Her Message to the World has come true. For herself, for Sigfrid, for all of them. But she does not flinch before the steady tread of her ap-proaching fate. She will not grovel. She cannot beg. She meets it head-on and defiant, like a female Prometheus.

There are, I do not doubt it, those who will read the play and then throw it down in outraged agreement with our heroine, the Lady in Black. But may I have a final word with them? She has gone on to be-come something of a television personality and I am hard at work on another play. And in the meantime we have become very good friends.

TERRENCE McNALLY

New York City
August 1965

THE PLAY

The Setting

A room. Two doors, left and right. At the rear of the stage there are stairs leading to a third and larger door. Beyond this door is the outside. The furnishings in the room — various sofas, chairs, small tables, etc. — are stark and modern. The style is anonymous, abstract somehow. Of special importance is a low table with an intercom system, phonograph, and tape recorder on it. There is a piano. And facing the rear wall and to one side is a very large chair. Whoever sits in it will be invisible to the audience. The lighting is white: a brilliant, blinding white which is of a uniform intensity throughout the room. There are no shadows or semitones.

The Players

FA, short, overweight, and almost bald. He is in his fifties.

RUBY, his wife. A good deal more youthful looking. She is larger, too.

SIGFRID, their son. Twenty-one years old, dark and good-looking.

LAKME, their daughter. Thirteen years old. She is wiry and tough, rather like a rooster.

GRANDFA, very, very old. But the eyes are quick and bright.

CLARENCE, early twenties, thinnish, irregular features.

AND THINGS THAT GO BUMP
IN THE NIGHT

ACT ONE

At rise the stage is empty. Absolute silence. Pitch dark. After a moment the red light on top of the intercom goes on and we begin to hear the terrible grunting and groaning noises of a person just waking up from a long and deep sleep. The sounds must be amplified to an almost unendurable volume. The theatre should reverberate. We hear a bed table laden with medicine bottles and knickknacks crashing to the floor. And then, after a yawn of agonizing dimensions, we hear:

RUBY'S VOICE

(*a pronouncement*) I'm awake. The Ruby is awake. *Buon giorno a tutti!* (*another huge yawn*) Correction: almost *buon giorno* and not quite *a tutti.* (*the lights begin to come up now: slowly, slowly, slowly*) Is everyone out there? . . the four of you? . . that's nice . . I like it when the four of you are out there listening to me . . and I'm all snuggled up . . broadcasting from bed. It comforts me, yes! (*lights up ever so slightly more*) Children, I have six toes! Look at them. One, two, three . . Come in here this instant and look at them! (*tiny pause*) Sigfrid? Lakme? Are you . . there? (*no response; Ruby laughs*) You little nippers! I know what you're up to. Pretending not to be there when I call you. Nasty nippers, naughty. Not nice. (*a pause; the light always slowly coming up*) I know you're out there, too, Grandfa. So shall we begin again? (*and now each time more floridly*) Buon giorno a tutti! (*pause*) Buon giornissimo a tutti! (*pause*) Buonissimo giornissimo a tutissimo! (*pause; then sudden, hard*) I SAID GOOD MORNING! ALL RIGHT, IT'S YOUR EVENING BUT IT'S

MY MORNING AND I SAID GOOD! (*pause*) I'm not amused by this. I warn you . . the four of you . . there will be retributions. I said I am not amused . . ANSWER! (*the lights are still coming up; Ruby's desperation is becoming more apparent*) I don't have six toes. I have eight! NINE! Sigfrid, you go right over to that intercom and answer me! Lakme, you too! (*the anger is steadily mounting*) You miserable . . you think it's so funny, well I do, too! If I ever thought you'd left me alone in this terrible house I'd . . kill myself! I suppose you'd like that! (*the lights are at full brilliance now; and then the terrified outburst*) I WON'T BE ALONE IN HERE! SOMEONE! SOMEONE COME IN HERE! . . PLEASE! (*Grandfa, scowling and dour, has come into the room in his wheelchair*) Who's that? . . Sigfrid, is it —? Lakme, you know better than to frighten me like this . . Fa, don't let them! Who is it? (*Grandfa is headed toward the intercom*) WHO IS OUT THERE??? SOMEONE . . PLEASE . . TELL ME WHO IT — (*Grandfa has snapped off the intercom*)

GRANDFA

Harpy! (*the room returns to utter stillness*) Oh am I ever glad this is my last night in this house. They don't know how glad I am. (*he is fiddling in a tote bag which he carries on one arm of his wheelchair*) No one knows how glad I am. (*produces a long strip of black knitting*) I don't know how glad I am! (*knits a moment*) My teeth in a goddamn cookie jar! (*Fa stirs in his chair at the rear of the stage; the first time we have noticed him. He will be reading a newspaper during the scene with Grandfa that follows.*)

FA

West.

GRANDFA

(*turning*) Son?

FA

It's moving west.

GRANDFA

I found 'em. And guess where the little monster hid 'em. The cookie jar. Not in the freezer again . . not like last time . . oh no, not her, not Lakme . . but the cookie jar.

FA

The government says it's moving west.

GRANDFA

(*crabbed*) What is? What's moving west?

FA

It.

GRANDFA

Poppycock! (*he can't get over it*) Eighty-five-dollar teeth she hides in a goddamn cookie jar! (*an appeal to some deity somewhere*) GODS!

FA

Listen to this. (*reads*) "A definite westerly movement in its western motion has been definitely defined," a high-ranking government spokesman who declined to reveal his identity told reporters today. "Alas," the anonymous spokesman added.

GRANDFA

And I say poppycock.

FA

The man in government said alas.

GRANDFA

The man in government is a politician. I'm an old man.

FA

So it's headed west?

GRANDFA

(*who often talks to himself*) He's also anonymous . . no, that's something in common.

FA

Which way is west?

GRANDFA

We are.

FA

Are you sure?

GRANDFA

We are the west, much good that ever did us.

FA

(*flat*) Oh. That's upsetting.

GRANDFA

It's disgusting.

FA

(*turning to another part of the paper, with great complacency*) Well here it's safe. No one's gonna die down here. Not in our sanctuary.

GRANDFA

You're damn right they're not. They're already dead.

FA

(*a weary rejoinder to Grandfa's protests*) It's only a room, Grandfa.

GRANDFA

Basement! It's not a room, it's a basement.

FA

Yes, Grandfa.

GRANDFA

Upstairs, now those were rooms, real rooms. But this thing, what you've built down here . .

FA

We're safe down here, Grandfa, and that's the most important thing these days . . to be safe. Everyone's doing it.

GRANDFA

I suppose so. I suppose you are safe down here. But safe from what?

FA

It, Grandfa, it.

GRANDFA

It . . IT!

FA

It.

GRANDFA

I hate this basement. I hate that fence up there. I hate the reason for them.

FA

You're malcontent.

GRANDFA

I'm old, damnit, there's a difference.

FA

(*folding the newspaper*) You've done your best, Grandfa, and what else can a man do but his best?

GRANDFA

I don't know . . I DON'T KNOW ANYMORE!

FA

(*settling deep in his chair for a long, long sleep*) What time are they coming for you?

GRANDFA

Early. As soon as the streets are open. This infernal curfew . . I could've gone tonight.

FA

(*covering a huge yawn*) We'll miss you.

GRANDFA

I won't. Should've done this years ago. Only I thought *you* had to put me to pasture. Didn't know I could do it myself. (*slight pause*) Well maybe you . . a little bit . . miss, I mean. Blood's blood. (*looks up from*

170

his knitting) . . I don't suppose you want to kiss me. (*the first snore from Fa*) SON!

FA

(*immediately responding, but groggy*) I'm listening, Grandfa.

GRANDFA

I said . . (*an old gentleman's embarrassment*) I said I didn't expect you wanted to kiss me.

FA

Now Grandfa!

GRANDFA

I didn't think so. (*slight pause*) It's been done before, you know.

FA

(*sleep overtaking him again*) Yes, Grandfa.

GRANDFA

It's a sign of affection . . a kiss is.

FA

Yes, Grandfa.

GRANDFA

And stop calling me that! That's their name for me.

FA

(*even sleepier*) We'll drive up every Sunday that it's nice.

GRANDFA

Well don't!

FA

. . every Sunday . . just like Ruby said . .

GRANDFA

You won't find me!

FA

. . every Sunday that it's nice . .

GRANDFA

I'll hide! I'll hide in a thicket!

FA

(*going fast now*) . . we'll find you . .

GRANDFA

You think . . you think!

FA

(*lapsing into sleep*) . . we'll find you . . Grandfa . . oh yes! . . we'll . . (*The snoring begins: an even rhythmic drone. Grandfa sits a moment. He is sad. Then he goes slowly over to Fa and puts his hand on Fa's shoulder. He looks at Fa. He does not move. There is a stillness.*)

GRANDFA

(*a gentle moan; a benediction; a forgiveness*) Oh. (*Now he moves away from Fa. Maybe he clears his eyes with his fist . . for perhaps there has been a tear or two. A pause. Now he is taking a writing book out of the tote bag. It is his Chronicle. He opens it, looks at his last entry, and then begins to write.*) "I am dying. It is acknowledged. I do not want to. It is not understood." (*Sigfrid is seen at the top of the stairs. He wears a heavy-knit, navy blue sweater with a large white "Y" on the front. He carries a football. He pauses there briefly.*) Life is . . it is not . . easy. It is not that.

SIGFRID

(*bounding down the stairs now, exuberant*) So they all went down to the seashore and . .

GRANDFA

(*at once, moving away from him*) . . and were drowned by their grand-father. Eavesdropper!

SIGFRID

No! They roasted wienies. They all went down to the seashore and had a wienie roast. Grandfa wouldn't drown his grandbabies.

GRANDFA

You don't know. You don't know what he wouldn't do!

SIGFRID

(*playing with the football, assuming a center's position*) And you're wrong about life, too, Grandfa. It's just one big fat snap! (*He shoots the ball between his legs. It hits Grandfa in the stomach with a thud. Sigfrid assumes an attitude of immense disappointment.*) Aaaaw! We could've had 'em, Grandfa. Some school try that was. Where's your oomph? You all out of oomph? (*Grandfa charges wildly at him with his chair*) Atta boy! That's the spirit.

GRANDFA

(*more sad than angry*) If I had a gun . .

SIGFRID

. . you'd shoot yourself! Now cheer up, Grandfa. It's your last night here.

GRANDFA

And I am jubilant!

SIGFRID

OK, I'm sorry. Peace?

GRANDFA

(*gruff*) Peace. (*and then*) Just a few more hours . . a few more hours in this room.

SIGFRID

Come on then, Grandfa, one last round of "Oh what a rogue and peasant slave am I."

GRANDFA

Not on your life.

SIGFRID

For old time's sake?

GRANDFA

I was good, Sigfrid. I was damn good. Those plays had stature. The characters had stature. They were the measure of a man. But now — (*cutting off abruptly, wheeling around in his wheelchair, looking in all directions*) All right, where is she?

SIGFRID

Who?

GRANDFA

That little troll child. Your sister.

SIGFRID

Lakme?

GRANDFA

Where is she? What direction is she going to come at me from this time?

SIGFRID

She'll be along. We got separated in the crowds. There's so many people out just before curfew, rushing back home.

GRANDFA

Any chance of her getting trampled to death?

SIGFRID

Not Lakme.

GRANDFA

Too bad. (*then*) What was the strategy for today? Today's bait?

SIGFRID

A football, Grandfa.

GRANDFA

A football!

SIGFRID

Well it worked. A football. A blue sweater. A little sister. And . . (*snaps his fingers*) we have a friend for tonight. His name is Clarence, Grandfa. And he sure has stature!

GRANDFA

Does it never stop down here with you people?

SIGFRID

Every night, Grandfa, someone every night.

GRANDFA

If you'd only —!

SIGFRID

(*hard*) Don't start in on me. (*then, gently*) Oh my Grandfa, my sweet and wondrous Grandfa, there are more things in heaven and earth than are dreamt of —

GRANDFA

In *your* philosophy, Sigfrid!

SIGFRID

You may not believe this, Grandfa . . I daresay you will find it incredible . . but the simple truth is that . . (*pantomimes very clearly the words "I love you"*) very, very much.

GRANDFA

(*fiddling desperately with his hearing aid*) What's that? What's that you said? (*It is a moment before Grandfa realizes what Sigfrid has done. They look at each other.*)

SIGFRID

I do. (*Lakme is heard at the top of the stairs. Her entrance is announced by the sound of a small child bawling her head off. The moment between Sigfrid and Grandfa is quickly broken.*) Enter one crocodile: tearful. (*Lakme appears, her face a study in childish misery. She sobs, howls, and in general carries on like there is no tomorrow. It is almost convincing. Her dress is tomboyish and appropriate for a thirteen-year-old. She might wear her hair in pigtails. She carries an array of photographic equipment: cameras, cases, etc. She is howling like a banshee, yet is perfectly capable of stopping should it be to her advantage. Sigfrid speaks with mock cheerfulness.*) Hello there, little one! What seems to be the trouble? You pick another fight with that German shepherd down the road? (*Lakme increases her howling*) Poor little Lakme. All forsook and chewed on. Comfort her, Grandfa.

LAKME

(*in heaving breaths between sobs*) Gran— Grandfa! . . Grandfa, Sigfrid tackled me! . . hard!

SIGFRID

(*mocking*) Not true, not true.

LAKME

He did! Look! (*she hunts for and finds a tiny cut on her knee*) See? . . see? (*Grandfa snaps his teeth at her: three times. Lakme continues in her normal voice; it is an ugly one.*) Where did you find those? . . hunh? Sigfrid, did you tell him where his teeth were?

SIGFRID

(*absolving himself with a gesture and then pointing to her injured knee*) That was quite a recovery . . even for you.

LAKME

(*tough*) Oh yeah? (*She begins howling again — though not quite so effectively as before — and limps her way over to Fa. Again she speaks in the congested voice.*) Fa! . . Sigfrid tackled — Wake up! (*furiously shaking him*) How are you going to have that heart attack if you sleep all the time? . . Hunh? . . LIAR! (*Sigfrid has been enjoying this enormously. Lakme turns on him now.*) Well it hurt!

SIGFRID

(*explaining to Grandfa*) It was nearly an hour ago. She said "ouch" . . that's all. And not one whimper all the way home.

LAKME

(*the anger dissipated into a general sulkiness*) Well you certainly don't expect me to waste my tears on you! A lot you care . . stinky! (*sits and examines the cut on her knee*)

SIGFRID

(*coming back over to Lakme*) How now, scab?

LAKME

There will be one! And I have a dance recital coming up next week . . two solos! It'll look terrible.

SIGFRID

Then you'd just better tippy-tap-toe your way into Ruby's bedroom and let her kiss it. That'll make it go away.

LAKME

(*flaring*) I don't tap dance! We do modern . . acrobatic modern.

SIGFRID

All right, then acrobat-modern your way in there . . slither.

LAKME

(*rolling down her pants leg*) You're such a cheat, Sigfrid. You say we're going to play touch football and then as soon as I get the ball you change it to tackle.

SIGFRID

And what about that stiff-arm? You practically gouged my eye out.

LAKME

That was different. That was a tactic. (*the little lady bit now*) Besides, if I were a twenty-one-year-old . . boy? Hah! . .

175

SIGFRID
(*he means this*) Watch it, Baby Snooks!

LAKME
(*continuing*) . . I'd certainly be embarrassed to be seen playing football in a public park with a thirteen-year-old child.

SIGFRID
Oh you would?

LAKME
Yes! And when the thirteen-year-old child just happens to be a thirteen-year-old girl . . !

SIGFRID
A what . . ?

LAKME
. . his own little sister, in fact . . well, that's just about the worst thing I ever heard of. And then hurling her to the turf like that . . a vicious tackle . . !

SIGFRID
(*suddenly on the defensive for the first time*) Now look, you little dwarf, you tripped. I didn't push you. You tripped.

LAKME
(*amazed that he could have taken her seriously*) I know that, stupid. Of course I tripped. Honestly, Sigfrid, you can be so dense sometimes. You know what a little liar I am.

SIGFRID
There's some jokes I don't like.

LAKME
(*with great affection*) You're such a dope. (*gets up to join him at the intercom and makes a final reference to her injured knee*) I don't mind helping you get the friend here so much . . I mean I know the reason for it. It's just the ploys you use. Couldn't we try another way? Like croquet or something? This really hurts. (*puts one arm affectionately around his waist*)

SIGFRID
(*into the intercom*) Hey Ruby! . . wake-up time! (*then to Lakme*) I can't help it. It's just my nature. I'm very . .

LAKME
(*anticipating him, so that they say the word together*) . . ployful! (*they laugh and jostle each other like the very best of friends, which, of course, they very often are*)

RUBY'S VOICE

(*on the intercom; it is very small, very frightened*) Sigfrid? . . is it you, Sigfrid? . .

SIGFRID

No, Karl Marx and Trotsky! Who do you think?

LAKME

Batman and Robin!

RUBY'S VOICE

(*with some relief*) Lakme!

SIGFRID

(*the little game over*) Come on, Ruby, hustle it.

LAKME

Wait'll you see him, Ruby! The friend.

RUBY'S VOICE

(*hell hath no fury*) . . you bastards! . . you utter, utter bastards! . . you think you're pretty funny, don't you? . .

SIGFRID

Ruby!

RUBY'S VOICE

. . had our little kicks for the evening . . hunh? . . we showed her what kind of games we can play . . we had ourselves one big fat laugh! . . HAH!

SIGFRID

Ruby, what — ?

RUBY'S VOICE

(*an explosion*) HOW DARE YOU PRETEND YOU'RE NOT OUT THERE! HOW DARE YOU!

SIGFRID

(*completely confused*) We didn't. I mean we weren't.

RUBY'S VOICE

Can you imagine what it's been like for me in here? Can you possibly conceive the terror of it? Of waking and thinking I was alone? Utterly, completely alone? And then hearing sounds . . and no answer, no answer at all? Can your pea-sized little hearts even begin to understand what an experience like that does to a person?

LAKME

I bet it was Grandfa playing tricks on her again. Say something to her, Grandfa.

GRANDFA

(*obligingly, loud and clear*) Harlot!

177

RUBY'S VOICE
I quivered . . yes! . . for fifteen minutes Ruby quivered!
LAKME
Can you picture it, Sigfrid? Ruby quivering?
RUBY'S VOICE
. . not knowing who was out there . . *what!* . . it could have been anything!
LAKME
(*acting it out*) The demon of death gulch! Aarg!
RUBY'S VOICE
That it was finally happening even! That it had come! Yes, I was that terrified!
SIGFRID
Ruby — !
RUBY'S VOICE
(*huge*) I WAS SO ALONE!
SIGFRID
(*cutting in, stern, to head off the outburst*) BUT YOU WEREN'T ALONE! (*a pause*) Ruby?
RUBY'S VOICE
(*a trifle disappointed*) I wasn't?
SIGFRID
You woke up early, that's all. No one had come down yet. Fa and Grand-fa must have still been in the upstairs dining room.
LAKME
Sigfrid and I were back here in plenty of time for your wake-up. We all were.
SIGFRID
If you were upstairs . . in one of the old bedrooms . . maybe there'd be some reason.
LAKME
I'm only surprised you didn't turn the fence on already!
SIGFRID
Christ, Ruby, it's a good thirty minutes till curfew!
LAKME
Sigfrid and I were on the streets . . we were outside . . where it can happen! . . and we're not all gone to pieces. (*a pause*) Ruby?
SIGFRID
Hey, Ruby. (*Ruby has come into the room behind them. She watches them a moment as they hover solicitously over the intercom.*)

178

AND THINGS THAT GO BUMP IN THE NIGHT

RUBY

(*flinging wide her arms and with purposeful, humorous exaggerations*)
ECCO LA MAMA! (*then, in a deeper voice*) If you ever do that again I will
take you upstairs and push you off the roof . . the four of you! (*advances
a step and again flinging open her arms*) GUARDAMI! (*another change of
voice*) Such bastardy, such unspeakable bastardy! (*a final step forward*)
ABBRACCIAMI! (*no one has moved toward her yet*) I said kiss me, damnit,
and I meant kiss me! (*Lakme crosses and gives her a rather perfunctory
kiss. Sigfrid stays where he is.*) Scorpions! (*A word now about Ruby's
appearance. It is a spectacular disappointment. Oh, the peignoir she wears
is fancy enough and there are many rings on her fingers and expensive
slippers on her feet. But Ruby herself will disappoint you. Her face is
without makeup and seems almost anonymous. The intense lighting in
the room, you see, washes the "character" out of her face so that it is
impossible to tell very much about her except that she is no longer young.
As for her hair, well she might as well be bald, for she wears one of those
wide elastic cloth bands women use to pull the hair back from their faces
before applying makeup. The appearance of her entire face, in fact, is
best suggested by this word "bald." Or "plucked clean." Or "erased." So
this, for the time being, is Ruby.*)

SIGFRID

Now if you'll just calm down, Ruby, and let me explain — (*Ruby makes
a sharp intake of breath*) Are you? Are you calm now?

RUBY

(*great dignity*) Considerably. And don't patronize.

SIGFRID

All right, now tell me what happened. Was it one of your dreams again?

RUBY

(*a deliberate sulk*) No.

SIGFRID

You're sure? You're sure it wasn't one of your nightmares?

RUBY

Yes, I'm sure and the word's *cauchemar*.

SIGFRID

Then you must have —

RUBY

(*imperial*) Say it!

SIGFRID

(*anything to accommodate*) Cauchemar.

179

RUBY
(*wincing*) *Mon dieu*, that accent!

LAKME
(*with great care and love for each syllable*) *Cauchemar.*

RUBY
Bravo, bravo, arcibravo!

LAKME
(*so in love with herself*) *Cauchemar!*

SIGFRID
Damnit Ruby! If you're not interested in this — !

RUBY
I am extremely interested!

LAKME
(*delirious*) *Cauche — !* (*Sigfrid slugs her*)

RUBY
What happened?

LAKME
(*not in a whine*) Sigfrid hit me.

RUBY
(*matter-of-fact*) Hit him back. (*Lakme does so. Sigfrid doesn't respond. They are used to this little ritual.*)

LAKME
I did.

RUBY
(*continuing where she left off now*) I am extremely interested, Sigfrid . . I am extremely interested as to why . . why with all the care, love, and protection I have lavished on you . . why with all the lovely and nice things I have given you . . your fabulous good looks, for example; courtesy of me, natch! . . why with so much . . with so many goodies in your little hopper . . why . . (*and with an abrupt change of voice*) you turned out to be such a miserable son of a bitch!

GRANDFA
(*to his private world at large*) I could answer that one! (*but he doesn't*)

SIGFRID
(*he's had it*) Christ!

LAKME
(*virtue triumphant*) That puts your little light under a basket!

RUBY
(*gently remonstrating*) Bushel, dear, bushel.

180

LAKME

(*discovering a delightful new word*) Bushel-basket! (*then, making it an expletive to hurl at Sigfrid*) Bushel-basket!

RUBY

(*stopping Lakme cold*) And that goes for you, too! You're both sons of bitches. You're all four sons of bitches. The whole world's sons of bitches! Except me. I'm nice. I like me. (*considers this a moment, then*) Sigfrid, look at you! . . that outfit . . is that what you wore? . . You're outlandish in that sweater! (*singing hilariously*) Boola, boola, boola, boola! Well I hope it worked! You did find someone in that getup?

SIGFRID

(*laughing, too, now*) Yes, monster mother. I found someone.

RUBY

Male or female? And do say male. It's been the little ladies, the little ladies nearly every night now.

SIGFRID

Well, Clarence is male, Ruby.

RUBY

Wonderful!

LAKME

(*sibilating*) Oh yes! Very male. Very definitely male.

RUBY

(*flat*) Oh. It's going to be one of —

SIGFRID

(*before she can finish it*) That's right, wonder mother, one of those nights.

RUBY

I don't approve, of course . . but *la vie n'est pas en rose.*

SIGFRID

You love it, you old bawd!

LAKME

We had a little trouble with him. He kept thinking better of it.

RUBY

(*dead serious*) But he's coming, Sigfrid? You're sure of it?

SIGFRID

He'll be here.

LAKME

He'd better be! Can you imagine it alone down here? Just the four of us? Without the friend? Yikes! (*gets up and wanders over to the tape recorder: in a moment she will have turned it on*)

181

RUBY

Oh it's going to be another lovely, lovely evening! I can feel it in my . . what, Sigfrid?

SIGFRID

(*playing along with her*) Fangs, Ruby, you can feel it in your fangs.

RUBY

Yes! Yes, I do!

RUBY'S RECORDED VOICE

(*on the tape recorder*) "The way we live. Message to the World Number 812."

LAKME

(*paroxysms of joy*) You taped another Message! Sigfrid, another Message to the World!

SIGFRID

You're such a pope, Ruby! You and your encyclicals. What's this one called?

RUBY'S RECORDED VOICE

"Final message. The summation."

SIGFRID

(*mimicking*) The summation.

RUBY

It's a closed book now as far as I'm concerned. See what you think.

RUBY'S RECORDED VOICE

(*a "quiet" voice, such as one uses when alone; yet with a full range of color and nuance; a sharp contrast with the often strident voice of the "live" Ruby we have been hearing*) "The way we live is compounded of love . . love which neither nurtures the receiver nor lays fallow the sender but will suffice for each . ."

LAKME

(*terribly put out*) Is this Message gonna be about love, Ruby? Ugh.

RUBY'S RECORDED VOICE

". . of hate . . and more of it than we can often cope with . . yes!"

LAKME

(*brightening*) That sounds more like you!

RUBY'S RECORDED VOICE

". . and of a numbing, crushing indifference . . an indifference which kills . . slowly, finally, totally."

LAKME

Bang, bang! You're dead.

SIGFRID

Sshh!

RUBY'S RECORDED VOICE

"And for which our cruelty (and pain now is our only reminder that we yet live) . . for which the cruelty we do unto each other is but a temporary antidote."

LAKME

Does that mean about the friend?

SIGFRID

(*not really listening to her, affected by the Message, looking at Ruby*) Yes . . no.

LAKME

Hunh?

RUBY'S RECORDED VOICE

"God . . gods . . some*one* . . some*thing* . . *whatever*: things done or not done and then called good or bad . . these *things* men speak of, attain to, do battle for . . the way we live does not involve us with them. They are the concerns . . no, were! . . were the concerns of peoples, nations . . yea, individuals . . who thought they were to prevail."

RUBY

(*a little strained, perhaps; Sigfrid doesn't take his eyes from her*) Quite biblical, don't you think? That "yea, individuals."

RUBY'S RECORDED VOICE

"We shall *not* prevail . . so be it. We shall *not* endure . . but who was ever meant to? And we shall *not* inherit the earth . . it has already disinherited *us*." (*A pause. Ruby moves as if to turn off the recorder. Sigfrid stops her.*)

SIGFRID

No.

RUBY'S RECORDED VOICE

"*C'est triste . . N'est-ce pas?*"

SIGFRID

C'est triste, Ruby.

RUBY'S RECORDED VOICE

"If we are without faith, we find our way in the darkness . . it is light enough. If we are without hope, we turn to our despair . . it has its own consolations. And if we are without charity, we suckle the bitter root of its absence . . wherefrom we shall draw the sustenance to destroy you."

SIGFRID

(*deadly*) You really went to town this time.

RUBY

(*faltering*) It was . . I . .

RUBY'S RECORDED VOICE

(*and this is the saddest part*) "Go . . seek not to know us . . to understand. The compassion of it will exhaust you and there is so little strength left us now . . so little."

RUBY

So little, Sigfrid!

SIGFRID

(*steel*) So little, Ruby.

RUBY'S RECORDED VOICE

(*very quickly, in an everyday tone*) "Spoken by me this December morning. Unwitnessed, unheard, alone." (*And now there is a good moment of silence. No one moves. The tape reels spin noiselessly.*)

FA

(*waking momentarily*) Good-bye, Grandfa . . Come and kiss me, Grandfa.

GRANDFA

(*Fa's had his chance*) I'm knitting. Knitting and listening to this harridan spout balderdash. You never heard such — (*but Fa is already asleep again*) Balderdash, Ruby! Pure tommyrot!

RUBY

(*switching off the recorder, making something of a moment of it, anything to break the mood in the room now*) Ecco la testimonia d'una traviata . . una testimonia nera!

LAKME

(*quite overcome by it all*) Nero? You mean *nerissimo*! Wow!

GRANDFA

(*grousing away in his corner*) Message to the World, she calls it. That's no message . . it's garbage, that's what it is . . pig food!

LAKME

(*trying to reconstruct a certain phrase*) "And if we are without faith . . we shall suckle? . ." Is that right, Sigfrid . . "suckle"?

GRANDFA

Yes, that's right. Suckle! Suckle your way like pigs!

LAKME

". . suckle our bitter root in the darkness"?

RUBY

(*throwing it away*) It has its own absence.

LAKME

Absence?

RUBY

(*trying to get it right for her now*) Consolations, then! It has its own consolations.

LAKME

Which has? Our bitter root or our darkness?

RUBY

(*irritably*) Well, something like that!

SIGFRID

How should Ruby know?

LAKME

She said it!

RUBY

That was this morning . . hours ago . . (*directly to Sigfrid*) centuries.

LAKME

(*satisfied with this*) That part about destroying you. That's the part I liked
best.

RUBY

You would. (*passing near Sigfrid*) Boola boola. (*sitting now*) I have such
a headache.

LAKME

You mean vapors. Ruby's evening vapors.

GRANDFA

(*they all love these word games*) No, vipers. She means vipers. Evening
vipers. The three of them.

RUBY

(*the game's over*) I mean vapors! (*with a wave of her arm*) Presto, cara,
presto.

LAKME

Wait'll you see this fink we got coming over here tonight. The friend. One
of those demonstrators.

SIGFRID

(*low*) We shall not prevail.

RUBY

Va! Fuggi!

LAKME

(*running on*) Finks! They're all finks. They're not going to change anything. Not with signs. Signs aren't going to make that thing out there go
away.

SIGFRID
We shall not endure.

RUBY
Fuggi, damnit, *fuggi*!

LAKME
(*stopped cold*) *Fuggi?*

SIGFRID
And we shall not inherit the earth.

RUBY
From *fuggire*: to make haste . . to pick up our little feet and vanish . . in other words, to scram!

LAKME
(*still puzzling*) *Fuggi* — ? (*she's got it*) Oh.

RUBY
Yeah, oh. *Piccola* nitwit.

LAKME
(*nice and prissy*) I'm sorry, Ruby, but we can't all of us be such opera queens. I mean some of us are normal. Some of us speak English when we want something. Some of us —

RUBY
Will you get in there and get that coffee?

LAKME
(*singing, anything to prolong her exit, Mimi's aria from* La Bohème) *Mi chiamano Lakme, ma il perche, non so.*

RUBY
Va!

LAKME
(*in a charming little voice*) *Vo.* (*She fairly twinkles through the door, stage right, and is gone. Even with Grandfa there, it is Sigfrid and Ruby alone now.*)

RUBY
(*after thinking it over a moment*) I am not an opera queen. Sigfrid, you don't think I'm an opera queen, do you?

SIGFRID
God knows you're some sort of a queen, Ruby.

RUBY
(*smiling, gritted teeth*) But not that.

SIGFRID
(*likewise*) You're in rare form tonight.

186

RUBY

(*hissing it, almost*) I'm just beginning! (*then turning and "seeing" Grandfa*) Grandfa! Sweetest old thing on two wheels! How old? Will you never tell us? Two hundred? . . three hundred? . . four?

GRANDFA

It's criminal how you abuse the gift of speech, woman!

RUBY

(*effusive*) Each day could be . . should be . . your very last . . but it never is. Keeping us in such suspense! Sly, sly, Grandfa.

GRANDFA

(*determined to be heard*) CREATURES LIKE YOU SHOULD HAVE THEIR VERY TONGUES CUT OUT!

RUBY

(*stopping her ears*) Grandfa! Don't shout at us like that. We're not the deaf ones; you are.

GRANDFA

Right out of your heads with a big rusty knife. (*rumbling on*) Message to the World! I never heard such contamination.

RUBY

We can't all be your beloved Shakespeare, Grandfa.

GRANDFA

I'll say!

RUBY

(*a little less playful here*) I meant it when I said it.

GRANDFA

So did he!

RUBY

Forsooth!

GRANDFA

And it didn't come out garbage!

RUBY

How you prate, nuncle, how you will prate!

GRANDFA

It was poetry. It sang!

RUBY

With a hey-nonny-nonny and a ho!

GRANDFA

Shakespeare respected words! And you know why? Because Shakespeare respected people! . . But you! . . this family! . .

187

RUBY
(*a little sorry she got into this*) You just put everything you're thinking about in that little book you're writing, Grandfa. Scribble it in your little novel.

GRANDFA
(*she has touched a sore point*) Chronicle! It's not a novel. It's a chronicle.

RUBY
Chronicles record the truth, Grandfa. Your book is full of lies. Therefore, your book is a novel.

GRANDFA
"Time Was: A Chronicle." A book of facts . .

RUBY
Not facts, Grandfa. Lies! Un-historical non-facts! Nonsense!

GRANDFA
(*never relinquishing the offensive*) Facts about you . . this family . . the truth!

RUBY
(*her last defensive*) That's wonderful, Grandfa. You go right on deluding yourself. Don't waste a minute! There's so little time left!

GRANDFA
(*not to be stopped*) I will! Old people remember, you know. They remember everything! That's their function . . to remember!

RUBY
(*retreating now*) Lakme! . . Where is that child?

GRANDFA
(*pursuing*) Only younger people don't like that! . . they don't like to remember . . they're afraid! . . facts frighten them . . memory frightens them . . old people frighten them!! This book frightens them!

RUBY
(*turning on him now*) Then won't you be happy to get away from us! Won't you be delirious up there on that little farm! All you old retired actors . . all you old Shakespeareans . . lolling around all day . . in wheelchairs . . being pushed! . . Just lolling around and mewling sonnets at each other all day long? Mewling sonnets over social tea biscuits and a drop of sherry? Won't that be fun? And doing real live theatricals for the Sunday visitors? Grandfa as Lear! Grandfa as Macbeth! Grandfa as Lady Macbeth! Well, why not? They did it in his time. They did it in that poet's time. And won't that be fun! Grandfa in a skirt with candle . . enters deranged . . *uno sonnambulo*! . . and tears the house down. Oh, you'll be very happy on that farm. I just know you will.

GRANDFA

(*a little sad now — his prospects are none too cheerful — but with simple dignity*) I have friends up there . . some . . old thespians like myself . . there's a few of us still left . . they say the food's not too bad . . the care . . I'll . . manage. (*a pause*)

RUBY

(*with more than a little desperation*) Isn't it wonderful, Sigfrid? . . at his age . . so spry!

SIGFRID

(*with a violence that has been building in him ever since Ruby's Message to the World*) LEAVE HIM ALONE, RUBY! JUST ONCE, LEAVE SOMEONE ALONE! (*Ruby, for the moment, is quite taken aback and absolutely speechless*) CHRIST, RUBY . . CHRIST! (*Sigfrid's explosion has produced a tense, angry silence. Grandfa has withdrawn and gone back to his corner. Sigfrid has moved away from Ruby who stands watching him, her own anger mounting. A long pause.*)

RUBY

(*with a repressed and terrible fury*) That wasn't called for, Sigfrid. That wasn't called for at all. (*Sigfrid is silent*) And take off that ridiculous sweater. You're home now. The camouflage is no longer necessary!

LAKME'S VOICE

(*a sudden intrusion on the intercom*) Hey, opera queen! Black?

RUBY

What?

LAKME'S VOICE

Your coffee. How do you want it? Black?

RUBY

No, blue!

LAKME'S VOICE

Well, sometimes you take a little brandy in it.

RUBY

(*always glowering at Sigfrid, never taking her eyes from him*) Brandy never changed the color of anything . . except maybe my teeth. (*then, directly to him*) Some people we don't humiliate each other in front of.

LAKME'S VOICE

So that's how you want it?

RUBY

Yes, that's how I want it! (*then again to Sigfrid*) We save that sort of thing for the friend.

189

LAKME'S VOICE

(*more confused than ever now*) With brandy? You want it with brandy?

RUBY

YES I WANT IT WITH BRANDY! (*snaps off the intercom*) Those are the rules, buster . . the way things are done . . and I think you'd just better stick to them. (*Ruby, restless as ever, moves away to center stage. Brooding. Silence.*)

FA

(*a terrified nightmare*) WEST, IT'S MOVING WEST! RUN, RUN FOR YOUR LIVES!

RUBY

(*with a somewhat forced gaiety*) What is? What's moving west? What is Fa mumbling about? (*No one answers. Long silence. A tension is building.*) It can get so silent down here . . so dead! I ask you: are we the only people in the world or are we not? Hmmm? Sometimes I think we are. I really do. (*Another pause. More silence. More tension. Then, going to Sigfrid and taking his lowered face in her hands, utterly without guile or a trace of anger*) Hey, I love you, prince. (*kisses him on the forehead*) No matter what I say . . although I meant it . . I do love you.

SIGFRID

(*quietly*) You should have seen the city today, Ruby. Outside. Sunlight. Ask Sigfrid what he saw. He saw people . . stumbling, wandering, milling . . masses of people. Outside movie theatres . . churches . . in the parks. Young men in tight pants . . old men in tight pants. Sigfrid saw a young girl nursing her baby. She had a growth on her neck. It was big. Like a grapefruit. It swayed when she walked. Tok-tok, tok-tok, tok. Butterflies . . pale yellow butterflies . . were hovering around them. Encircling them almost. One settled . . only for an instant . . near them, on them. The baby, startled, laughed then. Laughter. Tok. Then Sigfrid saw a crowd of people. They had an old man down behind a clump of bushes. They were kicking that old man. Some had knives. I'm sure they killed him. And then, coming back here, just a little while ago . . there was a girl standing crushed against me. We were facing . . there was no place else to look but at her . . we were so pressed, so close. She was ugly. She hadn't found someone. And she was crushing into me. "Take me with you. Let me be your friend tonight. Take me with you. Let me be your friend." That's all she said. She wasn't even crying. No one wanted her. She tried to follow me. Someone pushed her. On the stairs. She fell. Others fell on her. Stairs can be very crowded just before curfew. People can be trampled. (*short pause*) And everywhere

Sigfrid saw people marching, demonstrating, protesting. People saying
"No, No, No!" Sigfrid saw Clarence. (*another short pause*) That's what
Sigfrid saw today. All that. Out looking. With Lakme.

RUBY

(*a murmur*) How beautiful he is! . .

SIGFRID

(*looking directly at her now*) And then night after night down here in this
basement . . this stinking hole in the ground . . waiting for it to happen. Waiting for something to happen.

RUBY

. . how very beautiful!

SIGFRID

The way we live . . and Ruby acknowledges it. Ruby makes a Message.

RUBY

A prince, my son is a prince!

SIGFRID

(*wearily, he has tried to reach her*) Don't you understand, Ruby, don't
you understand anything? You went over the line with your goddamn
Message. (*he has gotten up and begun to move slowly out of the room*)

RUBY

(*to make him stay*) I was alone, Sigfrid! It was the strain — ! (*She breaks
off as Lakme enters with the coffee. But Sigfrid has gone.*)

LAKME

(*brightly*) *Ecco la Lakme!* (*taking a look over Grandfa's shoulder as she
passes him*) Message to the World? Hey, now Grandfa's started one! That
ought to be something. (*giving the coffee to Ruby*) Here, slurp. (*then,
throwing her arms around Ruby's neck*) Oh how much I love my Ruby!
Nobody loves their Ruby as much as I love mine.

RUBY

And my Lakme! How I love my little Lakme! (*then, hugging Lakme close
to her but her eyes looking to where Sigfrid left, as if she were trying to
reach him*) Both my children . . such beautiful children . . so strong
. . so . . *right.*

LAKME

(*seeking and finding a little girl's comfort in Ruby's arms*) That was a sad
Message to the World, wasn't it? The saddest one you ever made. They're
not usually so . . sad.

RUBY

(*holding Lakme close, but really an appeal to Sigfrid*) But not to frighten
you . . no! never that.

LAKME

But I do get so frightened sometimes, Ruby . .

RUBY

(*in a soft voice, almost to herself*) We all do, Lakme. We all do. (*The red light on the intercom has come on. Sigfrid is listening.*)

LAKME

Is that why, Ruby, you made the Message?

RUBY

(*her attention fixed on the intercom and Sigfrid*) In the morning . . early . . when you're sleeping . . the four of you . . and I'm alone . . sitting here . . thinking . . waiting for it to end, the night . . another night and it has not yet happened . . then . . when it's quiet . . no sounds . . no sounds at all . . I try to . . understand . . understand what has happened to us . . why . . and sometimes I have premonitions . . tremors . . not heart tremors . . nothing like that . . but soul tremors . . tremors of the soul . . when the very earth seems to rise up . . hover a moment, suspended . . somehow suspended . . and then fall back. (*short pause*) Sigfrid knows these moments, too.

LAKME

When we were little, you mean, Ruby?

RUBY

(*with a soft smile*) Yes, Lakme, when you were little and the wind blew and there was thunder. How Sigfrid howled when the shutters banged and the thunder clapped!

LAKME

But it's not that way now. Not when we're together.

RUBY

Remember, Sigfrid? Those nights? The howling, the hiding under the bed, the — (*the red light on the intercom has gone off*) It was the strain, Sigfrid! (*Ruby has gotten to her feet and taken a step toward the intercom, a movement which has dismissed Lakme rather abruptly from her place in Ruby's lap*)

LAKME

(*stung*) What's the matter now? Everybody's so moody in this family.

RUBY

(*pacing, a note of irritation in her voice*) Where's that draft coming from? Did someone leave a —? (*sees that the door at the top of the stairs is ever so slightly ajar*) Lakme, close the door!

LAKME

(*still sulking*) It's not time yet. Wait till curfew.

RUBY

I don't care what time it is. I don't want that door left open. Anytime!

LAKME

Well it is. It's open lots. We just don't tell you.

RUBY

Thank you. I hadn't known that. I'll see to it myself after this.

LAKME

That'll be the day!

RUBY

(*a quarrel is building*) I asked you to go up there and close it.

LAKME

How are we ever going to get any fresh air down here if we keep that door closed all the time? We'd all suffocate if we left it up to you.

RUBY

(*as her desire becomes more insistent, her tone of voice becomes more desperate*) I don't want that door left open.

LAKME

(*the voice getting meaner; victory is sweet*) People need air, Ruby. They have to breathe. Some people, that is. Normal people. I don't know about opera queens. I don't know what they use for oxygen. Arias, probably. Love duets!

RUBY

Please!

LAKME

(*giving no respite*) Of course we could all cut little gills in our necks and then flood this place and live like fish. I suppose then you'd be happy. All of us turned into a bunch of fishes!

RUBY

(*evenly*) It's simply that I feel safer when that door is closed . . that's all I meant . . that I would feel safer.

LAKME

But it can't happen until after curfew!

RUBY

They think.

LAKME

Well it can't.

RUBY

They only think!

LAKME

(*stubborn, but on less firm ground*) They're almost certain. It's never happened yet before. Besides, even when it does happ— . . I mean, if it ever happens . . how do we know it won't come right through that door and down those stairs? Right through! How do we know?

RUBY

Because the government —

LAKME

(*furious at herself, the situation, and the tears welling up within her*) The government! What do they know? What does anyone know? (*then, in a sudden outburst of rage*) What about last week, Ruby? Remember that little incident? You turned the electric fence on at noon! At noon! If that dog hadn't put his leg up against it to pee, Sigfrid and I would've both gotten it! You were afraid, so you turned the fence on at noon and nearly killed us! You've gotten so afraid, Ruby, you'll make it happen! You'll kill us you're so frightened!

RUBY

(*who has regained her composure, but with some effort*) Are you going to go upstairs and close that door or not?

LAKME

(*wild defiance*) NO!

RUBY

I see. I think you're going to regret this little interview.

LAKME

Oh am I now?

RUBY

Yes, are you now!

LAKME

Do tell! Do tell!

RUBY

I tell! I tell!

LAKME

You don't say!

RUBY

I say! I say all right!

LAKME

(*at once, determined to pursue the argument to the finish*) How? How am

194

I going to regret it? You going to have Fa spank me? Then first you'll have
to wake him and I doubt even you could wake Fa up.

RUBY

(*flaring briefly*) I don't want to!

LAKME

(*like machine-gun fire*) How else? How else am I going to regret it? Go
ahead. Tell me. Because I don't think I'm going to regret it at all.

RUBY

That will do, Lakme.

LAKME

(*still not satisfied with the blood she has drawn*) You never do anything,
you never go anywhere, you haven't been out of this house in . . years,
practically! All you do anymore is sleep in there in the daytime and then
come out here and sit up all night.

RUBY

I SAID THAT WILL DO!

LAKME

And look at yourself! Have you done that lately . . looked at yourself?
You used to be beautiful. You were a queen . . a real queen. But now!
(*quite matter-of-factly*) You've gone to pot, mother. That's what — (*A
buzzer sounds, loud, drowning Lakme out. It is a harsh, ugly, rasping
noise. Ruby chokes back a scream. Her knuckles whiten, she is holding
the arms of her chair so tightly. Lakme only marks time, ready to resume
speaking the moment the buzzer is silent. Five seconds of this terrible
sound. And then utter stillness. Lakme speaks at once.*) That's what I
think. You've gone to pot. (*then, getting up*) Come on. Fifteen minutes.
He'll be here. (*Ruby sits trembling; whimpering almost*) That was just the
warning buzzer, Ruby! It's fifteen minutes till curfew! That's exactly what
I was talking about! (*she goes to Ruby, embraces her, and continues with
enormous tenderness*) Look Ruby, I'll close the door. I'll turn the fence on
at curfew time. We'll be all safe and sound again. Even Grandfa wants the
door closed then and he's so old he might as well be . . dead! But he
still wants that door closed. Don't you, Grandfa? (*Grandfa looks up
from his journal, growls at her, and then resumes writing*) You just can't
be nice to that man. (*then, to Ruby, with a little laugh*) Besides, goose,
if we closed that door now our little friend might not think we were down
here and trot right back where he came from. Or what if he ran into the
fence while it was on? He'd end up like that dog . . sizzled! That would
be great . . just great! An evening without someone! You know what
happened the last time we tried that.

RUBY

(*very low, toneless, a private memory*) We nearly killed each other.

LAKME

You're telling me! And we certainly don't want that to happen again. Now, kiss-and-make-up, Ruby.

RUBY

(*the same*) Sigfrid actually had his hands around your throat. I almost let him.

LAKME

(*demanding*) Ruby! Kiss-and-make-up! Kiss-and-make — ! (*Ruby slaps her sharply across the cheek*)

RUBY

Kiss-and-make-up, Lakme. Kiss-and-make-up. (*Long pause. No one moves. Then, breaking the silence, Sigfrid's voice on the intercom.*)

SIGFRID'S VOICE

Ruby? . . Ruby?

RUBY

(*in a strange, almost monotone, voice which will seem all the more sinister because of its deadly calm; and all the while she talks to Sigfrid, she never once takes her eyes from Lakme*)

Yes, Sigfrid, Ruby's here.

SIGFRID'S VOICE

I'm all right now, Ruby.

RUBY

Yes, *caro*, yes.

LAKME

(*low, her eyes locked with Ruby's*) I knew you'd do that.

SIGFRID'S VOICE

Are you, Ruby? All right?

RUBY

Oh yes . . yes. (*And with slow, deliberate movements — almost like a priest performing some sacred rite — she loosens the hairband. Masses of hair tumble to her shoulders. This is the beginning of Ruby's Transformation.*)

LAKME

(*low again*) Sooner or later . . I knew you would.

SIGFRID'S VOICE

What you said . . about the strain . . (*Lakme is moving slowly up the stairs. When she gets there she will very quietly close the door.*)

RUBY

(*combing her hair out with long, slow strokes*) There is no strain . . not now . . in fifteen minutes there will be no strain.

SIGFRID'S VOICE

His name is Clarence.

RUBY

Clarence.

LAKME

Clarence. (*A pause. Lakme has closed the door.*)

RUBY

We are strong, children. In some ways we are strong.

SIGFRID'S VOICE

Clarence.

LAKME

The friend.

RUBY

It's only before that we are not so strong.

LAKME

Clarence.

SIGFRID'S VOICE

The friend.

RUBY

But soon . . in fifteen minutes . . then . . then we are strong. Fifteen minutes and we will be strong again. (*a pause*) There's only one trouble, Sigfrid . . just one. They always stay the night. They never leave. They always stay.

SIGFRID'S VOICE

I know.

RUBY

They never . . go out there.

LAKME

(*coming back down the stairs*) I think I know what you're talking about.

RUBY

Why, Sigfrid, why do we let them stay the night?

SIGFRID'S VOICE

You always said . .

LAKME

(*at the door*) I think I do. (*she is gone*)

SIGFRID'S VOICE

. . not to go too far.

197

RUBY

I did?

SIGFRID'S VOICE

We agreed on it. The three of us.

RUBY

I see. (*a pause*)

SIGFRID'S VOICE

Ruby?

RUBY

Yes.

SIGFRID'S VOICE

What are you thinking?

RUBY

That we might.

SIGFRID'S VOICE

Make him go out there?

RUBY

Yes.

SIGFRID'S VOICE

I don't know.

RUBY

It's a possibility.

SIGFRID'S VOICE

Yes.

RUBY

That way we would know . . for once and for all we would know what is out there.

SIGFRID'S VOICE

Yes.

RUBY

It would serve some . . purpose. The friend.

SIGFRID'S VOICE

Yes.

RUBY

Clarence. (*a pause*)

SIGFRID'S VOICE

We'll see, Ruby. All right? We'll see. (*The intercom snaps off. Ruby sits combing out her hair. A moment of silence. Then Grandfa begins to move in on her, slowly at first but then picking up speed.*)

GRANDFA

(*circling her chair, needling like a mosquito*) Who's it going to be, Ruby? Who's the victim for tonight? I know what goes on in here after I go to bed. I know. Thank God I never had to watch. Thank God for that. I thought I'd seen plenty in my time, but this . . . what you people do.

RUBY

(*lipsticking her mouth a brilliant red*) There are things, Grandfa, things which you do not understand.

GRANDFA

I understand corruption . . decay! I understand that!

RUBY

(*with studied disinterest as she continues making up*) Do you?

GRANDFA

I can smell it, woman! Smell it! There's a stench in this house. A stench of putrefying rot. Human rot! . .

RUBY

Things which you do not understand.

GRANDFA

(*not pausing*) And it's all here! Written down! The truth! Everything!

RUBY

We don't know those people. They're fictitious . . fabrications. They never existed.

GRANDFA

(*finding himself on the defensive*) You've made it that way. There was a time —

RUBY

(*with great force; she has no intention of continuing this conversation*) WAS! (*short pause*) There was a time, Grandfa . . was. (*Another pause; Ruby puts the final touches to her makeup. The Transformation is nearly complete.*)

GRANDFA

(*after a while; very sadly*) It wasn't meant to be this way.

RUBY

(*rather distantly*) Perhaps Grandfa . . just perhaps.

GRANDFA

(*his voice growing fainter*) Things weren't meant to be this way.

RUBY

But they are, *caro* . . they are.

GRANDFA

(*fainter still*) People weren't meant to be this way.

RUBY

(*with a sad mockery in her voice*) How, Grandfa, how were people meant to be? (*Grandfa scarcely tries to answer her question. She takes out a large and fantastic wig and settling it on her head, she faces Grandfa fully and repeats her question with a bitterness turned more against herself than him.*) Tell us, Grandfa. Tell us how people were meant to be. For we should dearly like to know. (*The wig is in place. The Transformation is complete now. The Ruby before us is utterly different from that "anonymous" woman of her entrance. What we see now is garish, hard, almost obscene. There is a pause.*)

FA

(*breaking the silence; in great terror; he is having a nightmare*) WEST! . . IT'S MOVING WEST!

GRANDFA

(*trying to answer Ruby now*) Not like . . not like you.

FA

RUN! . . RUN FOR YOUR LIVES!

GRANDFA

Like . . like here . . (*holds up his Chronicle*) as you were . .

RUBY

(*with the same sad mockery*) Imperfect? . . weak? . . afraid?

GRANDFA

(*low, but spitting it out*) Human, woman . . human! (POW! *A rubber-tipped toy dart has been fired through the stage right door hitting Grandfa squarely in the back of the head. The Chronicle falls from his hand. He does not turn to see who fired the dart. He knows. Lakme bursts into the room. She is in the highest spirits, dressed in her Green Hornet costume and ready for Clarence.*)

LAKME

Sic semper tyrannis! (*then, rushing toward Grandfa, doing a little dance around him*) The Green Hornet! Bzzzzzz! Bzzzzzz! (*Grandfa turns away from her and moves slowly toward the stage right door*)

RUBY

(*calling after him*) Why is it, Grandfa, why is it that you can be so quiet at times . . like a mouse . . a knitting mouse . . and at other times so noisy? Why is that?

LAKME

Hey, Grandfa! Aren't you going to chase me? Come on, try to run me down! (*Grandfa is gone*) What's the matter with him?

RUBY

Your Grandfa is suffering from an acute attack of how-it-was.

LAKME

Oh, he's off on that tack again! (*then, stopping to retrieve the Chronicle*)
Hey, Bede! You dropped your Chronicle, Bede! (*then, again to Ruby*)
The Venerable Bede. I know about him from school. He wrote chronicles, too.

RUBY

But your Grandfa is a novelist. The oldest first novelist in captivity. (*It might be remembered at this point that everyone, including Sigfrid, who has just entered through the stage right door, is in the sunniest of dispositions. Joy, for the moment, is abounding.*)

SIGFRID

(*dressed entirely in black now*) Guess what I spied? A tear on Grandfa's cheeklet.

RUBY

No!

SIGFRID

One large, goopy tear. Right here.

RUBY

Why, who would've thought the old man to have so much salt in him?
(*Sigfrid has joined Ruby while Lakme, to one side, begins to thumb through Grandfa's Chronicle*)

LAKME

(*reading from the Chronicle*) "Message to the World." That's all he
wrote: "Message to the World." And then it's blank.

SIGFRID

How do I look?

RUBY

Plumpish. Look how you stick out there. You used to have such a
firm stomach, Sigfrid. I'd never seen such firmness. Whatever happened
to it? You're all soft around there now.

SIGFRID

(*glumly regarding his waistline; maybe there is a hint, just a hint, of
flabbiness*) Well . . your bazooms have dropped.

RUBY

Well of course they have! There's no one I especially want to keep them
up for. (*Sigfrid, still concerned with the real or imaginary bulk at his
waistline, has begun a set of strenuous sit-ups. Lakme continues with the
Chronicle.*)

LAKME

(*it doesn't make any sense to her*) "Take me with you. Let me be your friend tonight." What is this stuff? (*turns to another place in the Chronicle*)

RUBY

What about me? How do I look? Apart from my fallen grapes, that is.

SIGFRID

(*always exercising*) You look . .

RUBY

Attention!

SIGFRID

. . Rubyesque.

LAKME

"Butterflies . . pale yellow butterflies!" Did you see this thing he's writing?

SIGFRID

Why don't you go put your costume on?

RUBY

I thought you told me it was going to be one of those nights?

SIGFRID

It is.

RUBY

Considering how long it's going to be before you need me . . considering the hour wait while you two play boy scouts . . I don't see what all the rush is.

SIGFRID

Well while you're waiting, sweetheart —

RUBY

(*perfectly aware she is interrupting*) Sigfrid, it just occurred to me! Whenever it's a girl you introduce her to me before you go in there and when it's a boy you don't want him to meet me until after. Why is that?

SIGFRID

It's the way things are done, Ruby.

RUBY

Oh?

SIGFRID

It's a heterosexual society we live in.

RUBY

Preposterous!

LAKME

Hey, Sigfrid! This part's about you. He wrote down all about you when you were little.

SIGFRID

As I was saying, *madre* . . while you're in your little boudoir getting up . . why don't you consider slipping into that *Walküre* outfit. You know, the one with the cast iron boobies and the winged helmet.

RUBY

(*correcting*) Wingèd. And thank you all the same.

SIGFRID

Ruby! You look so feminine in steel.

RUBY

No! It chafes.

SIGFRID

(*the last sit-up*) Suit yourself.

RUBY

Oh I will! I always do. (*Sigfrid gets up, paces a moment*)

LAKME

(*reading from the Chronicle*) "Sigfrid is a sickly child, prone to respiratory ailments. Sometimes his face and little hands turn an alarming blue. Ruby is heartsick." (*delves into the Chronicle again with renewed interest*) Did you used to be blue, Sigfrid? I didn't know that.

RUBY

Who is this friend, Sigfrid?

SIGFRID

His name is Clarence.

RUBY

I know what his name is. What I'm asking you is something about him.

SIGFRID

He says we went to school together. Up to the sixth grade. He insists we're old friends. Friend friends.

RUBY

I hope you told him.

SIGFRID

Well of course I did. Vicious gossip like that. I said, "Sigy-poo no have friends, Clarence. He have victims . . mice. But he no have friends. Especially since the sixth grade. Now he have mice."

LAKME

"We read Shakespeare together in the late afternoon. Sigfrid's enthusiasm is boundless. He has the makings of a poet. A poet's soul." You, Sigfrid, a soul? Hah!

RUBY

(*pacing, waiting*) Is he a clean person? This Clarence?

SIGFRID

Ruby!

RUBY

Well some of the people you've found lately are so . . well, there's something so grayish about them.

SIGFRID

Clarence isn't gray, Ruby. He's white. Lily, snow, virgin white. Clarence will come unto us . . in his whiteness . . and we shall be saved.

RUBY

Sigfrid, he's not a cleric! Some unfrocked something or other?

SIGFRID

He's one of the committed ones. Clarence believes in making this a better world. Clarence is deeply involved with that thing out there. Well, he was.

RUBY

Clarence is committed, therefore Clarence is clean?

SIGFRID

(*good-natured, checking his watch*) Merde, mamacita, merde. (*Sigfrid freezes*)

RUBY

(*at once, checking her watch*) Sigfrid!

SIGFRID

(*taut*) He'll be here.

RUBY

(*the same*) Two minutes, Sigfrid, two minutes till curfew.

SIGFRID

I said he'll be here, Ruby, and he will.

RUBY

(*almost a challenge*) An evening without someone, Sigfrid? (*Tense, awful pause. No one moves.*)

LAKME

Hey, Sigfrid. You used to write poetry! He wrote down a poem here. A poem you wrote.

RUBY

(*the threat is genuine*) Murder, Sigfrid . . an evening without someone? . . would it be murder?

SIGFRID

If . .

RUBY

Yes, Sigfrid?

SIGFRID

He'll be here. (*they are still frozen*)

LAKME

(*mostly to herself*) Did you really write this, Sigfrid? Did you used to write poems? Ugh!

SIGFRID

Shut up, Lakme!

LAKME

(*mean*) What did I do? (*she'll have her revenge*)

RUBY

(*with a resignation calculated to annoy Sigfrid*) Well, I think you'd just better run upstairs and lock up for the night. Turn the fence on. It's obvious he's not coming.

SIGFRID

I said he'll be here and he will.

LAKME

(*starting to needle now*) You want to hear some poetry, Ruby? You want to hear one of Sigfrid's finky poems?

SIGFRID

I said shut up.

RUBY

What we said, Sigfrid . . what we said about making him go out there . .

SIGFRID

(*curt*) No.

RUBY

. . assuming he ever comes . .

SIGFRID

No, I said.

RUBY

. . we'd know then . . what is out there . . it would end this . . wondering.

SIGFRID

I SAID NO!

LAKME

Nobody ever told us, Shakespeare, what a poetic genius you were!

SIGFRID

(literally counting the seconds till curfew) Come on, Clarence, come on!

RUBY

(with a strange smile, which becomes a laugh) Why, Sigfrid? . . Why not make him go out there? . . Murder? . . would that be murder, too? . .

SIGFRID

Jesus, Clarence, Jesus!

LAKME

(determined to get his attention) Poem by Sigfrid!

> Sky, a blue sky, the eagle soars.
> High soars, high soars the eagle.

SIGFRID

(turning to her, but not moving) Give that to me.

LAKME

(brazen, loving it) What kind of sores, Shakespeare? Big pussy ones?

SIGFRID

GIVE ME THAT BOOK!

LAKME

"Can I soar? Can I soar, too?" Suits us, Shelley. Take a big flying leap right off the roof!

SIGFRID

(going after her) You goddamn little bitch.

LAKME

(dodging him) You were some poet, Sigfrid. Some poet. You were a real Shelley. You are a Shelley! *(Sigfrid is strangling her. A sharp silence.)*

RUBY

(watching them, the cruel smile on her lips) Murder, Sigfrid? Would it be . . ? *(Sigfrid has gone far enough)* Sigfrid! *(a silence; then three long, heavy, metallic knocks from outside)* Allons, mes enfants, il faut commencer! *(short silence, again no one moves, again the three knocks)* IL FAUT COMMENCER! *(Sigfrid slowly takes his hands from Lakme's throat. An ugly moment of silence between them.)*

SIGFRID

(terrifying) Don't you ever . . ever! . . EVER! do that again.

LAKME

(a threat) That hurt, Sigfrid, that really hurt. *(the knocks again, more insistent this time)*

RUBY

(cutting them apart with her voice) The friend, Sigfrid! The friend is at the gate!

SIGFRID

Get the camera ready.

LAKME

I'll kill him!

SIGFRID

(*about to go upstairs*) And Ruby, do it right this time!

RUBY

(*again with the same strange, cruel mockery*) Murder, Sigfrid? Would it be murder? (*Sigfrid has disappeared up the stairs and out the door. Lakme, hard on his heels, stops at the open door, takes a picture with her camera and then runs back down into the room. The curfew buzzer sounds again; this time louder than before. Ruby and Lakme freeze. Ruby covers her ears with her hands. Five seconds of this terrible noise. Then silence. Ruby moves quickly toward the stage right door.*)

LAKME

(*following*) I'll kill him! (*Ruby is out*) Ruby? What's the matter, Ruby? (*Now Lakme is gone, too. The stage is empty. No sounds, nothing moves. Then, from outside, the sound of an enormous iron gate slamming shut. Reverberations. Then silence again. Footsteps are heard and a moment later Sigfrid is seen at the top of the stairs. He beckons with his arm for someone to follow him, then comes quickly down the stairs. He pauses a moment to pull down a lever on an electrical unit box. The lights dim ever so slightly and we hear a faint hum. And now Sigfrid has moved swiftly out of the room. Another brief moment of empty stage. Clarence, breathless and flushed, has appeared at the top of the stairs. He comes quickly into the room, closing the heavy iron door behind him.*)

CLARENCE

(*with a nervous laugh*) Whew! That was close. My bus . . I nearly missed it . . (*His voice trails off as he realizes he is alone in the room. We see now that he is carrying a large placard, the type that pickets carry, which reads: "There Is Something Out There."*) Sigfrid . . ? (*as he turns, we can read the other side of his placard: "We Shall Prevail." The curtain is beginning to fall.*) Gee, it's nice down here . . very nice. (*Clarence is coming down the stairs. Silence in the room. And now the curtain is down.*)

ACT TWO

At rise, the room is the same. As before, the lighting is white and brilliant. Clarence's placard, the "There Is Something Out There" side facing us, *rests against the wall near the stage left door. Clarence is alone in the room. He wears a woman's dress, but there is no mistaking him. We are perfectly aware it is a male in the wrong attire. We only wonder how he got there. His uneasiness in this strange and empty room is immediately apparent. His movements are tense and fidgety. He wanders. A long silence. And then a loud snortle from Fa in his chair. Clarence stiffens, retreats a little, pauses. Another snortle. Clarence is edging toward the chair. He is there. He looks down at Fa, hesitates, bites his lip, and then throws caution to the winds.*

CLARENCE
I'm Clarence. (*no response*) My name is Clarence.

FA
(*giggling foolishly*) Hello, Grandfa . . hello there!

CLARENCE
No, Clarence.

FA
Bye-bye, Grandfa! . . come and kiss me, Grandfa!

CLARENCE
Sir?

FA
(*almost a mumble*) West . . moving west . . unh . . (*lapses into a deep sleep — snoring sounds*)

CLARENCE
(*after a while; thoroughly miserable*) Oh, this is dreadful . . Sigfrid! (*and at once Grandfa comes through the stage right door; he has a suitcase*)

GRANDFA
(*a parody of senility*) Well well well. Looky here.

CLARENCE
Good evening.

GRANDFA
Fa! Wake up! Fa! We got company. Something of Sigfrid's. Something Sigfrid dragged home.

CLARENCE
I'm Clarence. My name is Clarence.

GRANDFA
Who?

CLARENCE
Clarence.

GRANDFA
You sure?

CLARENCE

Sir?

GRANDFA

Nice name.

CLARENCE

Thank you. (*pause*) It's English.

GRANDFA

What's that? You're English.

CLARENCE

No, my name. Clarence is English.

GRANDFA

And you? What are you? Or shouldn't I ask that question? (*laughs wildly; Clarence manages a weak smile*) You're the friend.

CLARENCE

Sir?

GRANDFA

The friend. You.

CLARENCE

Well, I'm *a* friend. I don't know if I'm *the* friend.

GRANDFA

You are.

CLARENCE

A friend of Sigfrid's.

GRANDFA

Ah yes, Sigfrid. Fine lad, fine lad.

CLARENCE

Yes, isn't he?

GRANDFA

Lakme, too.

CLARENCE

Lakme?

GRANDFA

His sister. Fine lad, fine lad.

CLARENCE

Fine *lad*?

GRANDFA

And let's not forget Ruby. Fine lads, all of 'em. You, too. Fine, fine lads and laddies.

CLARENCE

(*taking the suitcase and setting it down*) Here, let me take that for you.

GRANDFA

Thank you, thank you kindly.

CLARENCE

You're taking a trip?

GRANDFA

Off to the looney-bin, first thing in the morning.

CLARENCE

The where?

GRANDFA

The looney-bin. Bin for loons. I'm a loon.

CLARENCE

You're joking, of course.

GRANDFA

I don't know. I suppose that's why I'm a loon. (*laughs his wild laugh again; Clarence moves away from him, ever so slightly*)

CLARENCE

Gee, it's nice down here.

GRANDFA

We like it. It's nice and homey.

CLARENCE

That's what's so wonderful about it. It doesn't look at all like a basement. It's so . . so cheerful.

GRANDFA

Well, we've tried to brighten it up some. A little blood, a little spleen.

CLARENCE

(*trying for firmer ground*) Our sanctuary isn't half as nice. I mean, it's not even connected to the house. I guess you're Sigfrid's grandfather.

GRANDFA

(*enormously funny*) Who'd you think I was? His grandmother?

CLARENCE

(*laughing, too*) Well, not really!

GRANDFA

Oh, you're a droll one, you are.

CLARENCE

(*reckless*) Of course you might've been his aunt! (*the laughter is raucous, slightly hysterical*)

GRANDFA

Or his auntie! (*then, quickly, straight-faced*) Nice dress you got there.

CLARENCE

(*snapping to*) Sir?

210

GRANDFA

Eh? Sorry, I don't hear too well.

CLARENCE

I suppose you're wondering why I have this dress on.

GRANDFA

(*breezy*) Oh no! No no!

CLARENCE

Well you see —

GRANDFA

Happens all the time around here. If you're not one thing, you're t'other.

CLARENCE

Sir?

GRANDFA

You don't hear so well yourself. (*short pause*) Florence.

CLARENCE

Sir? (*then, correcting himself*) I beg your pardon?

GRANDFA

Florence.

CLARENCE

No, Clarence.

GRANDFA

Funny name for a young man.

CLARENCE

Clarence?

GRANDFA

No, Florence. Florence is a funny name for a young man.

CLARENCE

Yes! . . Yes it is. (*a pause*) I'm *Clarence*. My name is —

GRANDFA

(*crabbed*) I know what your name is. I was saying that Florence is a funny name for a young man. If your name was Florence, it would be funny. (*sweetly*) Nice frock, Clarence.

CLARENCE

Sir?

GRANDFA

(*thundering*) I SAID: NICE FROCK, CLARENCE!

CLARENCE

Oh.

GRANDFA

I haven't seen such a nice frock in a long time.

CLARENCE

Thank you. (*then, aghast*) Oh, but it's not mine.

GRANDFA

Finally!

CLARENCE

I lost my clothes. This is all I could find.

GRANDFA

Now I understand.

CLARENCE

I don't wear a frock . . a dress!

GRANDFA

Unless, of course, you've lost your clothes. Then you wear a frock.

CLARENCE

Well I certainly hope you don't think I came over here like this. A boy in a dress! That would be a sight!

GRANDFA

Oh yes! Indeed it would . . *is*, in fact.

CLARENCE

It's the craziest thing. Everything I had on when I got here . . gone! . . just like that. I can't understand it. I've looked everywhere.

GRANDFA

It's a careless generation, the younger one.

CLARENCE

My socks even.

GRANDFA

Well, you know the old saying: sooner or later we all end up in our rightful clothes.

CLARENCE

No, I never heard that one.

GRANDFA

Well, you trust in it. When all else fails, boy, trust in the old sayings and they'll never let you down.

CLARENCE

(*with a smile and a shrug*) Well, you certainly can't say I'm not a good sport about it. (*Grandfa seems about to leave the room. Clarence, with his back to him, continues with a relaxed genuineness we have not seen yet.*) Talk about giving the Movement a bad name! We've got a major demonstration in the morning. I'm a squadron secretary; I'll be leading an entire platoon. That's all we need at a time like this: a squadron secretary in a dress! There's enough opposition to us as it is. (*Grandfa is listen-*

ing to Clarence) We've actually been hooted. Physically attacked some-times. It's awful when that happens.

GRANDFA

(*a sad realization; softly, almost to himself*) You don't know what's going to happen, do you?

CLARENCE

(*without pause*) Why people should be against anyone trying to make this a better world, I'll never know. But they are . . Gee, I wish Sig-frid would come back.

GRANDFA

(*a weary sigh*) Go home, missy . . please . . go home.

CLARENCE

(*awkward*) It was such a coincidence . . running into each other like that this afternoon. We hadn't seen each other since the sixth grade. That's . . (*counting the years up on his fingers*)

GRANDFA

While there's time . . pick up your skirts and run along home.

CLARENCE

(*unable to prolong it*) I beg your pardon?

GRANDFA

You heard me . . maybe you didn't want to . . but you did.

CLARENCE

I . . no, no I didn't . . something about home?

GRANDFA

(*flat*) That's right. Something about home.

CLARENCE

Well? Well what?

GRANDFA

They'll devour you. Run, boy, I say run for your life. Get up those stairs and run.

CLARENCE

(*a little peevish*) I honestly don't know what you're talking about.

GRANDFA

I'm talking about what will happen to you if you stay here. He's already put you in a dress. But that was only a beginning.

CLARENCE

(*edgy*) I don't know what you're talking about.

GRANDFA

(*full voice*) I'm talking about you. Who you are! AND THEY WILL REVILE YOU FOR IT. That is their function! They'll make you want to die!

CLARENCE

(*ugly*) I DON'T KNOW WHAT YOU'RE TALKING ABOUT! (*a silence*)

GRANDFA

(*gently*) God help you, Clarence, God help you. (*The quiet is shattered by the horn fanfare announcing Norma's entrance from Bellini's opera. There is no specific source for the music. It is very loud. It will continue.*)

CLARENCE

(*distracted*) What? . . music . . the music . . where? . . Sir! (*Grandfa is headed for the door: slowly, slowly*) Wait! Where is everyone? . . What's going to happen? . . This music . . I didn't know what you were talking about . . I didn't know! . . please, stay! (*Grandfa is gone*) I didn't . . know . . (*He is alone. The music builds. At the first beat of the orchestral verse of the chorus, Lakme comes skipping into the room. She wears her Green Hornet dress and cape. As she skips about the room in time to the music, she scatters rose petals from a tiny basket. Clarence watches, stupefied, unable to speak. Sigfrid has entered directly behind her. He still wears his black shirt and slacks. But now he carries an enormous saber. He holds it out in front of him with great reverence, as if it were a sacred object. His expression and movements are solemn, trance-like.*) Where have you been? Sigfrid! Where?

SIGFRID

(*with a terrible, controlled fury*) Ruby! Her entrance!

CLARENCE

(*after he has recovered from this*) I . . I don't understand.

LAKME

(*helpful*) You'd better kneel. She won't like it if you don't.

CLARENCE

I . .

SIGFRID

(*the same voice*) Down! (*Sigfrid and Lakme kneel, facing the stage right door*) Down! (*Clarence kneels, too. The horn fanfare sounds again and Ruby makes her long-awaited entrance. It and she are spectacular. She is wearing an elaborate, flowing white dress, over which is a brilliant cape. She moves majestically to a spot center stage and stands there, motionless, until the music ends. Clarence, Sigfrid, and Lakme are almost prone on the floor, their heads bowed; they are not looking at her.*)

RUBY

(*after a pause, with an imperial gesture, Norma's opening recitative*) "Se-diziose voci —" (*She stops singing on the high note and yawns hugely, not*

*bothering to cover her mouth. Then she stretches, very slowly and yawns
again. Affected, and she knows it.) La Ruby non cantera stanotte.*

SIGFRID AND LAKME
(together, exaggerated cadences) Che peccato!

RUBY
E troppo stanca.

SIGFRID AND LAKME
Maledetto.

RUBY
E troppo vecchia.

SIGFRID AND LAKME
Poverina.

RUBY
(sitting) Buona sera a tutti!

SIGFRID
(low, to Clarence) Isn't she terrific? Didn't I tell you?

RUBY
Mi sento male. Mi sento noiosa. Mi sento many things. But most of all
mi sento blue.

SIGFRID
(the same) One in a million.

LAKME
One in ten million!

RUBY
(arms outstretched) Abbracciami, tesori, abbracciami.

SIGFRID
(excusing himself to Clarence) She wants to embrace us.

LAKME
No. she wants *us* to embrace *her.* There's a difference.

RUBY
*(taking Lakme and Sigfrid into her arms) Ah, mes enfants. Mes véritables
enfants. Comme je suis heureuse. Et comme je ne suis pas heureuse. Mais
ce soir . . peut-être . . je —* ("seeing" Clarence, she breaks off) Who is
that, please?

SIGFRID
Who?

RUBY
(pointing) That. That person.

SIGFRID
(terse whisper) The friend.

215

RUBY

Ah! *L'ami*. (*to Clarence*) *Nous vous avons attendé, chéri.*

CLARENCE

(*from across the room*) Hello. I'm —

RUBY

(*brightly*) We'll be with you in a moment, dear. Sweet dress and what a perfectly atrocious body!

LAKME

(*so knowing*) Sigfrid knows that, Ruby.

RUBY

I wouldn't have thought he was your type at all. Never in my life.

SIGFRID

It was the best I could do.

RUBY

It's the bottom of the barrel, Sigfrid. The veritable bottom of the barrel. This is hardly worth the effort.

SIGFRID

You try it next time, you think it's so easy. You try finding someone.

LAKME

As he said, it was the best he could do.

RUBY

(*with a sigh of finality*) *Ebbene, comminiciamo la commedia.*

LAKME

(*yelling to Clarence*) Hey! You!

RUBY

Not that way, Lakme. Properly, very properly. Sigfrid, he's your friend.

SIGFRID

Just . .

RUBY

Yes, darling? (*He only looks at her. She smiles up at him. Then Sigfrid goes over to Clarence, takes him by the arm and leads him back to Ruby. There should be a suggestion of royalty granting an interview during the next scene.*)

SIGFRID

Clarence, I'd like you to meet my mother. Ruby, this is Clarence.

RUBY

Enchantée.

CLARENCE

Enchanté.

RUBY

I beg your pardon?

CLARENCE

(*who doesn't speak French or Italian or anything*) *Enchanté?* (*Ruby shifts in her chair*) Please don't get up!

RUBY

(*settling back*) Oh I won't. I wasn't, in fact. But you sit down. Here . . on the friend seat.

CLARENCE

The what?

SIGFRID

Friend seat.

RUBY

Seat for friends.

SIGFRID

You're the friend. You.

CLARENCE

Oh. (*short pause; Clarence sits*)

RUBY

Halloween?

CLARENCE

Please?

RUBY

(*at once*) You've met our little Lakme? Our own *piccola cosa nostra?*

CLARENCE

No, I don't think so.

SIGFRID

In the park this afternoon. You left the demonstration and came over and played football with us.

LAKME

Attempted to play football with us. You're pretty stinky at it.

CLARENCE

Was that you?

RUBY

Lakme's thirteen. Aren't you, sweetheart? (*a pause*)

CLARENCE

I didn't recognize you in that . . dress.

RUBY

(*a little louder this time*) Lakme's thirteen. Aren't you, sweetheart? (*another pause*)

CLARENCE

I have a little sister.

SIGFRID

(*completely out of patience*) Lakme's thirteen. Aren't you, sweetheart?

LAKME

(*finally, remembering her cue*) Oh!

SIGFRID

Well it's about time!

LAKME

Well you changed the cue —

RUBY

Avanti, Lakme, avanti!

LAKME

(*a little aria directly to Clarence*) Thirteen! Thirteen years old and total monster. Have been for some time. I'm bright . . extremely bright. Close to genius, in fact. I know everything a thirteen-year-old girl isn't supposed to know. Even ninety-three-year-old girls aren't supposed to know what I know. I know so much they don't know what to do with me. "They" meaning everyone. Everyone outside this house. Ruby and Sigfrid are different. At least they hate me. (*appropriate comments from Ruby and Sigfrid*) I have talents. I must have. Only I don't know what they are yet. So I play the piano. Bach, mostly, but sometimes Mozart. My favorite thing in the world is the Green Hornet. He makes people tell the truth and goes "Bzzzz, bzzzzz" at them until they do. I do love the Green Hornet. My unfavorite thing is . . well, lots of things. Finks being in the vanguard. Fink! (*very fast now*) My favorite color is white . . because it's blank. Time of day: night . . blanker. Time of year: winter, blanker blanker. Fink! (*and now slower, languid*) Millions of tiny sprouts of golden hair on my legs and arms. In the sun they glisten. Breasts moving along nicely. Not much bigger than a scoop in a nickel cone right now. Eyes and teeth: sharp and healthy. Fink! (*fast again, the finale*) Other favorites — book: The Iliad; poem: The Rubáiyát . . yeah, the Rubáiyát! . . also "Sky, a blue sky, the eagle soars" . . it's by a certain Shelley I know . . movie: none. I never saw one. Ocean: the Dead Sea; tree: cactus; flower: lily; dress: the one with strawberries I wear on Fridays; painter: none . . well maybe Leonardo; color: black; food: fish; person: me. Fink! (*she finishes with a flourish; then, to Sigfrid*) "Lakme's a charming child. We're extremely fond of her." That's the cue, idiot!

RUBY

You've made a few changes in it, darling.

LAKME

(*so pleased with herself*) Unh-hunh!

SIGFRID

And one of them better go.

LAKME

Oh yeah? Which one? (*then to Clarence*) Sigfrid used to write . . (*hesitates, decides not to*) never mind . . (*She goes back to her place and sits. Awkward silence. Ruby snaps her fingers at Sigfrid.*)

SIGFRID

Clarence had quite a little tête-à-tête with Grandfa, Ruby.

RUBY

Yes, I heard them.

CLARENCE

. . heard? . .

RUBY

The intercom. We listen to everything. Poor Grandfa. Look, children, over there. His little bag's all packed. We're putting him in an asylum tomorrow.

CLARENCE

Yes, so he told me.

SIGFRID

Grandfa is insane.

CLARENCE

Yes, he told me that, too.

RUBY

He's written a novel.

CLARENCE

Oh. (*pause*) Is that what makes him insane? (*Ruby nods her head*) Oh. (*pause*) How does that make him insane?

LAKME

He thinks it's the truth.

CLARENCE

Oh. (*pause*) Well, lots of famous writers cracked up right toward the end. (*a joke*) Sometimes before!

LAKME

(*tight-lipped*) Grandfa isn't famous.

SIGFRID

(*the same*) Grandfa isn't a writer.

RUBY

(*the same*) Grandfa is insane.

CLARENCE

Oh. (*an extremely loud snortle from Fa*)

LAKME

And that's our Fa. Rip Van Winkle with a bad heart.

SIGFRID

Fa won't be with us much longer we're afraid.

LAKME

(*a horse laugh*) Afraid? Hah!

RUBY

It's imminent. We've been expecting the worst for quite some time now.

CLARENCE

That's awful.

RUBY

Yes, I suppose it is. But you see, Clarence, Fa has not been affectionate with us. He's slept, while we have . . how shall I put it? . . not slept.

SIGFRID

It's been a hard row to hoe without our *babbino*.

RUBY

Nevertheless we've managed, Clarence. Somehow we have managed.

SIGFRID

Triumphed, Ruby. Triumph is a better word.

RUBY

(*arms outspread to Lakme and Sigfrid again*) *Abbracciami ancora, tesori, abbracciami!* (*maybe they don't come this time*) Aren't they wonderful, Clarence? Aren't my babies wonderful?

CLARENCE

They're . . very nice.

RUBY

You use words so judiciously, Clarence. So judiciously. (*a pause; she snaps her fingers again*)

SIGFRID

(*the efficient host bit*) Drinks! I completely forgot. Ruby? What are you having!

RUBY

Cognac, a little cognac, darling. (*then, directly to Clarence*) *Je ne pouvais pas exister sans le cognac.*

CLARENCE

Yes.

SIGFRID

Lakme?

LAKME

A martini, stupid, what do you think? (*then, at once, to Clarence*) You should have seen your face when I came in here during Ruby's entrance. Stupefication!

SIGFRID

(*"rescuing" him*) Clarence? (*and before Clarence can answer*) You're not uncomfortable? Sitting there?

CLARENCE

(*crushed*) No, I'm fine, just fine.

SIGFRID

Let's see, does that get everyone? All-righty. And a pernod for me. (*he works at the bar*)

LAKME

(*who has been considering that word, "stupefication"*) Stupefaction. I can say stupefaction. Only I prefer stupefication. (*very virtuoso*) It's more stupefacient than stupefaction . . stupefication is. Stupid!

RUBY

That will do, Lakme. I should think that will do for quite a while now.

LAKME

I'm being nice. Aren't I? Aren't I being nice?

CLARENCE

(*to Ruby*) My little sister —

RUBY

(*beaming*) It's such a relief to see Sigfrid bring someone nice home for a change. We've had some of the most awful people here. Right where you're sitting. Riffraff! And if there's one thing I won't have in my basement, it's riffraff. Trash is all right . . and Sigfrid's brought home enough of it . . but I draw the line at riffraff . . Well do you blame me?

CLARENCE

It's not very pleasant.

RUBY

I wish you could have seen the girl he brought home with him last night. A belly dancer. An Arab belly dancer.

SIGFRID

She was amusing.

RUBY

I'm glad you thought so. The hair, Clarence. Horrible black hair. Everywhere. And the skin. Oily, oily.

221

SIGFRID

Olive, Ruby, an Arab's skin is olive.

RUBY

I call it oily. Now if that had been a real jewel in her navel . .

SIGFRID

Well Clarence isn't riffraff, Ruby.

RUBY

(*to Clarence, sharing an enormous joke*) Just trash? (*everyone laughs; Clarence manages a smile*) You don't say much, do you?

SIGFRID

(*coming forward with the drinks, passing them around; Lakme gets a Coke, of course*) Clarence is shy, Ruby. Clarence has a father who used to beat him as a child. Clarence has a mother —

CLARENCE

Sigfrid!

SIGFRID

Relax, sweetheart. It's no skin off your nose. You told me and now I'm telling them.

CLARENCE

That was . . different.

SIGFRID

Not really. (*continuing*) . . a mother who smothered him with affection. She still does, in truth. And Clarence works in the public library. It is not difficult, therefore, to explain why Clarence is shy. It is not difficult to explain Clarence. There are reasons for him. (*toasting*) Skoal, Clarence.

RUBY

Skoal, Clarence.

LAKME

Skoal, Clarence.

CLARENCE

(*instinctively raising his hand to drink*) Skoal. (*they drink to him*)

RUBY

(*reflectively*) There's something about you, Clarence . . I can't quite put my finger on it . . something about you that makes me think it's Halloween.

SIGFRID

It's the dress, Ruby.

RUBY

Mmm, I suppose it is.

SIGFRID

Clarence couldn't find his clothes. He asked if there wasn't something of yours he might put on.

CLARENCE

No!

RUBY

Well it is a bit damp down here this evening. You were afraid he might catch cold. I don't mind, do I?

CLARENCE

That's not true.

RUBY

(*running on*) Mind? Of course I don't mind. One thing life has taught me . . and perhaps this is all it has taught me . . is never to mind anything. Since I stopped minding, which was not so many years ago, I have . . on occasion . . been amused. And I suppose being amused is the closest thing left us to grace. (*then, directly to Clarence, with all her charm*) Don't you think so, Clarence?

CLARENCE

Mrs. . .

RUBY

Ruby. The name is Ruby.

CLARENCE

That's not true about . . I didn't ask to . .

RUBY

To what, dear?

CLARENCE

This . . this dress.

RUBY

(*placating*) Sigfrid's only joking . . maybe he's only joking . . either way, I know that. Besides . . hmm? (*Lakme is whispering into Ruby's ear. Ruby laughs and nods her head affirmatively several times. Meanwhile, Sigfrid joins Clarence, putting one arm affectionately around his shoulder.*)

SIGFRID

Ruby's a good sport. We all are. So you be one, too. Just . . relax.

CLARENCE

(*a whisper*) That was a lie.

SIGFRID

(*good-natured*) Oh, grump, grump, grump.

223

CLARENCE

Well it was. It was embarrassing.

SIGFRID

(*logically*) How can it be a lie when it's not true in the first place? . . Hunh?

RUBY

(*back to Clarence and Sigfrid*) I'm sorry. You were saying . . ?

SIGFRID

(*sweetly*) Clarence was just accusing me of telling a lie and I was explaining to him that it's not a lie unless it's true.

RUBY

Why of course! *Tout le monde* knows that. There's no point to a lie if it's not true. (*as before*) Don't you think so, Clarence? (*Lakme is at the rear of the room*)

SIGFRID

What's she up to?

RUBY

Lakme thought our little guest might enjoy a little music. Little guest, little music. One of the records, dear.

CLARENCE

Mrs. . . Ruby. It's just not true.

SIGFRID

Sshhh. You're going to like this.

RUBY

(*rising to the occasion, a command performance*) I had a career in grand opera, you know. I was a *diva* . . a *prima donna* . . quite one of the best. *La Regina dell'Opera*: me! Or as the children so idiomatically put it: I was an opera queen.

SIGFRID

That's idiomatic and literal both.

RUBY

(*not annoyed at his little interruption*) Well, to press on! I was beautiful then and there was music in my voice . . beautiful, beautiful music. I could sing anything . . and I often did. There was no role too high, too low, or too in-between. And on stage . . ah! on stage . . and you must believe this, I was beautiful . . so very, very beautiful. And now they are both gone: the beauty and the music . . dearly departed ornaments of my being. The one, frozen for a single terrifying instant, snatched from eternity, my eternity, in a red Moroccan leather album of yellowing photographs . . hundreds upon hundreds of them. The other, my voice . .

my beautiful voice . . echoes endlessly on the eroded grooves of a spinning black disc . . just this one. *Ascolta!* (*The music begins now. Instantly her mood lightens and her speech tempo becomes faster. The recording played should be that of an incredibly awful soprano singing an elaborate coloratura aria. Florence Foster Jenkins' recording of the Queen of the Night aria from* The Magic Flute *is suggested. The actress should "play" with the music at all times during the following speech: mouthing certain phrases of music, pausing in the speech to listen to certain phrases, conducting a little. One should never be too sure just how serious Ruby is about the recording, her career . . anything. Sigfrid and Lakme alternate between rapt attention and trying to keep a straight face. Clarence is flabbergasted.*) Aaaah! Wolfgang Amadeus! *Bravo, miei figli, bravi!* . . The unhappy mother, the enragèd Queen of the Night, swears vengeance and vows to deliver her daughter Pamina from her captor's hands . . Vengeance! . . This phrase: lovely, lovely. I sang this once in Moscow . . at the Bolshoi . . in Russian, no less . . those dreadful thick vowels . .

CLARENCE

(*in a whisper*) Is that really your mother — ? (*Sigfrid fiercely motions him to be silent*)

RUBY

After the performance I was delivered to my hotel in a troika drawn by several thousand delirious students who then proceeded to serenade me with folk songs from the streets beneath my windows . . I sat alone on my balcony . . it was a warm evening, warm for Moscow . . alone and weeping . . weeping and toasting them with vodka . . They sang until dawn . . I toasted till dawn . . when the Kremlin's domes first were flecked with the morning sun's gold. Here! The cadenza. Marvelous!

SIGFRID

(*a stage whisper to Clarence*) That's Ruby's Lucy Lammermoor mad scene dress.

CLARENCE

Oh!

RUBY

Once in Milano . . after my debut at the Scala in a revival of *La Cucaracha* . . revived for me, *ça va sans dire* . . the manager, the manager of La Scala, Milan, said to me: "Ruby, *tu hai la voce delle anime di purgatorio.*" . . Well, something like that. "You sing with the voice of the souls in purgatory!" You see, he'd heard the pain in my voice. *Verismo,* we called it. (*and now, acting it out*) This part, now! I would rush about the stage brandishing this enormous dagger. One critic said it was an awesome moment. Oh the memory of those nights! . . those days! The continental tours with Brunhilde, my Pekingese, and my three male secretaries! The steamer trunks stickered ten times over with those magic names: Paris, Rome, Vienna, London, Bayreuth, Peiping, Manila, Camden, New Jersey . . yes! Camden, New Jersey . . Athens, Napoli, Palermo . . Palermo where I first met Fa, after a Delilah at the Teatro Massimo. He'd come there to take away the olives . . Here! The *portamento*, Clarence, *il portamento!* . . Oh the glory! The glory! (*Her voice trails off and she is lost in revery, listening to the music with closed eyes, her head back. The music ends. There is a pause. Then Ruby opens her eyes and leans forward toward Clarence*) Well?

LAKME

Well?

SIGFRID

Well?

CLARENCE

I . . unh . . I . .

SIGFRID

Tell Ruby what you thought, Clarence. Go on.

CLARENCE

I . . I don't know very much about music. I really shouldn't venture to make a judgment.

SIGFRID

Oh go ahead, venture!

LAKME

(*singsong*) Nothing ventured, nothing gained.

CLARENCE

Especially opera. I don't know anything about opera. (*a weak joke*) Wagner wrote Puccini as far as I know. (*they are not amused*) Really . . I'm not qualified.

RUBY

(*edgy*) The quality of the voice, dear. We're interested in what you think of that.

CLARENCE

Oh . . that . . it was wonderful, Mrs. . .

LAKME

Ruby. Her name is Ruby.

CLARENCE

. . just wonderful.

226

RUBY

Yes?

CLARENCE

What else can I . . ? It reminded me of . . of a bird. A lark maybe. I don't know. But it certainly was wonderful. You're very talented. (*the three of them explode with laughter*) What? . . What's so funny? . . Did I say something wrong? . .

RUBY

(*rocking with laughter*) He's so pathetically polite.

SIGFRID

(*the same*) You're very talented, Ruby!

RUBY

And so patronizing.

LAKME

A bird! You reminded him of a bird.

CLARENCE

(*the light slowly dawning*) Oh . . I see . . that wasn't you!

LAKME

Do tell!

CLARENCE

(*joining in the laughter himself*) No wonder! . . well I'm glad it wasn't . . ha ha . . that was the worst thing I ever heard in my life . . ha ha ha . . it was awful . . where did you find that record . . who was she? (*abruptly, the laughter ceases and they stare fiercely at Clarence*)

RUBY

(*sharp*) A very dear friend.

CLARENCE

(*caught in mid-laugh*) Oh.

RUBY

A seventy-two-year-old lady.

LAKME

A seventy-two-year-old Negro lady.

SIGFRID

A seventy-two-year-old Negro servant from the deep Deep South.

RUBY

Seventy-two-year-old Negro lady servants from the deep Deep South who sing Mozart arias are not to be ridiculed. Ever!

LAKME

Racist! Dirty Nazi racist!

CLARENCE

(*thoroughly chastened*) I . . I didn't know.

RUBY

You may laugh with us, Clarence, at yourself . . but not at sweet old Aunt Jemina from the deep Deep South. (*again they explode with laughter. Clarence sits dumbly, not knowing what to do or say or think. Ruby leans forward to pat his cheek.*) Clarence! Where's that smile? That famous smile of yours? (*Clarence doesn't react*) Now! Together! Sing! (*She leads them in a rousing chorus of "For He's a Jolly Good Fellow." Suddenly the lights dim to half and hold there. The singing falters. Ruby is determined to finish the song, but for a moment she is the only one singing. Then Sigfrid joins in, rather limply at first, but soon belting it out with his full voice. Lakme has stopped singing altogether and moves away from the others. Even though her back is to us, we can tell from her heaving shoulders that she is fighting to hold back enormous sobs. The lights come swiftly back up to full, as Ruby and Sigfrid finish the song boisterously.*)

CLARENCE

I don't know what to think of you people. One minute you're friendly, the next you're making fun of me.

SIGFRID

(*poo-pooing*) Oh! Don't mind us. That's our way.

CLARENCE

Fun at my expense!

RUBY

(*looking across the room at Lakme*) Lakme!

SIGFRID

And whose fault is that? You admired the singing. A cat in heat, a God-knows-what, and you admired the singing.

CLARENCE

Because I thought it was . . I was only trying to be polite.

RUBY

Stop that, Lakme.

SIGFRID

So you made a fool of yourself? Oh baby, learn to laugh at yourself. Learn it quick. It's the only thing that makes sense anymore.

CLARENCE

I'm sorry, but I don't have a sense of humor.

SIGFRID

(*flip*) Neither do we. Think about that.

RUBY

Lakme, I asked you to stop.

SIGFRID

What's the matter with her?

RUBY

The fence. Something on the fence. Go to your room, Lakme.

SIGFRID

(*going to Lakme, not unkindly*) Come on, little one, calm down now.

LAKME

(*pulling away from him*) Keep away from me!

SIGFRID

We're here. We're all together. Don't —

LAKME

KEEP AWAY!

SIGFRID

It was only an animal. It's happened before.

RUBY

Make her go to her room, Sigfrid.

LAKME

I said keep away!

RUBY

(*delighted sarcasm*) Brave little Lakme. Fearless little Lakme. Our own little St. Joan of the underground. "Leave the door open, Ruby. It's fifteen minutes till — "

LAKME

Shut up, Ruby, just shut up!

RUBY

(*delighted with herself*) Coraggio, Lakme, *coraggio!*

LAKME

JUST DO WHAT YOU SAID YOU WOULD. MAKE HIM GO OUT THERE. BUT GET IT OVER WITH AND LEAVE US ALONE. JUST DO IT. (*she leaves quickly through the stage right door*)

SIGFRID

(*following*) Lakme!

RUBY

Sigfrid! Not yet.

SIGFRID

But she'll —

RUBY

Be all right.

SIGFRID

But she won't —

RUBY

She will. Sit.

SIGFRID

But —

RUBY

SIT! (*he obeys*)

CLARENCE

(*a voice in the void*) Is there anything the matter? (*a long pause*) Is there? (*Sigfrid snaps his fingers at Ruby*)

RUBY

(*abruptly*) Tell us about the way you live, Clarence.

CLARENCE

Sir? I mean . . (*laughs*) Excuse me.

RUBY

(*not amused*) The way you live. I want you to tell us about it.

CLARENCE

I don't understand. The way I live? Me?

SIGFRID

What you believe in, Clarence. A statement of principles . . life principles.

CLARENCE

Like my philosophy? Is that what you mean? My philosophy of life?

RUBY

(*an edge in her voice*) It's called the way you live.

CLARENCE

(*amused*) But why? I'm not even sure if I have one.

SIGFRID

You're alive, aren't you?

CLARENCE

Well yes.

RUBY

Then you have one.

CLARENCE

Well I suppose I do . . I must . . only I hadn't really thought about it.

RUBY

You gave Grandfa an earful.

CLARENCE

Please?

SIGFRID

(*always more conciliatory than Ruby*) Now's your opportunity, Clarence.

CLARENCE

What do you want with it? My philosophy of life?

RUBY

(*insistent*) It's called the way you live.

SIGFRID

We'd like to tape it.

CLARENCE

Tape it? You mean on a — (*Sigfrid nods*) But why would anyone want to do a thing like that? Tape someone's philo— . . way he lives?

SIGFRID

Ruby collects them. All our guests do it. She's looking for the answer.

RUBY

I have the answer. I'm looking for corroboration. I find it consoling. Usually.

CLARENCE

(*a little intrigued with the idea*) You mean we'll probably end up saying the very same thing? Or just about?

RUBY

Or just about. (*Sigfrid has been setting up the recorder*)

RUBY'S RECORDED VOICE

(*very loud*) ". . wherefrom we shall draw the sustenance to destroy you . ."

RUBY

On "record," dear, not on "playback." (*Sigfrid now sets a microphone in front of Clarence*)

CLARENCE

(*to Ruby*) That was you. Was that from your . . ? (*noticing the microphone*) Is this what I talk into? I feel like I'm on the radio. Gee, I bet I make a mess out of this. (*Sigfrid motions for silence and points to the spinning reels*) You mean I'm on already? Heavens! I'm really not prepared, you know. (*a pause*) Unh . . unh . . the way I live . . no, let me start again . . unh . . (*takes a deep breath*) The Way I Live . . The way I live is . . the best I can do. I try. I mean I really try. And I think I am improving. I think I am becoming a better human being day by day. I really do . . Anyway, I'm trying. (*then, turning to Ruby and*

231

Sigfrid) This is awful. I told you — (*they motion him to continue*) I believe in . . well lots of things. (*short pause*) And I think it's sad that we
can't enjoy these things the way we were meant to. Because of . . the
circumstance. (*shorter pause*) I love life. I suppose that's a corny statement . . I know how fashionable it is to be morose these days . . but
I do. I really do love it. There are just too many good things in the world
not to want to be alive. Just think of all the beautiful things men have
made. Music, art, literature . . Shakespeare alone is a reason to be
alive. How could anyone not want to be alive after there's been a Shakespeare on this earth? Someone who writes poetry? I can't imagine it. And
even if I've never seen it real . . and maybe I never will . . how could
anyone not want to be alive when there is a city in Italy named Florence?
How could they? Just knowing about Florence! . . what it means to us
that it's there. That there was a Florence, is and will be. It . . it makes
the rest of this planet tolerable. Florence is why we're alive. It's what
we're about. (*a pause*) And the things you can do! The simple things.
What about them? Just to take a walk even. It can be wonderful. Or to
be by the sea and feel that air on your face and see what the horizon
means. You can actually see the curve of the earth. Just what they taught
you in school and it's true. That's a wonderful thing to see for yourself.
Or just to sit in a park . . with the sun spilling all over you . . watching
the people. The other people. They're not you, and that's what's so beautiful about them. They're someone else. Sit and wonder who they are.
What they ate for breakfast, what paper they're reading, where they live,
what they do . . who they love. And that's another reason. Everybody
loves somebody . . or they will . . sometime in their life. (*a pause*)
Anything that makes you want to live so bad you'd . . you'd die for
it . . Shakespeare, Florence . . someone in the park. That's what I
believe in. That's all. That's the way I live. (*a silence*) Was it all right?
(*Sigfrid turns off the recorder*)

RUBY

Shakespeare, Florence, and someone in the park. That was nicely spoken,
Clarence.

CLARENCE

I sort of enjoyed it once I got into it. What happens now? With the tape,
I mean.

SIGFRID

(*almost mechanical, his mind elsewhere*) We put it aside . . save it . .
keep it for reference.

232

CLARENCE

Were they very similar? Yours and mine?

RUBY

Not quite, Clarence . . not quite.

CLARENCE

Did you . . ? (*giggles*) did you like it? (*looks from one to the other*)

RUBY

Sigfrid?

SIGFRID

There is a sadness, Clarence, there is a sadness in what you said.

CLARENCE

Sadness? . . No!

SIGFRID

There is a sadness.

RUBY

(*edgy, suspicious of this change in Sigfrid's mood*) What are you doing, Sigfrid?

SIGFRID

(*simply*) I don't know.

CLARENCE

(*trying to relieve the tension*) Well sure, there is sadness in the world. Lots of it. Everyone knows that.

SIGFRID

Do they?

CLARENCE

I do.

SIGFRID

The sadness of Shakespeare . . the enduring sadness of Florence . . and the necessarily greater sadness of someone in the park.

CLARENCE

I . . I don't understand.

SIGFRID

(*turning directly to him*) And that is the sadness of Clarence. (*then, to Ruby*) Maybe we could stop now, Ruby. Maybe we don't have to finish it tonight. (*Ruby snaps her fingers at him, hard*) For whose benefit? His?

RUBY

Yours!

CLARENCE

(*another try*) Sigfrid, what happened after the sixth grade? After they . .

233

RUBY

(*making him say it, to goad Sigfrid*) After they what?

CLARENCE

Expelled him. What happened then?

RUBY

Nothing.

CLARENCE

(*to Sigfrid*) Nothing?

RUBY

Nothing.

CLARENCE

Well something . .

SIGFRID

Nothing! . . this! . . nothing.

CLARENCE

(*after an awkward silence, one final try*) Well anyway . . and this is another nice thing . . I should've taped it . . another very un-sad thing . . sometimes you run into an old friend. A friend you haven't seen —

SIGFRID

I am not your friend, Clarence. I am . . I am not that either, but I am not your friend. (*a pause*) And that is the sadness of Sigfrid. The sadness of being him. (*rises*) Gently, Ruby, gently.

RUBY

Sigfrid?

SIGFRID

(*his answer to this*) I'll be here . . when it's time . . I'll be here.

CLARENCE

Sigfrid, where are you going?

SIGFRID

You'll see. (*and then*) Despair, Clarence, despair.

CLARENCE

Is something going to happen?

SIGFRID

You might say that. (*and again*) But despair, Clarence, despair. (*he is going*) And gently. (*he is gone*)

CLARENCE

(*to no one in particular*) I hate surprises. (*A very long silence. Ruby slowly takes off her wig. Next she will remove her cape.*) I wrote a poem once. For my mother. On her birthday. When I was little. "God bless the Lord, God bless my mother. She has good things in her oven." She's al-

234

ways saved it. (*a pause*) What did Sigfrid mean? . . about the sadness? And to despair? (*another pause*) It was unfortunate.

RUBY

(*rather distantly at first*) What was?

CLARENCE

That they expelled him. Sigfrid was very popular at that school.

RUBY

(*with an almost grotesque emphasis on the word*) Lots of things . . are unfortunate.

CLARENCE

(*in solemn agreement*) The Situation. You mean the Situation.

RUBY

(*flat*) That's right . . the unfortunate Situation. (*and then, reading from Clarence's placard*) "There Is Something Out There."

CLARENCE

"We Shall Prevail."

RUBY

I beg your pardon?

CLARENCE

Turn it around. The other side's a little more optimistic. It's what we believe in.

RUBY

(*reading from the other side of the placard*) "We Shall Prevail." Will we, Clarence?

CLARENCE

I think so. (*warming to his subject, his favorite, not hearing her*) It's been this way so long now . . I suppose it would be easy to get depressed. Do you realize there are children who have never seen a sunset and the moon only in the daytime when it's not really the moon . . the way it should be the moon?

RUBY

(*low; he doesn't hear this*) Lakme.

CLARENCE

(*running on*) Though actually, if I had a choice, I think I'd rather see an eclipse of the moon than the moon itself. From what I've read —

RUBY

(*cutting in now*) Once.

CLARENCE

You've seen one? What's it like, an eclipse?

RUBY
Dark.
CLARENCE
(*disappointed*) Oh.
RUBY
It was in Florence.
CLARENCE
You've been to Florence!
RUBY
It was lovely.
CLARENCE
Everything is was now. (*the lights suddenly dim to half*) The lights again! Something's happening to the lights! (*the lights come back to full*) See how jittery I am? Something happens . . a little thing like the lights . . and I think it's started to happen . . that it's finally out there. If we only knew when . . It's this waiting that's so terrible. And we don't even know what it is we're so afraid of!
RUBY
We know it's out there. That's enough.
CLARENCE
And if you went out there to find out . .
RUBY
Yes?
CLARENCE
(*looks at her*) Dead. You'd be dead.
RUBY
But you'd know, Clarence. Then you would know what is out there.
CLARENCE
And then you'd be dead.
RUBY
What would it take, Clarence, to make someone go out there?
CLARENCE
(*who doesn't like this part of the conversation*) You'd have to be crazy or something.
RUBY
Or something.
CLARENCE
I don't know.
RUBY
Despair, Clarence. Sigfrid said despair. (*another pause*)

CLARENCE

What do you think it is?

RUBY

I don't know.

CLARENCE

Don't you have any idea what it's like?

RUBY

I said I don't know!

CLARENCE

Oh.

RUBY

Does that disappoint you?

CLARENCE

(*it does, of course*) No. It's just that I'm so frightened of it. Aren't you frightened of it?

RUBY

If it gives you any pleasure to know this, Clarence, I am terrified beyond belief, and, occasionally, out of my mind. (*the lights dim again, hold a moment, and then come back to full*)

CLARENCE

(*more frightened this time*) What's happening? The fuses keep blowing!

RUBY

It's not the fuses. It's those dumb stray animals wandering into the fence.

CLARENCE

You mean it's . . electrified?

RUBY

We have to keep people out somehow. There are signs posted at regular intervals. You don't approve I suppose?

CLARENCE

No . . it's just that . . well how often does it happen?

RUBY

Four or five a night. Dogs . . cats . . an occasional parrakeet. The city picks them up the next morning along with the garbage. Of course if Darwin were right the animals should have learned to read those signs by now.

CLARENCE

It shouldn't be like this . . fences, basements, curfews.

RUBY

Well it is.

CLARENCE

And it's because it is this way and it must not be that I'm so concerned. You can't be indifferent to these things. People have to care . . passionately!

RUBY

(*who has been moving about the room and now holds up a sock which she has "found" under one of the sofa cushions*) Passion . . ah yes, one must have passion . . where would we all be without passion? (*she has "found" another sock now*)

CLARENCE

(*a little nervous; those are his socks*) Don't you care about . . (*gestures vaguely toward the outside*) things?

RUBY

The only issue of passionate concern in this family . . the only one any of us really cares about . . is who's going to get who: where, when, and how. (*holds up a pair of garishly-patterned undershorts*) Did you ever in your life? (*laughs*) I'm sorry, Clarence. You were saying?

CLARENCE

(*a certain smugness will begin to creep into his voice*) I was talking about something else. Those are social relations . . personal problems . . neuroses. I was talking about more universal themes . . the ones that really count.

RUBY

Oh? And what are they? (*she has put the socks and undershorts next to where Clarence is sitting*)

CLARENCE

(*terribly uncomfortable*) Life . . survival . . that thing out there . . I don't know.

RUBY

(*helpful*) The big things?

CLARENCE

Yes.

RUBY

The major issues of our times?

CLARENCE

That's right.

RUBY

And not . . how shall I put it? . . personal unpleasantness?

CLARENCE

Especially not that. People think too much about themselves these days.

That's all they think about. They encourage their neuroses. They coddle them, if you ask me.

CLARENCE

RUBY

Well we'll certainly put a stop to that.

CLARENCE

I hope I'm not sounding smug or anything.

RUBY

You? Smug? Clarence!

CLARENCE

I have that tendency. (*but plunging right ahead with it*) All it is actually is a question of people allowing themselves to become involved . .

RUBY

Commitment!

CLARENCE

(*a little surprised at this*) Yes! But how did you know what I was —

RUBY

That is the word for you people? The committed ones? But committed to what exactly?

CLARENCE

(*shrugging*) Anything.

RUBY

(*obviously teasing*) To an asylum, like Grandfa?

CLARENCE

(*laughing*) No! Something . . large!

RUBY

Elephants are large. Are you committed to elephants?

CLARENCE

(*the same*) You know what I'm talking about. Something larger than my-self . . something . . I don't know . . purer! . . a cause, an ideal . .

RUBY

Well if that's all that being committed is . . being purer than someone who isn't . .

CLARENCE

I didn't mean it exactly like that.

RUBY

(*not stopping for him*) . . I suppose it's better than nothing. I suppose it's better than us.

CLARENCE

Nowadays people are all hunched over their navels when they have the stars to reach for.

RUBY

Had.

CLARENCE

I beg your pardon?

RUBY

Had the stars to reach for.

CLARENCE

(*sadly*) Yes, had.

RUBY

"Everything is was now." Those are your words. (*nailing him*) Then what's the point, Clarence? The point you people are trying to make?

CLARENCE

(*very directly*) If I didn't believe that I could do something about that thing out there . . if I didn't believe the Movement could do some good . . if I didn't believe that people . . if they tried, really tried . . could change things . . if I didn't believe all that, I'd . .

RUBY

Yes?

CLARENCE

(*beginning to understand the word now*) Despair.

RUBY

(*almost a dare*) And then . . you'd go out there? (*a pause; Ruby is standing over him, her hand on his cheek; she speaks softly*) Soon, Sigfrid, very soon now.

CLARENCE

(*losing ground fast*) Maybe I'm not as aggressive as I'd like to be . . outgoing. I'm more introspective.

RUBY

(*with the velvet glove*) But committed.

CLARENCE

I try to be.

RUBY

Dedicated.

CLARENCE

That, too.

RUBY

No distractions.

CLARENCE

(*his back to the wall*) Well sure. You can't worry about these things twenty-four hours a day.

RUBY

(*deadly*) I didn't think so.

CLARENCE

(*simply*) I know you don't like me. What I don't know is why. (*but too late; Ruby has already begun it*)

RUBY

(*the coup de grace, but gently, almost sadly at first*) I mean there you were, Clarence: marching around town all afternoon in this nippy weather . . Marching and waving your little sign and being committed and all. Being purer! That's what I call a big day. You needed a distraction after an afternoon like that. No wonder you toddled over to the curb when you saw that good-looking son of mine giving your little sign the once-over. No matter how committed you are, you certainly don't pass up a good-looking distraction like Sigfrid without at least inquiring. After all, he might be committed, too! Only in this case he wasn't. He most certainly wasn't. (*acting out the dialogue, slowly becoming uglier*) "Hello there. I'm looking for something larger than myself. What about you?" asks the commitment. The distraction only smiles but does not answer. They never do. (*breaking the mood a moment*) I know this scene well. (*then, resuming*) And now the distraction, still smiling . . always smiling . . beckons with his head and begins to move away. "But I'm committed. I can't go with you!" cries the commitment. What to do? What to do? And as he stands there . . soon to be alone . . his feet numb with cold . . watching the commitments march up the street one way and the distraction walk slowly down it the other . . he remembers those immortal words of Clarentius, the saddest commitment of them all: "You can't worry about these things twenty-four hours a day." Hey! Distraction! Wait for me! (*she whistles with two fingers in her mouth, and then breaks into laughter, prodding Clarence in the ribs*) Wasn't it that way, Clarence? Wasn't it?

CLARENCE

(*immobile, shattered, quiet tears*) That isn't everything about me. There's more.

RUBY

That boy of mine may be a lousy commitment but he's one hell of a distraction.

CLARENCE

THAT ISN'T EVERYTHING!

RUBY

(*fast and tough*) Look, sweetheart, it's not like outside down here. You check the guilt baggage at the front door when you come into the house. We deal with what's left us . . not what we'd like to add to the mythology. It's a subtraction process and if the answer is zero . . that's okay, too. Now you just be a sweet little distraction and simmer down.

CLARENCE

I'm not a distraction!

RUBY

You're just someone who happened in off the street, all committed up for Halloween? Is that it?

CLARENCE

NO!

RUBY

(*making him look on her face*) "And someone in the park!" That's your commitment. Not Shakespeare, not Florence, not what's out there, but someone in the park! And that someone happened to be Sigfrid!

CLARENCE

(*broken now*) I didn't come here for that.

RUBY

But Sigfrid wanted it that way. So you let him.

CLARENCE

I didn't want him to.

RUBY

But you let him. Oh Clarence . . Clarence, Clarence, Clarence.

CLARENCE'S RECORDED VOICE

(*a mocking echo, from no specific source*) Oh Sigfrid . . Sigfrid, Sigfrid, Sigfrid.

RUBY

I beg your pardon? (*Clarence neither answers nor looks at her. Sigfrid and Lakme enter through the stage right door. He carries a slide projector. She, a movie screen.*)

LAKME

Here we are. Ready to go. Did you two have a nice talk while we were gone? Did Clarence try to convert you to the cause, Ruby?

RUBY

Sshh! The Clarence is temporarily out of commitment.

LAKME

Aaaaaw!

SIGFRID

I gave you some advice, Clarence. I hope you took it.

CLARENCE

I'd like to go home, please.

SIGFRID

Then I guess you didn't.

CLARENCE

I'd like to go home.

SIGFRID

(*an exaggerated transition*) But love-blessing! Lakme's produced an entertainment . . a sight and sound entertainment . . especially for you.

CLARENCE

(*each time more emphatic, but never rising*) I would like to go home!

RUBY

I must say your mood's improved.

SIGFRID

You think? (*then*) Do you know what Clarence did, Ruby? He told his father I was a girl. Me. Can you imagine it? And he told his mother he was coming over to see a boy.

RUBY

Oh I see! His daddy lets him sleep with girls and his mummy lets him sleep with boys. They're a very conventional pair, your parents.

CLARENCE

(*strong, for him*) Stop it!

RUBY

That's right, Clarence. Tell us off.

CLARENCE

(*standing*) I'd like my clothes, please. My own clothes.

SIGFRID

But buttercup, you're in them.

CLARENCE

WHERE ARE THEY?

SIGFRID

(*mocking*) Hoo hoo! Hoo hoo!

LAKME

(*simultaneous*) Arabella's in a huff. She's huffled!

SIGFRID

We're getting waspish. Oh oh oh oh!

CLARENCE

I don't have to stay here.

LAKME

Oh yes you do. (*mock horror*) There is something out there! Grr!

CLARENCE

Not if I can find my clothes I don't.

LAKME

Poor lady, poor lady Godiva.

CLARENCE

Do you know where they are?

SIGFRID

Pout, pout, pout. Pretty Alice Pout.

CLARENCE

Stop that! I'm not pouting. I'm getting mad. And my name's not Alice.

SIGFRID

Sorry, Joan.

CLARENCE

(*the explosion*) WHERE ARE MY CLOTHES!

SIGFRID

(*ugly, ugly, ugly*) WHERE'S YOUR SENSE OF HUMOR YOU MEAN!

LAKME

THAT'S WHAT YOU'RE LOOKING FOR!

SIGFRID

YOU CAN'T LIVE WITHOUT A SENSE OF HUMOR! NOT ANYMORE! NOT NOW!

LAKME

DOPE!

SIGFRID

SO WHERE IS IT! HUNH! HUNH! HUNH! (*quietly, and with a hideous calm*) You've also got a lousy body.

LAKME

Skin and bones.

SIGFRID

(*he means it*) Shut up, Lakme.

CLARENCE

(*pathetic*) I didn't say you hid them.

SIGFRID

We did, of course.

CLARENCE

I didn't accuse you.

SIGFRID

Maybe you should've. (*Clarence makes a sickened, moaning sound. Sigfrid continues, almost gently.*) You're rather a toad, aren't you?

CLARENCE

I'm . . I'm just not strong. But I think things!

SIGFRID

Yes, I suppose you do. (*a pause*) What was that word, Clarence?

CLARENCE

(*almost inaudible*) Despair.

SIGFRID

I can't hear you, Clarence.

CLARENCE

Despair.

SIGFRID

I still can't —

CLARENCE

Despair! *Despair!* DESPAIR! (*he is silent*)

SIGFRID

Very good, Clarence, very good.

RUBY

(*not breaking this mood*) Shakespeare, Florence, and someone in the park. Two are names and one's a person. Right, Clarence? . . right?

CLARENCE

(*numbed*) Right. (*a pause; Lakme, Sigfrid, and Ruby are ready now and return to a lighter mood*)

RUBY

Lakme, what's the name of your production?

LAKME

"The Way You Live."

RUBY

The way who lives, dear?

LAKME

Him!

RUBY

Clarence! It's about you. Lakme's entertainment is about you.

LAKME

(*finishing the arrangements*) OK. You ready, Sigfrid?

SIGFRID

All set.

RUBY

(*clapping her hands*) It's beginning, it's beginning! Can you see all right from there, Clarence? (*Sigfrid sits where he can control both the slide projector and the tape recorder; Lakme sits at the piano*)

LAKME

"The Way You Live. Clarence Fink: This Is Your Life." Lights! (*All the lights in the room go off except for a dim spot on Clarence, who sits with his back to the movie screen. Not once will he look at it. Throughout the scene that follows our concentration is on Clarence live on the hassock and Clarence on the screen. The voices of Sigfrid, Lakme, and Ruby are but sounds in the dark. Lakme narrates over the musical commentary.*) Lakme Productions bring you "The Way You Live" . . an entertainment conceived, produced, and directed by Lakme Herself. Visuals and audio by Sigfrid Simp. With occasional shrieks, howls, and whoopings by Ruby Rat. Clarence Fink! This is your life! (*The picture on the screen comes sharply into focus now: we see Clarence marching along with his poster*)

SIGFRID

There you stand, Clarence Fink. A young man of bold convictions and forthright ideals. Admired . . loved . . respected even by all who know you. As you march boldly into the future, wagging your sign behind you . .

LAKME

Wagging your commitment!

SIGFRID

. . do you remember, beneath that façade of confidence and bright hope . . do you remember, Clarence Fink, do you remember this? (*the slide changes to a wretched dwelling*) Ruby!

RUBY

It was a miserable beginning.

SIGFRID AND LAKME

Aaaaw!

RUBY

Oh yes! The palace had seen better days. The windows all were broken and the great marble floors were cracked and stained. Your mother, good queen Nefertiti, was reduced to taking in dirty linen. (*a rather whorey nude with enormous breasts*) That's her, Sigfrid! That Arab girl you had here last night!

SIGFRID

Olive-skinned. What did I tell you?

LAKME

Will you look at those knockers!

RUBY

Lakme!

LAKME

Sorry.

SIGFRID

Tell us about Clarence, Mrs. Fink. In your very own words. (*falsetto*) "He was a good boy. Bright, too. Walking at five years, talking at ten. Caught him once doing nasties behind the barn when he was fifteen, but other than that . . I love him, still do, always will, I 'spose."

RUBY

And your Pa, Old King Cole . .

SIGFRID AND LAKME

. . that merry old soul! . .

RUBY

. . was putting on the airs! (*a Prince of the Church in all his finery*) Mr. Fink?

SIGFRID

(*exaggerated basso*) "I'd as soon hit him as spit on him." (*real voice*) He's a mean man, your daddy. Ruby!

RUBY

Out of such squalor, out of such filth . . can any good come unto our little Clarence?

SIGFRID AND LAKME

Yes!

RUBY

You dreamed of a house . .

LAKME

. . a beautiful house . .

SIGFRID

. . high, high on a hill. (*the slide changes to a stately home*)

RUBY, SIGFRID, AND LAKME

Our house!

RUBY

Fa, we simply must have those hedges trimmed.

SIGFRID

And you dreamed of the people in the beautiful house high, high on a hill. (*we see Ruby, Sigfrid, and Lakme*)

RUBY, SIGFRID, AND LAKME

Us!

SIGFRID

That's a rotten picture of me, Lakme.

RUBY, SIGFRID, AND LAKME

How to get there? How to meet them? How?

SIGFRID

You came to the big city. It was cold and you were lonely. You drifted, spent hours at the movies, took odd jobs. (*the Radio City Rockettes*) But nothing seemed to last.

RUBY

You were searching . .

SIGFRID

You were groping . .

RUBY

He was *searching* . .

LAKME

For someone . . something . .

SIGFRID

For anyone . . anything . .

RUBY

In other words . .

RUBY, SIGFRID, AND LAKME

COMMITMENT! (*piano fanfare, great applause; the slide changes to Sigfrid dressed in the collegiate sweater he wore in Act One*)

RUBY

Your salvation was just around the corner . .

LAKME

. . your commitment! . .

RUBY

. . well at the curb, actually . . and you went right over to it. (*Sigfrid and Clarence talking on the street*) SNAP! And the poor little fishy gobbled up the big bad worm.

SIGFRID

Commitment thy name is Sigfrid! (*piano fanfare; applause; Sigfrid and Clarence outside the house*)

RUBY

Shakespeare, Florence, and someone *from* the park! (*piano fanfare; applause; Sigfrid and Clarence going into the house*)

LAKME

There is something out there. We shall prevail! (*piano fanfare; applause which quickly fades as we see Clarence by a bed unbuttoning his shirt; gasps, clucking of tongues, etc.*) This is the beginning of the sexy part. I used an F15 lens.

SIGFRID

Clarence Fink, stand up and take a bow!

AND THINGS THAT GO BUMP IN THE NIGHT

RUBY AND LAKME

A committed bow! (*The lights on Clarence grow perceptibly brighter. From this point on, the slides are shown more rapidly. The "slide" directions that follow are merely an indication of where we generally are in the sequence.*)

RUBY, SIGFRID, AND LAKME

Speech! Speech!

CLARENCE'S RECORDED VOICE

"I'm . . well I guess slender is the word . ."

LAKME

See, Clarence? Sight and sound. (*Clarence barely responds to the sound of his own voice; his head, shoulders only sag even more*)

CLARENCE'S RECORDED VOICE

"I take after my mother. He's enormous . . my father is. You should've seen him when he was young. He played football in school." (*Clarence with his shirt fully off*)

RUBY

(*awed by the sight*) Oooooooooooo!

SIGFRID

Aren't those pectorals something, Ruby? Pret-ty snazzy!

RUBY

These are wonderful pictures, Lakme, just wonderful.

LAKME

Thanks.

CLARENCE'S RECORDED VOICE

"I'd like to have a better build. Broader shoulders, better arms."

RUBY, SIGFRID, AND LAKME

Sweet Clarence. Sweet, sweet, sweet. (*Clarence taking off his pants*)

CLARENCE'S RECORDED VOICE

"But you can't have everything. I mean, I've got a fairly good mind. I'm not manual labor, that's for certain. I'll never dig a ditch. And there are worse places than the public library." (*Clarence with his pants off*)

RUBY

That's what we always say.

CLARENCE'S RECORDED VOICE

"Sigfrid . . are you glad I'm here?"

SIGFRID

Sure I'm glad. Why not?

CLARENCE'S RECORDED VOICE

"I'll probably lose my rank for leaving the parade like that. They're very strict. Once you begin a march you're expected to finish it."

RUBY

But you can't worry about these things twenty-four hours a day. Right?

SIGFRID AND LAKME

Right!

CLARENCE'S RECORDED VOICE

"What if they demote me? I'm a squadron secretary."

SIGFRID

You can be our squadron secretary.

CLARENCE'S RECORDED VOICE

"Oh well, I'll tell them I got sick or something."

RUBY

Or something.

CLARENCE'S RECORDED VOICE

"I doubt if they'll check up on me."

SIGFRID

Now that's what I call commitment! (*Clarence taking his socks off*)

LAKME

Clarence wanted to wear his socks to bed.

RUBY

I can see that, dear. Sshh!

SIGFRID

I think it's uncouth to wear one's socks to bed.

RUBY

Well you! (*Clarence's clothes tidily arranged on a chair*) What's happening now? Where's Clarence?

LAKME

Where do you think?

SIGFRID

Sshh!

CLARENCE'S RECORDED VOICE

"Sigfrid, do you ever get lonely? I mean for someone more than just a friend? . ."

RUBY

You mean someone in the park, dear.

SIGFRID

He means me.

AND THINGS THAT GO BUMP IN THE NIGHT

CLARENCE'S RECORDED VOICE

"Someone you can really be with . . I do. Sometimes . . you may think this is silly . . but sometimes at night I cry about . . about being lonely . . (*Sigfrid, Ruby, and Lakme begin a steady chant of the word "uncommitted," whispering but steadily growing louder*) at night . . when I can't sleep . . and that thing is out there . . I get frightened . . and I cry . . I get frightened . . and I'm lonesome and I cry . . (*Sigfrid has set the tape recorder at a faster speed; Clarence's recorded voice takes on a ridiculous tone*) Maybe I talk too much but . . I don't feel safe most places . . I'm nervous . . I feel cold sort of . . but not here . . oh, no, not here . . I feel safe here . . it's warm . . very, very warm . . Oh Sigfrid . . Sigfrid, Sigfrid, Sigfrid."

LAKME, RUBY, AND SIGFRID

(*mimicking in unison*) Oh, Sigfrid . . Sigfrid, Sigfrid, Sigfrid. (*At this moment, which has been building up inside him ever since this sequence began, Clarence stands with an incredible look of pain and terror on his face. At the same instant, his face appears on the screen in close-up with exactly the same expression on it. The two faces should seem to overlap. Clarence gives an animal howl from the guts and suddenly he has bolted across the room and we hear his footsteps running up the stairs. A moment later we hear the iron door opening. A long silence in the dark room. The only light comes from the slide of Clarence's face.*)

SIGFRID

(*after a pause, tentative*) Ruby?

RUBY

(*steel*) He'll be back, Sigfrid. Clarence will be back.

SIGFRID

But maybe he —

RUBY

(*strong*) Clarence will be back.

CLARENCE'S RECORDED VOICE

"I don't want to ever go home. I could stay heeerrree fooooorrrrevv — " (*the tape drags to a halt; the lamp in the projector goes out; absolute darkness now*)

SIGFRID

(*after another pause*) Ruby?

RUBY

It was one of the animals, Sigfrid.

SIGFRID

Maybe not.

RUBY

The friends always stay the night, Sigfrid. They never go out there.

SIGFRID

(*a decision*) Lakme, get the flashlight.

RUBY

The light will come back, Sigfrid. It always does.

SIGFRID

I'm going up there.

RUBY

It was one of the animals, Sigfrid.

SIGFRID

We don't know, Ruby. WE DON'T KNOW! (*Sigfrid and Lakme rush up the stairs*)

RUBY

Sigfrid! Lakme! Come back here! Don't leave me alone down here! SIGFRID! LAKME! IT WAS ONE OF THE ANIMALS! PLEASE! (*silence, darkness, the hysteria is mounting*) You miserable . . you goddamn miserable . . I WON'T BE LEFT ALONE DOWN HERE! (*Grandfa enters with a flashlight. He shines it directly into Ruby's face. The moment the light hits her, she begins on a hysterical laughing jag.*) Murder, Grandfa? . . would it be murder? . . if we made him go out there? . . Grandfa? . . murder? (*Grandfa moves the light to the top of the stairs. Sigfrid is standing there, carrying Clarence's body. Ruby's laughter builds and builds.*) It was one of the animals, Sigfrid. What did I tell you? It was one of the animals. (*The laughter, completely out of control and hysterical, continues. Sigfrid is coming slowly down the stairs with Clarence in his arms. Tableau. The lamp in the slide projector comes back on and once again we see Clarence's face. The tape recorder starts playing.*)

CLARENCE'S RECORDED VOICE

". . ever and forever and forever. I don't want to ever go home . ."

FAST CURTAIN

ACT THREE

At rise, the room is again the same. But now the slide of Clarence's face dominates the stage. The picture is enormous, filling the entire rear wall. A person will seem very small standing next to it. Candlelight, black crepe . . maybe. Fa is still in his chair, the top of his head or perhaps one arm barely visible to the audience. He snores. There is a coffin: black, stark. It is Clarence's. Ruby sits, center stage, rigid, immobile. Sigfrid and

Grandfa are at opposite sides of the stage, each with his back to her and to each other. Lakme stands looking down at Clarence. It is a formal grouping. After all, the final, grimmest ritual is being played out now. There is a stillness in the room we have not heard before.

CLARENCE'S RECORDED VOICE

". . and that's another reason. Everybody loves somebody . . or they will . . sometime in their life. (*a pause*) Anything that makes you want to live so bad you'd . . you'd die for it . . Shakespeare, Florence . . someone in the park. That's what I believe in. That's all. That's the way I live. (*and then, with that foolish giggle in his voice*) Was it all right?" (*A long silence. Ruby rises, moves slowly to the projector and turns it off. The picture of Clarence fades.*)

LAKME

(*looking down at Clarence*) The way his eyes are open . . just like the dogs' are.

SIGFRID

(*not turning*) Go to bed, Lakme.

LAKME

I never saw dead before.

SIGFRID

Lakme.

LAKME

People dead.

RUBY

(*who has moved back to her place center stage*) "Was it all right? (*slowly shaking her head*) And that is the lesson of him, Sigfrid. Not the sadness.

LAKME

Just like the dogs' are!

RUBY

(*controlled, yet with apparent difficulty: she cannot, will not, must not acknowledge Lakme's anguish and terror*) We must move now toward some . . understanding.

LAKME

Ruby, his eyes!

RUBY

(*blotting that voice out of her consciousness*) The strong have survived . . the weak have not . . and what is there more to say.

LAKME

Ruby!

253

RUBY

(*gaining in strength, finding it in what she says; at the same time fighting her own emotion*) There are those who remain . . and those who do not . . it is that simple. There is strength and there is weakness and there is only they. But oh! such a din there is when they collide! There is trembling . . there is clamor . . there is a spasm of the earth. There is struggle. (*and then this keening, lacerating howl*) THERE IS EXULTATION!

LAKME

(*an involuntary cry of terror*) Exultation!

RUBY

And then . . there is this . . how it ends . . the silence. This is how the world is. This. And so be it.

GRANDFA

(*very sad, very low, and very far away*) No.

RUBY

(*almost to herself*) An understanding. Yes. (*then, directly to Lakme*) The lesson of Clarence, Lakme. (*Lakme only looks at her with wild, accusing eyes*) The strong have survived . . the weak have not . . and what —

LAKME

I don't like dead. I don't like him to be dead.

RUBY

Those who remain . . and those who do not . . it —

LAKME

(*her voice always rising*) I don't want him to be dead. I don't want anyone to be dead . . ever!

RUBY

(*the façade of strength is cracking*) There is strength and weakness . . and there's only they!

LAKME

Dead is bad, Ruby . . you didn't tell us . . you didn't tell us how bad dead was.

RUBY

(*faltering*) Those who remain, Lakme! Think of those who remain!

LAKME

(*unrelenting*) I don't like it . . dead. I don't like it at all!

RUBY

There is . . exultation, Lakme!

LAKME

WHY DIDN'T YOU TELL US? WHY DIDN'T YOU TELL US HOW BAD DEAD WAS?

RUBY

(*breaking, opening her arms to Lakme*) I couldn't . . not until now . . now, this night.

LAKME

(*with a sharp cry, rushing into Ruby's arms*) JUST TELL US WHY!

SIGFRID

(*very low*) Answer her, Ruby . . answer us.

RUBY

(*comforting Lakme in her lap, her eyes beseeching Sigfrid to understand with her*) Some things can't be told, Lakme . . best not . . or answered. They just . . happen.

LAKME

(*her head buried in Ruby's arms*) Dead? You mean dead?

RUBY

(*her eyes on Sigfrid*) The silence. And there is only the silence.

LAKME

(*calmer now*) But Clarence . . that thing out there . .

RUBY

(*at once and with strength*) People like Clarence don't need something out there to come to a bad end. (*she must make this point*) People like Clarence don't even need us. They find it on their very own . . even in broadest daylight . . under the bluest skies. They sniff it out . . hunt and scratch for it under every stump and log until they finally dig it up like some rotten truffle. IT IS THEIR PROPENSITY. They are attracted to a shabby, dismal, futile end as surely as . .

SIGFRID

(*alone and far away*) We are.

RUBY

Are not, Sigfrid. As surely as we are not. (*she should be center stage now*) Consider the Clarences of this world . . and they are out there . . just as he was . . millions upon millions of them . . no different — not really — from this one . . consider these Clarences . . consider them objectively . . with neither tears nor laughter . . but objectively . . and you will know this: that no good will come to them.

SIGFRID

(*with a sad smile . . perhaps*) Objectively. The most important emotion . . objectivity.

RUBY

They . . just as he . . do not understand what we have understood and

255

we have . . will . . ARE DETERMINED to survive them. Understood that there is no —

SIGFRID

Shakespeare . . Florence . . someone in the park.

RUBY

(*with finality*) Anything. Just . . us.

GRANDFA

(*again and always as from afar*) "If they live long and in the end meet the old course of death, mankind will all turn monsters."

RUBY

And then, there is this, Lakme . . how it ends . . the silence.

LAKME

The silence, Ruby.

GRANDFA

(*his voice always the most remote and distant sounding*) "I'll never care what wickedness I do if this man come to good."

RUBY AND LAKME

(*low, in unison*) This is how the world is. This. And so be it.

GRANDFA

(*responding with all the force an old man can summon*) NOOOOOOO!

RUBY

(*with quiet strength now; the crisis has passed; only this remains to finish it*) The litany, Sigfrid. Shall we begin now?

SIGFRID

(*low*) I can't do it, Ruby.

RUBY

After this lesson of Clarence must come our litany of the strong.

SIGFRID

I SAID I CAN'T DO IT.

RUBY

(*with a soft, cruel laugh*) You will, Sigfrid. Sooner or later . . you must. With me, Lakme. (*Sigfrid still does not, will not turn to her. Lakme, however, is kneeling at her feet and looking up at her. Ruby has taken a deep breath and now begins a kind of chant.*) Fear is not strong.

LAKME

(*with the same cadences*) Fear is not strong.

RUBY

Fear sickens.

LAKME

Fear sickens.

RUBY

Fear corrupts.

LAKME

Fear corrupts.

RUBY

We were not strong . .

LAKME

We were not strong . .

SIGFRID

(*almost feverish*) Words . . these words! . .

RUBY

. . once!

LAKME

. . once!

SIGFRID

. . all my life I've heard these words!

RUBY

(*her voice always rising*) But we have dealt with fear . .

LAKME

But we have dealt with fear . .

SIGFRID

(*turning on and to Ruby, trying to shatter the rhythms of the litany*) No! It has dealt with us. Warped . . maimed . . MUTILATED!

RUBY

(*at once, in deadly combat*) . . not succumbed to it.

LAKME

. . not succumbed to it.

SIGFRID

We have succumbed. We're suffocating with fear.

RUBY

(*relentless*) But dealt with it.

LAKME

Dealt.

SIGFRID

(*trying to break through to Lakme*) Don't listen to her.

RUBY

(*stronger in his moment of weakening*) Because we had to.

LAKME

(*breaking out of the cadence of the litany: a simple concern for her brother now*) We had to, Sigfrid.

257

SIGFRID

Close your ears to her!

RUBY

(*never breaking the cadence of the litany; forcing it, in fact*) Because demands were made on us . .

LAKME

We agreed, Sigfrid. The three of us. The way we live . . remember?

SIGFRID

(*close to the breaking point*) WE ARE NOT LIVING AND WE HAVE MURDERED FOR IT. WHY, RUBY, WHY!

RUBY

Because we could no longer cope with it.

SIGFRID

(*now*) OURSELVES! ! !

RUBY

(*tremendous*) IT! ! ! BECAUSE WE COULD NO LONGER COPE WITH IT! ! !

LAKME

(*shrinking*) I'm frightened, Ruby. I'm frightened.

SIGFRID

(*a prayer, a desperate prayer*) Please . . someone . . make it stop!

LAKME

Ruby!

SIGFRID

Let it stop.

GRANDFA

(*on the alert, moving in now*) Go on, Sigfrid.

RUBY

(*after blood*) What stop, Sigfrid? Let "what" stop?

SIGFRID

Us . . everything . . this . .

RUBY

What else is there, Sigfrid?

SIGFRID

I DON'T KNOW . . SOMETHING . . SOMETHING ELSE. THIS ISN'T ENOUGH.

RUBY

(*rapping it out*) IT WILL SUFFICE!

SIGFRID

It's a mechanism, the way we live. That's all it is . . a machine. It runs us. Sitting here . . night after night . . pretending —

AND THINGS THAT GO BUMP IN THE NIGHT

RUBY

(*always attacking*) No, Sigfrid, no pretending!

SIGFRID

PRETENDING! Pretending not to feel . . to live. Rituals . . requiems . .
litanies . . friends. Devices! Excuses for living. (*making her*) LOOK AT
HIM! LOOK AT CLARENCE! That is the way we live . . the result of it.

RUBY

(*making him*) Death, yes! But his! Sigfrid, not ours!

SIGFRID

(*breaking away from her*) WE DON'T LIVE ANYMORE. WE . .

GRANDFA

Go on, Sigfrid, finish it.

SIGFRID

(*with a terrible anguish*) WE DO! WE ARE NOT ALIVE DOWN HERE . . WE
ARE!

LAKME

What's Sigfrid doing?

SIGFRID

(*the breath coming in gulps now, harder and harder for him to breathe;
convulsive, almost*) This room . .

LAKME

Is something bad happening?

GRANDFA

Yes! oh thank God yes!

SIGFRID

This room . .

RUBY

(*harsh*) You won't win him, Grandfa. I won't let you.

LAKME

It is something bad.

SIGFRID

This rooooooom! . .

GRANDFA

(*at once, hoping Sigfrid will turn to him and not Ruby*) Say it, Sigfrid!

SIGFRID

. . I am safe in this room.

GRANDFA

No, Sigfrid, not safe. Save yourself from it.

RUBY

(*the enemy is Grandfa but never taking her eyes from Sigfrid whose back is to both of them*) He can't, Grandfa.

SIGFRID

And there is the need for this room! The need for it.

GRANDFA

(*insistent, strong*) Ask questions, Sigfrid. There are answers.

RUBY

He already has them!

SIGFRID

This room . .

GRANDFA

Other answers!

RUBY

Other answers are called Clarences!

SIGFRID

. . nothing happens in this room. Nothing. Except us. Us. We happen. HAPPEN.

RUBY

(*always topping him*) And we are the victors, Sigfrid. Remember that.

SIGFRID

(*his voice rising, too*) This room . .

RUBY

Remember who we are. We are the victors!

SIGFRID

(*overlapping with her*) . . there is death in this room!

GRANDFA

Then go out of here. Go up!

RUBY

Down, Sigfrid, our way is down!

SIGFRID

This room . .

RUBY

(*picking it up*) There is exultation in this room!

SIGFRID

. . I AM SUFFOCATING IN THIS ROOM. Suffocating on that presence. There. (*pointing to Ruby*) That response to that thing without a name. That alternative to looking on its face. That consequence of being down here. That death!

RUBY

(*rising to her full strength now, overwhelming*) Without me, Sigfrid, without me . .

SIGFRID

I would be free of all this. I could hope to be free. Dare to.

GRANDFA

(*a Dies Irae voice*) Dare it then, Sigfrid! (*Sigfrid suddenly bolts for the stairs; Ruby freezes*)

RUBY

(*terrified*) Noooo! (*but halfway up the stairs he stops — a silence*) You can't.

GRANDFA

Go on!

RUBY

(*the venom and contempt are mounting again*) There's your fear . . your sadness . . your rage. Those stairs and what's beyond them.

SIGFRID

(*writhing, pitiful*) This room! . .

GRANDFA

Dare it!

RUBY

Accept!

SIGFRID

. . I would be out of this room!

RUBY

(*relentless*) The answer to your questions is down here, Sigfrid. With me! I have that answer. I have become that answer!

SIGFRID

(*his eyes always on the door; wanting to move, but motionless; a command, yet pleading*) Open.

RUBY

(*using the words like a sledgehammer*) I am your sadness! I am your rage! And yes! yes! I am your fear!

SIGFRID

Open!

GRANDFA

Sigfrid, dare it!

RUBY

But consider, consider how I grow strong! That I remain right! That I triumph!

SIGFRID

(*coming to a climax*) Open!

GRANDFA

(*the same*) Dare it!

RUBY

(*the same*) I AM OUR STRENGTH.

SIGFRID

OPEN!

RUBY

I AM OUR LOGIC!

SIGFRID

OOOPPPEEENNN!

RUBY

I AM OUR TRIUMPH — ! (*Her mighty howl withers into a stifled moan. Sigfrid has bolted up the stairs and thrown open the door. There is an immediate, terrible silence. Ruby and Lakme freeze. Even Grandfa winces with fear. Only Sigfrid, at the top of the stairs, his back to us, moves: his entire body heaves as he gulps in the outside air. A very long silence.*)

SIGFRID

(*turning back into the room*) We are . . outside, Ruby.

RUBY

(*staring straight ahead, never at the door*) Yes. (*silence*)

SIGFRID

I . . did it, Grandfa.

GRANDFA

(*the same as Ruby*) I know. (*silence*)

SIGFRID

Are you . . cold, Lakme?

LAKME

Ruby . . Ruby's shivering.

SIGFRID

I know. (*silence*) We are outside then. (*silence*) Nothing.

GRANDFA

Nothing.

SIGFRID

Nothing.

LAKME

Ruby's shivering.

RUBY

(*a moan*) Close . . please close.

SIGFRID

It's dark out here . . all stillness . . no sounds at all.

GRANDFA

Yes.

SIGFRID

I thought there would be . .

GRANDFA

What?

SIGFRID

Something.

RUBY

(*again*) Cloooose!

SIGFRID

(*dawning on him*) The fence.

LAKME

(*trying to soothe her*) Poor Ruby . . poor.

SIGFRID

We have no need of a fence. (*low, but decisive*) Lakme. (*she turns from Ruby and looks up at him*) Turn off the fence.

LAKME

The . . ?

SIGFRID

(*calm*) Off . . yes.

LAKME

(*recoiling*) But . .

SIGFRID

(*terrifying*) OFF! (*Lakme obeys, then goes quickly back to her place with Ruby; the room will seem even stiller than it did before*) Yes . . now. (*and at once there is a rapid, rustling sound: almost like the beating of wings, but not specifically that; it grows loud quickly and passes quickly*)

SIGFRID

(*in the silence that follows*) Grandfa?

GRANDFA

I don't know, Sigfrid.

SIGFRID

It . . passed . . us.

GRANDFA

Yes.

263

SIGFRID

Will it . . ? (*the sound again: louder, more terrifying than before; no one moves*)

RUBY

(*trying to drown out that sound*) CLOOOOOOOOOSSSSE! (*sharp silence*) Are we still . . ?

SIGFRID

Yes, Ruby.

RUBY

. . out there?

SIGFRID

Yes.

RUBY

(*as if she's been punched in the stomach*) Ooooh!

SIGFRID

(*going to her now*) And you will look with me. Give me your hand. (*grabs her wrist*) The victors are not afraid. Together they will look. (*leading her toward the door*)

RUBY

No, Sigfrid!

SIGFRID

(*unrelenting, a momentum of cruelty building*) The strong have survived, the weak have not and what is there more to say? LOOK.

RUBY

(*trying to break away*) Sigfrid!

SIGFRID

(*forcing her to stand with him before the door*) There is strength and there is weakness and there is only they. LOOK.

RUBY

I will not!

SIGFRID

The survival of the strong. It is that simple. LOOK.

RUBY

I have looked!

SIGFRID

(*brutal*) THEN LOOK AGAIN. WE ARE THE VICTORS NOW AND TOGETHER WE SHALL LOOK AT WHAT IS OUT THERE!

RUBY

NOOOOOOOOOOOOOOO! (*they break apart; there is a pause*)

SIGFRID

(*very low*) The survival of . . the strong.

LAKME

(*a concern for Ruby*) Sigfrid —

SIGFRID

(*in command now, exercising it*) I WILL NOT CLOSE.

LAKME

I'm frightened, too!

SIGFRID

(*cruel*) I WILL NOT! (*playing with them*) Except for . .

LAKME

Who?

RUBY

Whoooooooo?

SIGFRID

(*simply*) Clarence.

RUBY

(*at once*) Ask him, Clarence!

LAKME

Clarence is . .

SIGFRID

(*howling it*) DEAD! (*manic*) Then what did Sigfrid mean by that? (*a new sound now — it could be the wind, or it might be a moan, human, animal, something in pain; low at first, then rising*)

GRANDFA

The wind.

SIGFRID

Something. (*a beat, then very softly*) "For he's a jolly good fellow, for he's a jolly — " Sing with me! "For he's a jolly good fellow." SING! (*he is standing over Ruby and Lakme now, shouting out the song*) "For he's a — !" WITH ME! SING! (*a crescendo of sound; then, sharp silence*) Sigfrid's shivering . . warm him . . please . . warm.

RUBY

I . . am . . alone.

LAKME

Me, too . . me, too.

SIGFRID

(*looking down on Clarence*) What did you want from me, Clarence who was so simple for us? . . who stumbled against the fence and did not go

265

out there? . . who could have told us something? . . who was pointless? Simple, stumbling, pointless Clarence . . WHAT!

RUBY

It . . is . . dark . . here.

LAKME

Yes . . yes.

SIGFRID

He feels your hand, Clarence. It's cold, Clarence. Dead, Clarence.

RUBY

It . . is . . silent . . here.

LAKME

(*her arms around Ruby*) I'm here, Ruby . . I'm here.

SIGFRID

Someone in the park is very cold now. He was always warm until you
came here . . He wrote a poem once. He was . . like you. Warm him
then . . please . . warm. Someone who wrote a poem.

GRANDFA

(*who has come over to Sigfrid and put his hand on Sigfrid's shoulder*)
Sigfrid — !

SIGFRID

(*tremendous*) I HAVE OPENED AND YOU MUST WARM ME!

LAKME

(*scarcely daring*) Ruby, are we . . ?

RUBY

(*toneless*) Yes.

LAKME

. . dying?

SIGFRID

Shakespeare . . Florence . . and someone in the park.

GRANDFA

Yes.

SIGFRID

Anything that makes you want to live so bad you'd die for it.

GRANDFA

Yes.

SIGFRID

Die . . for us, Clarence.

GRANDFA

(*gently*) Sigfrid.

SIGFRID

(*sudden, ugly*) DIE FOR US! (*the breath coming harder now*) You said men could change things. You believed that. Then change this. Change now. Change or tell me to close!

GRANDFA

I can't.

SIGFRID

(*turning on Grandfa*) Then what, Grandfa! What was that word if he couldn't change? That word we made him say?

GRANDFA

Despair.

SIGFRID

(*his voice rising*) I can't hear you.

GRANDFA

(*low*) Despair.

SIGFRID

You're shouting!

GRANDFA

Despair.

SIGFRID

YOU'RE BREAKING MY EARDRUMS!

GRANDFA

(*almost inaudible*) Despair. Despair. Despair.

SIGFRID

(*keening*) DESPAIR! There was warmth in our despair. And none, none in his. Tell me to close!

GRANDFA

(*sudden, lacerating*) I WILL NOT DESPAIR! (*enormous; it is the most important — the only point really — that he can make*) IT'S OUT THERE FOR ALL OF US. (*a silence; he has been heard*) It's out there for all of us.

SIGFRID

Then what's the point of going on with it?

GRANDFA

To stand up to it!

SIGFRID

From a wheelchair?

GRANDFA

Does there have to be a point to everything? Is that what men insist upon these days?

267

SIGFRID

(*in spite of himself*) I suppose not, Grandfa. I suppose not if you're nine thousand years old and you're standing up to it sitting down in a wheelchair. Then I suppose there doesn't have to be a point to anything. (*a pause; then low, very low*) Even dying.

RUBY

(*low, gasping*) Finish it, Sigfrid, finish it then.

SIGFRID

You're a Clarence, Grandfa. That's who you are. Clarence thought he could change things. Clarence even thought he could change us. Wasn't that sweet of him, Grandfa? And wasn't that sad. Sweet Clarence, sweet Grandfa. Sad Clarence, sad Grandfa. He couldn't do it, Grandfa. And neither can you. Things are the way they are. We are the way we are. Look what it took Clarence to find out he couldn't change anything . . most of all himself. He stomped all over town . . stomp, stomp, stomp . . bells ringing, banners waving . . his own little children's crusade . . ta ta ta ta ta! Wanting to change things. And all he accomplished was this. Why he didn't even accomplish me. (*the viciousness, the hysteria are mounting now*) I buggered him, Grandfa. I buggered him good. We can't have buggered saints, now can we, Grandfa? We're sorry, Clarence, but your bid for martyrdom has been rejected. It was a real good try, baby, but you just didn't have the stuff. This is the court of last resort down here and you and your ideals . . your buggered ideals . . have been found lacking. They lack the substance, they lack the granite, they lack the simple facts of life. The facts of you! AND I WILL CLOSE! (*And with a cry he has rushed up the stairs and slammed shut the mighty door. All external sounds cease at once. Ruby begins heaving great breaths. She is coming back to life . . inflating, like a balloon. Sigfrid, from the top of the stairs, without pause and not breaking the tempo and emotion of the preceding speech, continues.*) Yes, we're horrible. We have made that choice. This house is horrible. But none have built a stronger one. The way we live is horrible. Then teach us your way. But don't send us this for an answer . . don't send us a Clarence. It simply won't do. And know this first . . before you send us another Clarence . . AND THERE WILL BE MORE OF THEM . . know! Know this horribleness. Know this room without windows. Know Clarence who does not move. Know Fa who meant nothing. Know that thing out there without a name. Know us. KNOW! (*and now, facing full front, his fists clenched*) All right, Ruby! We may resume now! (*he has begun the litany*) With hands!

RUBY

(*new strength surging in her*) Ah!

SIGFRID

. . with mind! . .

GRANDFA

(*low, his head bowed*) No, Sigfrid.

SIGFRID

(*relentless, moving down a step with each phrase of it*) . . with passion! We have managed an existence!

RUBY AND LAKME

(*picking it up now*) An existence!

SIGFRID

. . an arrangement . .

RUBY AND LAKME

. . an arrangement . .

SIGFRID

. . an arrangement that works . .

RUBY AND LAKME

Yes!

SIGFRID

. . something for us!

RUBY AND LAKME

Us!

SIGFRID, RUBY, AND LAKME

We have done that . .

SIGFRID

(*almost to the very front of the stage now*) . . done that! . .

SIGFRID, RUBY, AND LAKME

AND WE HAVE SURVIVED YOU! (*These last words were very loud: shouted almost. Now there is a sharp silence. No one moves. There should be the suggestion of a tableau. The moment looks and feels like the end of the play. A long pause. Then Ruby, abruptly breaking this mood, crosses the stage and turns on the overhead lights. After so much darkness, the room should seem unbearably bright.*)

RUBY

(*at once, her old self: all energy and triumph restored now, as if the preceding had never happened*) Your *viola da gamba* lesson, Lakme. Is it tomorrow or the day after? I can never remember which.

LAKME

(*a dead voice*) Tomorrow. The day after. I don't know.

269

RUBY

Put something on the phonograph. Something exhilarating. "La Grand Messe des Morts" should do very nicely. (*Lakme does not move*) I understand the Libyans are agitating for land reforms. Or isn't that what they're saying? It's so difficult to keep up these days . . turmoil under every bushel. Bushel-basket, Lakme. Bushel-basket? (*no response; silence*) I am an admirer of the works of Miss Jane Austen. In rereading . . oh you know that book . . I was struck by the similarity of her writing to the music of Mozart. Each so precise, so balanced . . so controlled, that's the word! Don't you think so? Sigfrid? (*no response; silence*) Grandfa! Will you favor us with one of your dramatic recitations? And may I suggest the Richard II deposition scene? It should have particular significance for you this evening.

GRANDFA

(*who has never taken his eyes off Sigfrid, even though Sigfrid has his back to him*) There was a time, Sigfrid —

SIGFRID

(*without turning*) Was. I was choking on that word. The time is. I am.

RUBY

(*still with Grandfa; trying to end his exchange with Sigfrid*) No? An old trouper like you passing up an opportunity for a gala farewell performance? *Ein kleiner Schwanengesang?* Grandfa!

GRANDFA

(*still to Sigfrid, quiet anger*) It didn't mean anything to give in to it like this.

SIGFRID

It meant a lot, Grandfa. It meant Ruby is right. It meant Clarence is dead. It means we are down here.

GRANDFA

(*harsh*) I'm down here, too!

SIGFRID

(*simply*) Yes.

RUBY

(*alone, restless, inner tension building*) What shall we do now? No music, Grandfa won't recite, *les enfants sont* sulking . . look at Clarence the rest of the night? (*And somewhere, in the nethermost regions of the theatre, there sounds a faint, dull* thump. *Silence. No one moves. All eyes go to the door and hold there. A quiet terror. A pause. And again that sound, ever so slightly louder. Lakme has begun to move slowly out of the*

270

room. *Ruby is abstracted, looking at the door, yet wanting to hold Lakme close to her.*) Lakme! (*opens her arms to her but Lakme does not come*)

LAKME

I wish . .

RUBY

I know.

LAKME

(*she means this*) I wish we hadn't done this tonight.

RUBY

(*who must ignore this*) Now say good-bye to Grandfa. He won't be here in the morning. (*Lakme crosses to Grandfa*)

LAKME

(*simply*) Grandfa. (*he does not look at her*) We'll miss you. And I hope you'll be very happy wherever it is you're going. I hope — (*turning wildly on all of them*) I HOPE YOU DIE ON THAT FARM! I HOPE WE ALL DIE! (*She is gone. Brief silence. And again the thump. Each time a little louder, a little closer.*)

RUBY

Sigfrid? (*he looks at her*) Nothing.

SIGFRID

What, Ruby?

RUBY

Nothing. (*Sigfrid is moving out of the room now*) Sigfrid! (*he turns*) Please.

SIGFRID

It's late.

RUBY

Just a little while longer. (*The thump. It is becoming increasingly difficult not to acknowledge it.*)

SIGFRID

(*alone, remote, as they all are now, his eyes fastened on the invisible rooms above them*) There is a room up there with a bed in it. My bed. My bed before . . this.

GRANDFA

(*low, almost toneless, reading from his Chronicle*) "Sky, a blue sky, the eagle soars."

RUBY

(*by herself, center stage, hoping against hope the thump will not sound again*) Sigfrid, do you remember when — (*the thump*)

SIGFRID

I had a quilt on that bed . . a quilt with calico patches. Every night . .

271

even the very coldest . . I would sleep with the windows open. They were that warm . . my bed and my quilt with the calico patches.

GRANDFA

"High soars, high soars the eagle." (*the thump, still louder, more compelling, more terrifying*)

RUBY

(*the terror mounting*) Make it stop, Sigfrid!

SIGFRID

And I would dream . . real dreams. I would dream of Persia and flying carpets and every far-off place I'd ever read of.

GRANDFA

"Can I soar? Can I soar, too?"

SIGFRID

I *could* dream of them under my quilt with the calico patches all snuggled deep in my soft warm bed.

GRANDFA

"For my longing is as great." (*a terrifically loud thump; each of them, in his fashion, starts perceptibly.*)

SIGFRID

WE ARE CLOSED! (*pause*) And we will never open . . again . .

GRANDFA

(*very low, closing the Chronicle*) "For my longing is as great." (*Silence. And then yet another thump. It is loud, very loud. It is a moment before the sound fades away.*)

RUBY

(*in the silence that follows*) Sigfrid? (*he looks at her, but she will not acknowledge what she has just heard*) Nothing.

SIGFRID

What, Ruby?

RUBY

Nothing! (*he turns from her and is on his way out*) Sigfrid! (he stops but *does not turn to her*) Five minutes? (*he starts to go again*) SIGFRID! (*again he stops, but again he does not turn to her*) What will become of us?

SIGFRID

(*after a moment*) Nothing.

RUBY

No?

SIGFRID

We will continue. (*and again the thump*)

272

RUBY

Yes?

SIGFRID

Ask Clarence. (*he is going*) We will continue. (*He is gone. The thump. Ruby and Grandfa are alone.*)

RUBY

We will continue. Did you hear that, Grandfa? Sigfrid said we will continue. (*The thump. Grandfa has begun and will continue very slowly to tear the pages, one by one, from the Chronicle.*) And that nothing will happen to us. Ask Clarence, he said. (*the thump, each time a little louder now*) But Clarence doesn't have anything to say. Clarence is dead. (*The thump*) Then what did Sigfrid mean by that? (*The thump; then, like lightning*) I AM NOT A STUPID PERSON. WHAT OTHER ALTERNATIVES WERE THERE? (*The thump*) We are eagles, Grandfa, we are. We have, you see, some stature. We are not little people. We are not pathetic people. There is something heroic about us. (*The thump*) WE ARE SAFE. DOWN HERE WE ARE SAFE. (*The thump*) Ask Clarence? I have nothing to ask Clarence. I'll tell him. Tell him something he should have known. For all his talk about commitment, we were, after all, as it turned out, the committed ones. We were. (*The thump*) IT WILL PASS. THIS THING WILL PASS US BY. (*The thump*) You see, Clarence, we, too, have taken a stand against these things, only we have acted on it. We have acted accordingly. We are no longer life-size. We are larger than you. We have transcended — (*an enormous* THUMP; *she falters, then forces herself to continue*) We have survived everything and we shall survive now this night. We are prepared for now this night. Our lives were meant for it. It is our meaning. We are vindicated . . now this night . . finally . . totally . . we are vindicated now this night! (*the thud; terrifying, overwhelming, crushing, like a hard punch in the stomach; no reverberations; a dull, hard, crunching thud*) SIGFRID SAID WE WILL CONTINUE! . . WE . . WILL . . CONTINUE! (*And again that devastating sound. And now silence, a very long one. Grandfa lets the pages of the Chronicle fall from his lap and begins a slow, slow exit. Without moving, numbed and toneless, Ruby continues.*) Grandfa? (THUMP) Sigfrid? (THUMP) Lakme? (THUMP) Fa? (THUMP) No one? . . No one! . . NO ONE! (THUMP, THUMP, THUMP. *A very, very long silence. Sigfrid and Lakme come slowly into the room. They stop at the door and look at Ruby. No one moves. Silence.* THUMP. *Silence. Ruby has moved almost somnambulistically to the tape recorder. The wheels are spinning.*)

RUBY'S RECORDED VOICE

".. who thought they were to prevail. We shall *not* prevail . . so be it. (THUMP) We shall *not* endure . . (THUMP) . . but who was ever meant to? (*Ruby is walking slowly back to her place in the center of the room*) And we shall *not* inherit the earth . . it has already disinherited us. (THUMP. THUMP. *Ruby sits. Staring straight ahead, not looking at them, she extends one hand each to Sigfrid and Lakme who come forward and sit one to each side of her. They do not move.*) If we are without faith, we find our way in the darkness . . it is light enough. (THUMP) If we are without hope, we turn to our despair . . (THUMP) . . it has its own consolations. And if we are without charity, we suckle the bitter root of its absence . . wherefrom we shall draw the sustenance to destroy you. Go . . seek not to know us . . to understand . . the compassion of it will exhaust you and there is so little strength left us now . . so little. (*Ruby, Sigfrid, and Lakme never move. Even their eyes do not move. They stare straight ahead and nothing more. The lights are beginning to fade.*) Spoken by me this December morning. Unwitnessed, unheard, alone." (*The Thump. Silence. No one moves. The Thump. Silence. The Thump. Fa snortles. The Thump. Silence. The* THUMP. *And silence. The stage is completely dark. THE THUMP.*)

CURTAIN